Fluvial Forms and Processes

David Knighton

Senior Lecturer in Geography
University of Sheffield

Edward Arnold

A division of Hodder & Stoughton

LONDON NEW YORK MELBOURNE AUCKLAND

© 1984 David Knighton

First published in Great Britain 1984
Reprinted, 1987, 1989, 1992, 1993

Distributed in the USA by Routledge, Chapman and Hall, Inc.
29 West 35th Street, New York, NY 10001

British Library Cataloguing in Publication Data

Knighton, David
  Fluvial forms and processes.
  1. Rivers
  I. Title
  551.48'3   GB1205

ISBN 0-7131-6405-0

To my mother, for all her help and encouragement

Typeset in 10/11pt Times by Colset Private Ltd, Singapore.
Printed and bound in Great Britain for Edward Arnold, a division of Hodder and Stoughton Limited, Mill Road, Dunton Green, Sevenoaks, Kent TN13 2YA by Athenaeum Press Ltd, Newcastle upon Tyne.

Contents

List of symbols

a	coefficient in width-discharge relation
A	cross-sectional area
A_b	channel capacity (bankfull cross-sectional area)
A_d	drainage basin area
$\overline{A}_u$	mean drainage area of streams of order u
b	exponent in width-discharge relation
B	bifurcating link, per cent silt-clay in channel banks
c	coefficient in depth-discharge relation
C	cis link, Chezy coefficient, concentration of solutes or solids
CT	cis-trans link
d	mean depth
d_{max}	maximum depth
D	bed material size
$\overline{D}$	mean grain size
D_d	drainage density
D_x	grain diameter $\geq$ x per cent of bed material sample
D_{50}	median grain size
f	exponent in depth-discharge relation
ff	Darcy-Weisbach friction factor
F	Froude number
g	gravitational acceleration, coefficient in slope-discharge relation
h	height above datum
H	bed height above datum
j	exponent in suspended load-discharge relation
k	coefficient in velocity-discharge relation, constant
$\overline{l}_i$	mean interior link length
L	distance downstream
$\overline{L}_u$	mean length of streams of order u
m	exponent in velocity-discharge relation, mass
M	magnitude, weighted per cent of silt-clay in channel perimeter
n	Manning resistance coefficient, constant
N_u	number of streams of order u
P	length of wetted perimeter
P_m	mean annual precipitation
q	discharge per unit width
q_{sb}	Q_{sb} per unit width
q_{ss}	Q_{ss} per unit width
Q	stream discharge
Q_b	bankfull discharge
Q_d	dominant discharge
Q_{diss}	dissolved load
Q_m	mean annual discharge
Q_{ma}	mean annual flood

Q_p	peak discharge
Q_s	sediment load/discharge of bed-material load ($= Q_{sb} + Q_{ss}$)
Q_{sb}	bed load discharge
Q_{ss}	discharge of suspended fraction of bed-material load
Q_{susp}	suspended sediment load
Q_2, Q_{15}, Q_{50}	discharge that is equalled or exceeded 2%, 15% or 50% of the time
$Q_{2.33}$	discharge with a return period of 2.33 years (mean annual flood)
r	coefficient in suspended load-discharge relation
r_c	radius of curvature
R	hydraulic radius
R_e	Reynolds number
R_B	bifurcation ratio
s	channel gradient, energy gradient
S	source link, channel sinuosity
S_y	mean annual sediment yield
t	time
T	trans link, tributary link, recurrence interval
TB	tributary bifurcating link
TS	tributary source link
u	stream order
u_*	shear velocity
u_{*_0}	threshold shear velocity
v	mean velocity, stream order
v_{cr}	critical velocity
w	width
w_b	bed width
x	distance, variable
x_c, X_c	critical distances
y	exponent in relation of Manning's n to discharge, channel form variable, water depth
z	exponent in slope-discharge relation
α	downstream rate of change of bed material size, coefficient
β	exponent
γ	specific weight of water
δ	downstream rate of change of channel gradient
η	eddy viscosity, measure of grain packing
θ	dimensionless shear stress, local path direction, slope angle
λ	meander wavelength
λ_*	path wavelength
μ	link magnitude, molecular viscosity
ρ	water density
ρ_s	sediment density
σ	sorting coefficient
τ	shear stress
τ_0	boundary shear stress
τ_{cr}	critical shear stress
ϕ	angle of repose and friction
ω	stream power per unit width, maximum deviation angle
ω_0	threshold unit stream power
Ω	stream power

Acknowledgements

The author and publishers would like to thank the following for permission to include copyright figures:
J.E. Abbott (fig. 3.8b); George Allen & Unwin (fig. 4.17); Almqvist & Wiksell (fig. 5.9): American Geophysical Union (figs. 4.3c, 2.5a, 3.7a); The American Journal of Science (figs. 5.1c, 5.6a); The American Society of Civil Engineers (fig. 2.6c); Annals of the Association of American Geographers (fig. 5.5b); R.A. Bagnold (fig. 3.9b); Blackwell Scientific Publications Ltd (fig. 4.16e); B.J. Bluck (fig. 4.15c); Colorado State University (figs. 2.8, 2.12c); W.H. Freeman & Co. Publishers (fig. 4.12a); The Geographical Association (fig. 4.14c); The Geological Society of America (figs. 2.7, 2.9, 4.9b, 4.10b, 4.13a, 4.14b, 5.10), V.R. Baker and GSA (fig. 5.7), E.A. Keller and GSA (figs. 4.9a, 4.13b) and M.G. Wolman and GSA (fig 4.3a); J.M. Grove (fig. 5.1a); Hydrological Sciences Journal (fig. 3.7d); Journal of Fluid Mechanics (fig. 4.10c); Journal of Hydrology (figs. 2.5b, 3.7e, 4.3d, 4.10d); The Institute of British Geographers (figs. 4.12, 5.4, 5.6b); L.B. Leopold (fig. 4.18c); Macmillan Journals Limited (figs. 3.7c, 4.9d); Methuen & Co. Ltd and the US National Academy of Sciences (fig. 5.2); S.A. Schumm (figs. 4.10b, 5.10); United States Department of the Interior (figs. 4.5b, 4.8, 3.4c, 4.15b, 4.10a, 3.3c, 4.11d, 5.3, 5.8a, 4.9b, 4.16f, 4.15a); John Wiley & Sons Ltd (figs. 2.5a, 5.1b, 5.2, 4.18a, 4.18b); N. Wrigley and Pion Publishers (fig. 4.11d) and D. Zaslavsky (fig. 2.6c).
Detailed citations may be found by consulting captions and References.

I would also like to express my thanks to the following for their assistance at different stages of production: David Stoddart, who first invited me to write the book; the various staff in the Departmental and Drawing Offices of the Department of Geography at Sheffield, who typed the manuscript and prepared the diagrams; my publishers, Edward Arnold, who kept the wheels in motion; and my wife, Celia, who has been a constant source of help. One outcome of writing this book may be a mixed blessing – I agreed to give up smoking once it was published. Life could be hell for a while!

David Knighton
Sheffield
June 1984

1
Introduction

Rivers are a dynamic and increasingly important part of the physical environment. Their behaviour is of interest to a wide variety of concerns, ranging from flood control, navigation and water resource development to recreation. They represent a potential threat to human populations and property through floods, drought and erosion. They therefore have political, social and economic as well as physical relevance.

Rivers are essentially agents of erosion and transportation, removing the water and sediment supplied to them from the land surface to the oceans. They transport on average over 10,000 million tonnes of material each year (Meybeck, 1976). Water flow is one of the most potent forces operating on the Earth's surface both in terms of the total energy expended and the total amount of debris transported. In performing their erosional and transportational work, rivers have developed and continue to develop a wide range of network and channel forms. The character of those forms relative to the underlying behaviour of natural streams is the principal concern of this book.

Rivers usually have well-defined spatial boundaries and can usefully be regarded as open systems in which energy and matter are exchanged with an external environment. The character and behaviour of the fluvial system at any particular location reflect the integrated effect of a set of upstream controls, notably climate, geology, land use and basin physiography, which together determine the hydrologic regime and the quantity and type of sediment supplied (Figure 1.1). Downstream controls such as base-level are also important. Climate is of primary significance in that it provides the energy for the most important processes and, in combination with vegetation, directly influences basin hydrology and rates of erosion. Geological variables are less easily quantified but can have far-reaching effects at a variety of scales, particularly in constraining the nature and level of fluvial activity. In addition to these natural controls, man's influence is becoming increasingly relevant through river regulation schemes and changing patterns of land use. With the marked increase in dam construction since 1945, up to 20% of total stream runoff is now regulated in Africa and North America, with comparable figures of 15 per cent and 14 per cent for Europe and Asia respectively (Beaumont, 1978).

Rivers are dynamic entities whose characteristics vary over time and space with changes in the environmental controls. The large range of scales over which channelled flow occurs, from small headwater streams to major rivers, creates problems of adequate sampling and of establishing general principles. The choice of an appropriate time scale has been a source of continuous debate amongst geomorphologists as it influences our conception of equilibrium within streams, the relationship of cause and effect, and the significance attached to the magnitude–frequency characteristics of process action. In considering the conflict between

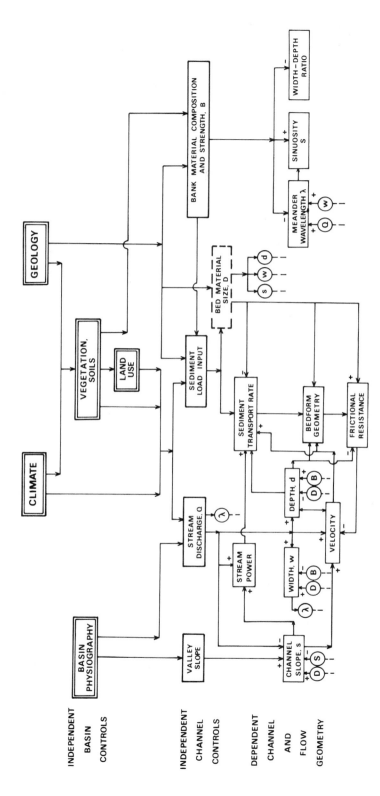

Fig 1.1 Interrelationships in the fluvial system. Direct relationships are indicated by + , inverse ones by − . Arrows indicate the direction of influence.

short-term equilibrium and long-term evolution, Schumm and Lichty (1965) suggested a tripartite division into cyclic, graded and steady times with corresponding periods of about 10^6, 10^2 and 10^{-2} years. Progressive change over cyclic time is seen during the shorter span of graded time as a series of fluctuations about a mean state underlying which is the time-independent state of the system during steady time (Figure 4.2). Since most measurements are made in the short term, the problem exists of extrapolating results to longer time periods.

Strong links are apparent between spatial and temporal scales of investigation. Emphasis on the details of process action at the small scale gives way to consideration of form development at the large scale as the effects of past and present processes become increasingly difficult to differentiate over longer timespans. A wide range of scales may therefore be regarded as appropriate, with reconciliation of the gap between our understanding of process at the small scale and form development at a larger scale being achieved at some intermediate spatial and temporal scale.

In many ways the approaches adopted by various groups differ in the significance given to change over time. At one end of the spectrum are mathematicians and physicists concerned with the development of rational theory with which to explain the detailed mechanics of flowing water. The more pragmatic engineering approach has focused on stream behaviour over relatively short timespans of 10^1 – 10^2 years or less with the sediment transport problem being a primary concern, especially as it applies to the design of stable channels. To this end the Anglo-Indian school of engineers developed a set of semi-empirical equations, known collectively as 'regime theory' and intended for use in the construction of irrigation canals.

Geomorphologists, at least in the first half of this century, have been more interested in long-term development and in the reconstruction of events assumed to have led to the present, an approach owing much to the influence of W.M. Davis's cycle of erosion. Dissatisfaction with the levels of explanation achieved by this approach led in the post-war period to a greater concern with the action of contemporary processes and their relationship to form. With the rapid expansion in the use of statistical techniques, functional relations were sought between form and process variables. The emphasis has thus shifted from the broad temporal and spatial scales of the denudation chronologist to the short time and small space scales more familiar to the engineer. Although a specific concern with river channel form and process has been the major outcome of these changes in approach, the historical element remains an important part of the geomorphological perspective (Schumm, 1969, 1977).

No one approach could be successful in describing and explaining all aspects of natural river systems. One major distinction can be drawn between *empirical* and *theoretical* approaches. The first chiefly involves the collection and analysis of field data in order to establish relationships between form variables or between a form variable and factors summarizing some aspect of process. Paramount among the large range of relationships which could be used has been the power function,

$$y = \alpha x^\beta \tag{1.1}$$

where y is a variable dependent on x and α and β are coefficients to be determined (Figure 1.2). Nowhere is this more apparent than in the hydraulic geometry approach pioneered by Leopold and Maddock (1953) as a means of describing stream response to changing discharge both at particular cross-sections and in the downstream direction. The equation is flexible and easily linearized but whether in

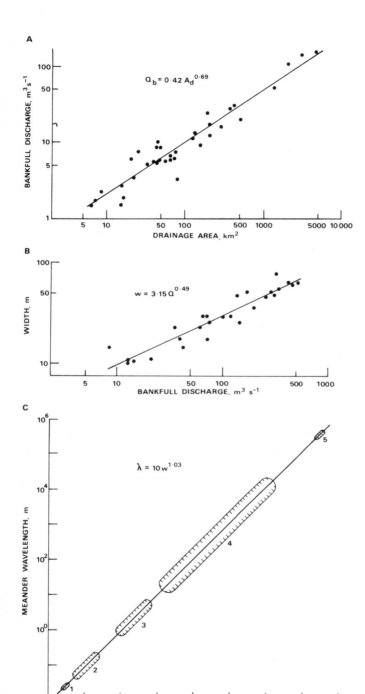

A

BANKFULL DISCHARGE, $m^3 s^{-1}$

$Q_b = 0.42 A_d^{0.69}$

DRAINAGE AREA, km^2

B

WIDTH, m

$w = 3.15 Q^{0.49}$

BANKFULL DISCHARGE, $m^3 s^{-1}$

C

MEANDER WAVELENGTH, m

$\lambda = 10 w^{1.03}$

CHANNEL WIDTH, m

its simple bivariate (1.1) or extended multivariate form, its adoption has not always been adequately justified. Although techniques of analysis have become more sophisticated, the procedure remains largely inductive with the attendant problem of making generalizations from empirical results founded usually on a restricted sampling base. A strong statistical relationship sometimes gives the illusion that explanation has been achieved, and that the effects of underlying processes have in some way been captured when often the independent variable is merely a surrogate for some aspect of process. Despite these shortcomings, the empirical approach has been dominant in geomorphology and has provided valuable insights into the working of the fluvial system. Results of this form are an important preliminary step but, to be of lasting value, need to be embodied within a theoretical structure, even if only qualitatively.

The more deductive *theoretical* approach has as its main aim the formulation and testing of specific hypotheses based on established principles, and involves the construction of models of varying complexity. With the relative lack of established theory, geomorphologists have drawn on the experience gained in allied fields, notably hydraulic engineering, and have frequently argued by analogy between geomorphic and other systems (e.g. Leopold and Langbein, 1962). Characterized by complex interactions of many variables (Figure 1.1), the fluvial system is eminently suited to the adoption of modelling strategies in which some degree of abstraction or simplification is introduced. Again a distinction can be made, between deterministic and probabilistic approaches.

Deterministic reasoning is based on the belief that physical laws control the behaviour of natural systems and that, once the laws are known, that behaviour can be predicted exactly or to a satisfactory level of accuracy for a given set of conditions. Thus, in view of a minimum area being required to support a unit length of channel (the concept of a constant of channel maintenance), Schumm (1977, p. 63) has argued 'that the drainage network develops in response to material erodibility and to the eroding force applied to the surface of the basin in a deterministic manner'. The basic equations used in modelling are: (i) the continuity equations for water and sediment, (ii) the flow momentum equation, and (iii) a sediment transport equation. Whereas (i) and (ii) are well defined theoretically, being based respectively on the Principle of Mass Conservation and Newton's second law of motion, many sediment transport equations include empirically derived coefficients. Deterministic modelling has been used in a wide range of contexts: from channel initiation (Smith and Bretherton, 1972) and drainage network development (Horton, 1945) to the prediction of cross-sectional form (Li *et al.*, 1976) and bed topography in meander bends (Bridge, 1977). It is possibly most useful when dealing with relatively small-scale problems. As situations become more complex, they are increasingly difficult to represent in terms of a set of closed equations and predictions consequently become less reliable.

There appear to be two main arguments behind adoption of an alternative, *probabilistic*, strategy in model building. First, the natural world is so complex that a

Fig 1.2 Power-function relationships:
A. Relationship of bankfull discharge to drainage area, Upper Salmon River, Idaho (data of Emmett, 1975).
B. Relationship of channel width to bankfull discharge, British rivers (data of Nixon, 1959).
C. Relationship of meander wavelength to channel width: 1 = stream plate experiments (Gorycki, 1973); 2 = solution channel meanders in limestone; 3 = supraglacial stream meanders; 4 = river meanders; 5 = meanders in Gulf Stream (Zeller, 1967).

complete deterministic explanation can never be achieved even though each process may be deterministic, a view neatly summarized by Shreve (1975, p. 529): 'Geomorphic systems are descendants of antecedent states that are generally unknown, and they are invariably parts of larger systems from which they cannot be isolated . . . . a probabilistic theory that takes account of the *apparent randomness* is evidently a necessity, because if our theories are to succeed, they must reflect the world as it is, not as we would like it to be.' The second argument goes one step further in not only recognizing an apparent randomness in physical systems but claiming that randomness is an inherent property of such systems. Physical laws are regarded as not sufficient by themselves to determine the outcome of system interactions however detailed are the observations. This view which clearly conflicts with the deterministic standpoint is a central theme in much of the theoretical work carried out by Leopold and Langbein who intended that *inherent randomness* should be a basic principle governing behaviour in the fluvial system. Whatever view of randomness is taken, probabilistic methods have been widely used in the fluvial context, notably in the analysis of drainage networks and the development of minimum variance theory (Langbein, 1964a).

Very real problems exist in modelling a complex physical system whatever framework, deterministic or probabilistic, is adopted and most progress is likely to be made with a mixed approach. Considering the inherent variability of natural streams, physical modelling provides an opportunity for scaling down space and accelerating change over time in order to identify detailed interactions. In this area the laboratory flume has occupied a pre-eminent position even though it too has quite stringent limitations (Maddock, 1969). Scale modelling is essentially an empirical exercise whose value in a geomorphic context is limited by the extended time and space scales common to geomorphological problems. Despite the use of various modelling strategies, geomorphology remains essentially a field science. With the ultimate objective of explaining the behaviour of natural streams, field observations provide the data necessary for empirical relationships and the testing of models, subject always to the constraint of sampling over an adequate range of spatial and temporal scales with minimum disturbance to a system in which single effects are seldom the result of single causes.

2
Drainage networks

In the fluvial system the transfer of water and material from land surface to oceans is characterized by a tendency toward increasing concentration and organization. A spatially diffuse input in the form of precipitation and weathered material is combined via a system of hillslopes and a network of channels into a single output at the mouth of a drainage basin. Available in a hierarchy of sizes, the drainage basin is typically a well-defined topographic and hydrologic entity which is regarded as a fundamental spatial unit (Chorley, 1969). While the links between slopes and channels in the movement of water and material through the drainage basin should be recognized at the outset, even though those links tend to become much weaker for larger streams with well-developed flood-plains, the intention here is to focus on the channel networks themselves, firstly as regards their properties and secondly as regards their possible modes of evolution. While the first can be determined from the analysis of existing networks, the second can rarely be observed directly and explanations of evolutionary tendencies often depend on the results of network analyses.

Network analysis

In the absence of definitive theory, drainage network analysis has until recently largely been an empirical and inductive procedure. It has been used not only for the express purpose of identifying structural characteristics but also as a basis for demonstrating the effects of environmental controls on the fluvial system, for suggesting how networks might evolve, and for predicting basin output variables such as stream discharge which are related to the net. The provision of an adequate data base is therefore critical, involving the problems of consistent sampling and channel definition (Jarvis, 1977).

Because channel delineation in the field is time-consuming, most network analyses have been based on data derived from topographic maps which at best represent an 'average' stream network. The main issue is the unambiguous definition of fingertip tributaries and their headward limits, a problem complicated by short-term fluctuations in stream-head position (Gregory and Walling, 1968) and by the distinction between perennial, intermittent and ephemeral streams. The common practice is to take the blue-line network at an appropriate map scale, usually 1:25,000 in Britain, as the initial basis. Various methods for extending that network have been suggested, with the contour-crenulation method as the most popular, but their reliability can be highly variable, leading to inconsistency. Different methods or even different operators using the same method can produce large discrepancies, particularly in the length properties of headwater streams. Consistent and objective criteria for channel definition are needed if comparisons of results from different sources are to be meaningful.

Drainage network composition

Two themes dominate the early approaches: the importance of time and geologic structure. The classification of streams by such terms as consequent, subsequent and obsequent, to which Davis (1899) attached evolutionary significance, reflects an early recognition of a hierarchical structure in drainage networks. Zernitz (1932) collated an elaborate set of terms and type examples intended to show the effect of geology (and topography) on drainage patterns. Thus, for example, dendritic networks reflect a relative lack of geologic control, while trellis networks develop in areas with parallel belts of dipping strata having differential resistance to erosion. Applicable largely at a regional scale, such classifications are essentially qualitative.

Two related concepts introduced by Horton (1945), *stream order* and *drainage density*, laid the foundation for modern network analysis. Their development has tended to follow separate paths, with emphasis respectively on the internal composition or the overall geometry of networks.

Drainage network composition refers to the topologic and geometric properties of networks. Horton's intention was to replace previous qualitative descriptions of drainage basins and their constituent networks with quantitative ones in which a hierarchical structure was explicitly recognized. The basis for a typical Horton analysis is a method of classifying segments of stream channel according to their hierarchical position in a network by means of stream order. Assuming no triple junctions within an essentially dendritic network, the system of stream ordering (now most commonly by Strahler's (1952) modification of Horton's method) involves the following rules:

(i) fingertip tributaries originating at a source are designated order 1;
(ii) the junction of two streams of order u forms a downstream channel segment of order $u + 1$;
(iii) the junction of two streams of unequal order u and v, where $v > u$, creates a downstream segment having an order equal to that of the higher order tributary v (Figure 2.1A).

The distinction between the streams of order u in (ii) and (iii), classified respectively as order-formative and order-excess by Jarvis (1976), underlines one serious drawback of the ordering system. Besides violating the associative law of algebra, rule (iii) is out of accord with physical reality. Properties such as stream discharge can change when a lower order tributary enters a higher order stream but the order of the main stream may remain unaltered. This problem has partly been resolved by an alternative method which uses link magnitude as its basis (Figure 2.1B).

The immediate outcomes of Horton's ordering scheme were the laws of stream numbers and stream lengths, to which a third, the law of drainage areas, was later added (Schumm, 1956). These so-called laws of drainage network composition (Table 2.1) approximate to geometric progressions of inverse (law of stream numbers) or direct (laws of stream lengths and drainage areas) form. Plots of log N_u, log $\overline{L}_u$ and log $\overline{A}_u$ against stream order (u) are therefore approximately linear (Figure 2.2). Except in conditions of strong geologic control, the three ratios (R_B, R_L and R_A) tend to have relatively narrow ranges of 3–5, 1.5–3.5 and 3–6 respectively (Smart, 1972), suggesting either an underlying regularity in network structure or a lack of sensitivity on the part of the parameters.

A parallelism in the plots of mean stream length and mean drainage area against stream order suggested to Schumm (1956) a direct proportionality between the first two variables, leading to the concept of a *constant of channel maintenance*.

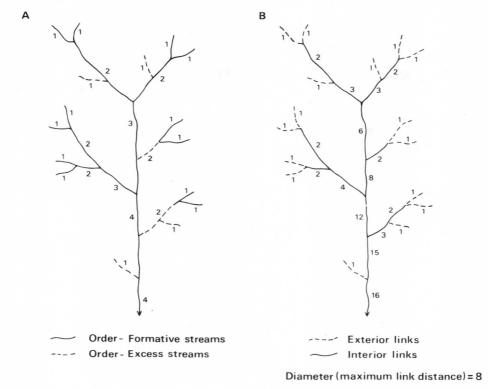

Fig 2.1 Systems of stream ordering:
A. Channel segments ordered by the Horton system as modified by Strahler (1952).
B. Channel links ordered by magnitude.

Table 2.1 Laws of drainage network composition

	Ratio form	Functional form	Author
Law of stream numbers	$\dfrac{N_{u-1}}{N_u} \simeq R_B$	$N_u \simeq \alpha_1 e^{-\beta_1 u}$,	Horton (1945)
		where $\beta_1 = \ln R_B$	
Law of stream lengths	$\dfrac{\overline{L}_u}{\overline{L}_{u-1}} \simeq R_L$	$\overline{L}_u \simeq \alpha_2 e^{\beta_2 u}$,	Horton (1945)
		where $\beta_2 = \ln R_L$	
Law of drainage areas	$\dfrac{\overline{A}_u}{\overline{A}_{u-1}} \simeq R_A$	$\overline{A}_u \simeq \alpha_3 e^{\beta_3 u}$,	Schumm (1956)
		where $\beta_3 = \ln R_A$	

Symbols: $N_u, \overline{L}_u, \overline{A}_u$, are respectively the number, average length and average drainage area of streams of order u; R_B, bifurcation ratio; R_L, stream length ratio; R_A, drainage area ratio; $\alpha_1, \alpha_2, \alpha_3$ are coefficients

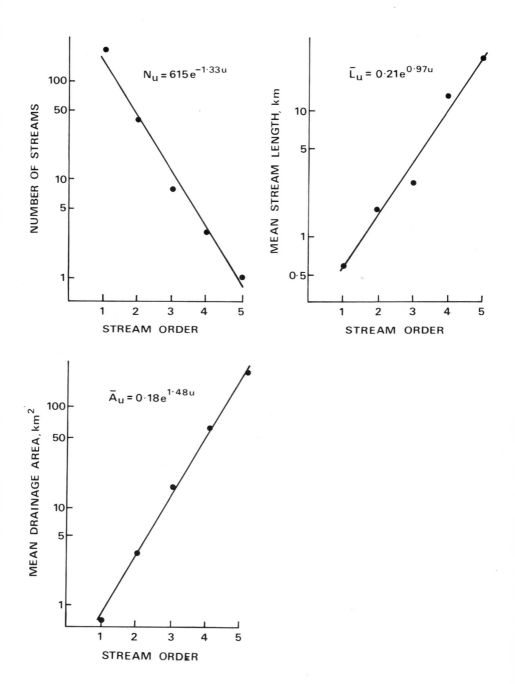

Fig 2.2 Laws of drainage network composition, Bollin-Dean network.

Although the constant can be interpreted as the intercept value in a log-log relationship of basin area to cumulative stream length (Strahler, 1957), the concept is more general than that. It implies that, for a given set of environmental conditions, a minimum area is required for channel initiation and as such represents an important principle in network evolution.

This theme of area–length association has been variously extended, notably by Hack (1957) in an empirical relationship of mainstream length (L) to drainage basin area (A_d),

$$L = 1.4 A_d^{0.6} \qquad (2.1)$$

which appears to hold for a wide range of conditions (e.g. Shimano, 1975; Newson, 1978). In common with Schumm's constant of channel maintenance, it has been interpreted in terms of network evolution. That the exponent is 0.6 rather than 0.5 suggested that drainage basins elongate with increasing size and that therefore headward extension is a dominant mode of network growth. However, the exponent value may not be independent of basin size (Church and Mark, 1980).

The general applicability of the laws of network composition, demonstrated over a period of more than 20 years, implied a degree of organization in network structure not otherwise apparent. Each stream order has a characteristic number of channels, length and drainage area. Horton regarded the laws as deterministic statements about natural networks, related through network development to the action of physical processes. However, they are essentially empirical relationships with small but systematic deviations from straight lines. Much of the regularity in the parameters, notably R_B and R_L, is a consequence of the ordering scheme which is too insensitive to variations in physical controls and which therefore tends to obscure fundamental properties of drainage networks. Nevertheless, stream order remains useful as a crude index of basin size for descriptive purposes.

Repetitious application of Horton's methodology has been largely superseded by the broader-based *probabilistic-topologic approach* pioneered by Shreve (1966) and Smart (1968), which takes account of the randomness as well as the regularity in network structure. New models of network composition, namely the random topology and random link length models, have been proposed and new network variables defined, two developments which are closely related but logically independent of one another. To date, the main emphasis has been on topologic and length properties of networks.

The Strahler stream segment has been replaced as the basic unit of network composition by the *link*, defined as an unbroken section of channel between successive nodes (sources, junctions or outlet). An *exterior link* extends from a source to the first junction downstream and therefore corresponds to a first-order stream, while an *interior link* connects two successive junctions or the last junction with the outlet. A network with M sources thus contains 2M – 1 links, M being exterior and M – 1 interior. The most important topologic parameters are link *magnitude* and network *diameter* (Figure 2.1B). The magnitude of a link is the number of sources upstream: thus an exterior link has a magnitude of 1, an interior link a magnitude equal to the sum of the magnitudes of the two links at the upstream end, and a network with M sources a magnitude of M. The additive property of magnitude overcomes the problem with stream ordering noted earlier. Diameter is the maximum link distance in a network and is a measure of the longitudinal extent of the network, with mainstream length as its geometric analogue. In a network of

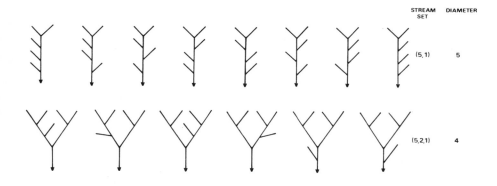

STREAM   DIAMETER
SET

(5,1)   5

(5,2,1)   4

Fig 2.3 Schematic diagram of the N(5) = 14 topologically distinct channel networks (TDCN) of magnitude 5. The networks fall into two distinct stream set and diameter classes. In a topologically random population these 14 networks should be equally probable.

magnitude M ($= 2^{\alpha} + \beta$, where $\beta = 1, 2, \ldots, 2^{\alpha}$), it has a maximum value of M and a minimum of $\alpha + 2$ (Knighton, 1980a).

The probabilistic-topologic approach is founded on two basic postulates:

(i) In the absence of strong geologic controls, natural channel networks are topologically random (Shreve, 1966); that is, all *topologically distinct channel networks* (TDCN) of a given magnitude are equally probable;

(ii) The exterior and interior link lengths of drainage networks developed in similar environments have separate statistical distributions that are approximately independent of location within the basin (Shreve, 1967; Smart, 1968).

These two assumptions are reminiscent of Horton's laws in dealing respectively with topologic and length properties, but their implications are far wider. The random model is an attempt to establish a theoretical framework for the explanation and prediction of drainage network composition.

The idea of topologically distinct networks is based on the fact that networks with the same number of sources have similar topologic complexity (i.e. the same number of links and junctions) but are nevertheless distinguishable topologically. The number of TDCN for a given number of sources, N (M), is defined by

$$N(M) = \frac{1}{2M-1} \binom{2M-1}{M} = \frac{(2M-2)!}{M!\,(M-1)!} \tag{2.2}$$

Thus the numbers of TDCN, or the ways in which the links can be interconnected, for magnitudes one to six are 1,1,2,5,14 and 42 respectively. Figure 2.3 illustrates the 14 possible TDCN for magnitude 5 networks. The only complete test of the random topology model (the first postulate) requires a random sample of networks of a certain magnitude, which are grouped into their respective TDCN classes to form an observed distribution which is then tested against the theoretical equifrequency distribution. For M > 5 the sample sizes required to satisfy statistical tests are so large that a regrouping of TDCN becomes necessary. Direct tests have consequently been limited to networks of low magnitude. The need to aggregate TDCN represents a major drawback to the effective testing of the random topology model since regrouping loses information.

Table 2.2   TDCN of magnitude 12 grouped into stream sets

Stream sets	Number of TDCN (N)	Probability of each stream set (P)
N(12,6,3,1)	2	0.00004
N(12,6,2,1)	24	0.00041
N(12,6,1)	16	0.00027
N(12,5,2,1)	1 080	0.01837
N(12,5,1)	1 440	0.02450
N(12,4,2,1)	3 360	0.05716
N(12,4,1)	13 440	0.22862
N(12,3,1)	26 880	0.45725
N(12,2,1)	11 520	0.19596
N(12,1)	1 024	0.01742
Total	58 786	1.00000

Note: P = N/58 786

One regrouping method is based on stream sets which are defined in terms of Strahler stream order (Figure 2.3). The number of TDCN having $n_1, n_2, \ldots, n_{U-1}$, 1 streams of order $1, 2, \ldots, U - 1$, U respectively is given by

$$N(n_1, n_2, \ldots, n_{U-1}, 1) = \prod_{u=1}^{U-1} 2^{(n_u - 2n_{u+1})} \begin{pmatrix} n_u - 2 \\ n_u - 2n_{u+1} \end{pmatrix} \qquad (2.3)$$

Values for equation (2.3) are listed in Table 2.2 for magnitude 12 networks which have 10 possible stream sets, each with an associated probability. Using equation (2.3), Shreve (1966) was able to show that the most probable stream sets closely approximate Horton's law of stream numbers. The obvious question is: how can natural networks simultaneously satisfy Horton's seemingly deterministic law and the random topology model of equiprobable TDCN? One implies a sense of regularity in network structure and the other an absence of regularity. However, there is no real contradiction (Jarvis, 1977). Horton's law is not a law in the strict physical sense but merely a statistical relationship describing the most probable state of network composition. The random topology model provides a theoretical explanation for the clustering of bifurcation ratios about 4.

Despite problems of effective testing and some minor deviations from expectation (e.g. Abrahams, 1975), results tend to confirm the overall validity of the random topology model when tested at the network or TDCN scale, even in areas of strong geologic control (Mock, 1976). However, at the more detailed link level, significant departures from topologic randomness have been noted. In comparing sets of dendritic and trellis networks, Mock (1976) found that the latter differed significantly from random at the link level but hardly at all at the TDCN level. Geologic factors tended to produce an excess of lower magnitude links. Although the first postulate excludes geologic control, this contrast in result emphasizes a need for caution when testing the random model at different scales. Classifying interior links (Figure 2.4A) as either *cis-links* (tributaries at either end of the link enter from the same side) or *trans-links* (tributaries at either end enter from opposite sides), James and Krumbein (1969) found that cis-links were less numerous than expected, a result confirmed in some (e.g. Smart, 1978) but not all cases (e.g. Dunkerley, 1977). Flint (1980) has pursued this theme in focusing on the spatial arrangement of tributaries along trunk channels and again non-random

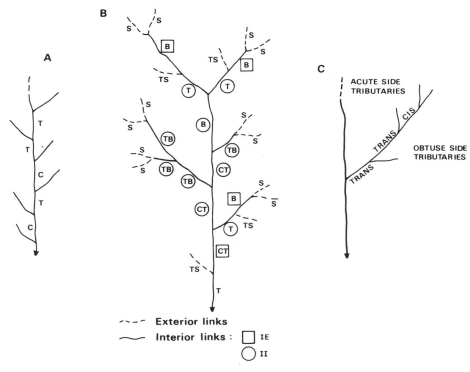

Fig 2.4   Classifications of channel links:
A. Cis (C) and trans (T) links.
B. Source (S), tributary source (TS), bifurcating (B), tributary (T), cis-trans (CT), and tributary bifurcating (TB) links as defined by Mock (1971). Interior links can be classified as IE or II depending on whether they join an exterior or an interior link at their downstream end (Smart, 1978).
C. Tributary arrangements (Flint, 1980).

tendencies have been identified, related partly to the constraints of limiting basin size. In addition, the sequence in which tributaries of different size enter a main stream appears not to be random because of the spatial requirements of different tributary sizes (Figure 2.13; Jarvis and Sham, 1981). The entry of a small tributary has little effect on the size of the next tributary downstream but large tributaries preclude development of another large tributary in their immediate vicinity on the same side of a main stream and consequently tend to be separated in a downstream sequence. These examples do not constitute overall rejection of the random model but rather illustrate how the probabilistic-topologic approach allows greater insight into the spatial pattern of drainage than is possible with the stream ordering approach (Jarvis, 1977).

The random model has been concerned not only with topologic but also with length properties of drainage networks. Smart (1968, 1972) derived a random link length model in which the mean stream length of order u ($\bar{L}_u$) is expressed in terms of stream numbers:

$$\bar{L}_u = \bar{l}_i \prod_{a=2}^{u} (N_{a-1}-1)/(2N_a-1) \qquad u \geqslant 2 \qquad (2.4)$$

where $\bar{l}_i$ is the mean interior link length and N_a is the number of streams of order a. The model explains the behaviour of ordered stream lengths and reveals that, as with the law of stream numbers, Horton's law of stream lengths is largely a result of applying the ordering scheme to a topologically random network.

The model rests on the assumption that interior link lengths are random variables independent of location in the basin or any topologic property such as stream order or link magnitude. Tests made in several ways cast doubt on the general validity of this assumption. Firstly, interior link length tends to increase with both stream order (Ghosh and Scheidegger, 1970) and link magnitude (Smart, 1978), although results are not always consistent. Secondly, the length of both exterior and interior links appears to increase with the magnitude of the link joined downstream (Abrahams and Campbell, 1976; Smart, 1981). Since the magnitude of the link joined downstream would tend to increase with distance from the headwaters, a locational influence on link length is implied. Thirdly, sources of variation in link length have been identified within exterior and interior link types.

In comparing the length distributions of cis and trans links, James and Krumbein (1969) found that their networks exhibited a systematic deficiency in short cis links. Differences in link length properties occur between the link types suggested by Mock (1971; Figure 2.4B; Table 2.3). For six drainage systems in eastern Australia, Abrahams and Campbell (1976) showed that source (S) links are significantly shorter than tributary-source (TS) links, a distinction which becomes sharper further downstream in the network as the latter join progressively higher magnitude links. As regards his classification of interior links, Mock (1976) noted a relation between link type and mean link length with length increasing in the order: bifurcating (B), cis-trans (CT), tributary bifurcating (TB) and tributary (T) links. Both results have been confirmed elsewhere (Smart, 1978, 1981). In addition, a subdivision of interior links into those which join an exterior (IE) or interior (II) link at their downstream end (Table 2.3) has shown that the latter tend to be significantly longer (Smart, 1978).

Table 2.3 Classifications of link types

| Author | Type of link | Definition of link type having magnitude μ | |
		Magnitude of upstream links	Magnitude of downstream link
Mock (1971)	Exterior		
	Source (S) link	—	1
	Tributary-source (TS) link	—	> 1
	Interior:		
	Bifurcating (B) link	$\frac{1}{2}\mu$	$< 2\mu$
	Tributary-bifurcating (TB) link	$\frac{1}{2}\mu$	$\geqslant 2\mu$
	Cis-trans (CT) link	$\neq \frac{1}{2}\mu$	$< 2\mu$
	Tributary (T) link	$\neq \frac{1}{2}\mu$	$\geqslant 2\mu$
Smart (1978)	Interior:		
	IE	$\geqslant 1$	1
	II	$\geqslant 1$	> 1

The main implication of these varied results is that the geometric structure of channel networks is more complex than the random model would at first suggest. In terms of the major categories of exterior and interior links, link lengths are not independent random variables drawn from common populations. Large differences in link length distributions occur between link types, related possibly to the magnitude of the link joined downstream (Smart, 1981) and therefore to location within the network. Little theoretical work exists at this detailed scale, however, and most of the reported deviations from expectation are based on empirical observations of natural networks, which are subject to sampling and measurement constraints. In particular, link length studies are dependent on the accuracy with which the networks are initially delineated, a significant problem in the case of exterior links whose sources are rarely well defined on topographic maps. Despite these drawbacks, the random model has provided a valuable basis for analysing the length properties of drainage networks. Departures from the model have yet to be fully explored but do suggest processes of network development altogether more detailed than previously perceived.

In the past 15 years the analysis of drainage network composition has experienced a profound change in methodology with the development of the random model and the derivation of new network variables. Increasingly attention has focused on network properties at the fundamental link level. The random topology and random link length models provide explicit null hypotheses or statistical standards against which natural networks can be compared. Many of the relationships previously obtained have been explained theoretically, notably Horton's laws of network composition and Hack's (1957) mainstream length–basin area relation (Shreve, 1974), and the prediction of new relationships is confidently expected (Smart and Werner, 1976).

Reservations have been expressed about the geomorphologic relevance of the probabilistic-topologic approach on the grounds that general explanations of network structure in terms of geomorphic processes cannot be expected if networks are indeed topologically random (Werritty, 1972; Kirkby, 1976). However, significant departures from expectation have been identified, at the detailed scale in particular, which can be explained in terms of network growth processes and geologic influences which act as partial constraints (Mock, 1976). Also, many attributes of drainage networks such as link drainage areas, link slopes (Flint, 1974, 1976) and channel orientation remain to be fully explored (Jarvis, 1977). The main emphasis to date has been on topologic and stream length properties. Future work may well concentrate on the interrelationship of network structure and the hydrologic processes which ultimately control it. The probabilistic-topologic approach provides a basis for these developments while emphasizing the need to take account of the apparent randomness as well as the regularity in a system governed by many unknowns.

Drainage density

Except in one or two cases (e.g. Smart and Werner, 1976), few attempts have been made to integrate the stream ordering and drainage density concepts introduced by Horton (1945). Drainage density (D_d), defined by

$$D_d = \frac{\Sigma L}{A_d} \tag{2.5}$$

where ΣL is the total channel length in a basin of area A_d, is regarded as the most important areal measure of network geometry in that it expresses the degree of basin dissection by surface streams and hence links the form attributes of the basin to underlying processes.

Drainage density has various connotations. In one sense it reflects the complex interaction of those factors which control surface runoff and consequently varies over space and in the long term with changes in the controlling variables. In another it has causative significance in determining the efficiency with which surface runoff is discharged from an area during individual storms. Eight-fold variations in drainage density have been reported from a single catchment as the network expanded and contracted in response to short-term fluctuations in precipitation (Gregory and Walling, 1968). In dealing with the permanent rather than instantaneous wet-channel network, the problem is to explain the spatial variation of drainage density in terms of controlling variables whose individual influences are difficult to isolate because of interactive effects. Unfortunately the theoretical background is somewhat limited and the main approach has been empirical, based largely on data from mid-latitude areas. Such an approach again suffers from the problem of channel definition and network delineation when obtaining representative values and comparing densities from different map series. The range of drainage density values is wider than Horton originally supposed but, of 42 areas listed by Gregory (1976), only 13 had densities greater than 15 km km^{-2} and only five densities greater than 20 km km^{-2}.

Two sets of factors determine drainage density: those which govern the amount and quality of water received at the surface, and those which control the subsequent distribution of that water, its availability for channel cutting, and erodibility. The first is climatic, while the second includes a complex mix of lithologic, vegetational, edaphic and topographic influences. A global synthesis is inhibited by the overall lack of data but broad trends can be identified, especially as regards the first group.

Drainage density is broadly correlated with mean annual precipitation (Figure 2.5A). Maximum values occur in semi-arid areas where also the range of drainage density is greatest. In those areas the proportion of precipitation receipt which flows as surface runoff and which is therefore immediately available for erosion is greater than in more humid environments. Drainage density decreases in more arid and more humid areas because of reduced runoff potential and the impeding effects of vegetation respectively, although values may increase again in the seasonally humid and humid tropics where mean annual precipitation exceeds 1500 mm (Abrahams, 1972). It is no coincidence that this global pattern of drainage density variation is similar to that proposed for sediment yield (Langbein and Schumm, 1958; Figure 2.5A), especially as regards the correspondence of their respective maxima. High sediment yields reflect increased channel development and a more efficient drainage system.

The choice of mean annual precipitation reflects more the availability of data than causative significance since there is no *a priori* reason why it is physically the most relevant rainfall variable. Rainfall intensity may be a more appropriate parameter in that it influences the short-term availability of water for channel cutting, especially during infrequent storms. Chorley and Morgan (1962) attributed a difference in mean drainage density between two areas of high relief (Dartmoor, England and the Unaka Mountains in the south-eastern United States with density values of 2.1 and 6.9 km km^{-2} respectively), both with a complete vegetation cover, to the contrast in rainfall intensities. Aside from the question of operational definition, the problem is to determine the magnitude of rainfall intensity which is largely responsible for initiating and maintaining channels. Networks appear to be closely related to conditions of maximum runoff. Seasonality is yet another factor of importance, especially in combination with rainfall intensity, since markedly seasonal climatic regimes tend to have high drainage density values. Clearly the hydrologic input having the dominant influence on drainage density is difficult to isolate empirically when the several rainfall variables are so highly intercorrelated. Indeed the dominant control could vary from one climatic province to another and may only be isolated through deterministic modelling of the kind suggested by Kirkby (1978).

The effectiveness of precipitation in producing runoff can be expressed by Thornthwaite's P-E index, a measure of moisture availability for plant growth. In the most complete empirical study of drainage density variation, Melton (1957) identified the P-E index as the single most important variable. As the index increased over the range of 12–110 drainage density decreased (Figure 2.5B), which Melton interpreted as indicating the efficacy of an increasing vegetation cover in controlling erosion. In contrast, Madduma Bandara (1974) found a positive correlation between the two variables for Sri Lankan basins where the index varies from 86 to 373. The implication is that, beyond a critical value of effective precipitation (80–90), the relationship changes from negative to positive (Figure 2.5B) because further increases in precipitation cannot be countered by similar increases in the vegetation cover, a result which has an obvious parallel in the tendency for drainage density to rise where mean annual precipitation exceeds 1500 mm.

The effects of vegetation itself are difficult to isolate because they are bound up with those of climate and soil cover. The large differences in erosion rates between vegetated and unvegetated slopes point to the major influence of the presence or absence of vegetation on surface water erosion. Drainage density is highest in areas of sparse vegetation and also tends to decline as the extent of the vegetation cover increases (Melton, 1957). However, once a more or less complete cover exists, differences in vegetation density appear to have little further effect on drainage density, provided the infiltration capacity is high enough to preclude Horton overland flow (Dunne, 1980).

Climatic characteristics, operating partly through their influence on vegetation, have a dominant control on drainage density variation at the global and regional scales. Inter- and intra-regional differences, which tend to be smaller than those between climatic provinces (Gregory and Gardiner, 1975), can be attributed to lithologic and topographic factors, especially in so far as they affect the infiltration–runoff relation. Bedrock permeability influences the relative amounts of surface and subsurface flow so that less permeable rock types which favour lower infiltration are commonly associated with higher drainage densities (Gregory and Gardiner, 1975). Increasing aridity may accentuate the effect of bedrock differences which are not always apparent (Carlston, 1966). In humid areas in particular, where channel formation is strongly related to subsurface water movement, lithology influences drainage density through its effect on the intensity of chemical weathering and hydraulic conductivity in both the main mass and the vicinity of channel heads (Dunne, 1980). Certainly lithologic contrasts can determine the short-term response of drainage density during occasional storms (Day, 1980).

The distinction between wet-weather and perennial networks underlines the dynamic quality of drainage density and the need to establish theoretically the

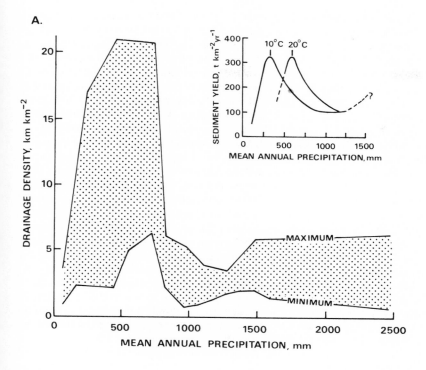

A.

B.

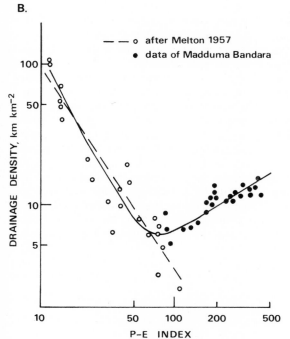

Fig 2.5 Variation of drainage density:

A. In relation to mean annual precipitation with corrections for basin size (after Gregory, 1976). The inset shows a relation of sediment yield to mean annual precipitation for two mean annual temperatures (after Langbein and Schumm, 1958).

B. As a function of precipitation-effectiveness (after Madduma Bandara, 1974).

magnitude-frequency characteristics of rainfall (and therefore runoff) events controlling channel formation. While the drainage density determines the flows in the short term, the flows determine drainage density in the longer term through environmental factors whose intercorrelations complicate empirical attempts to isolate individual effects based on inter-area comparisons. Correlative structures of the kind envisaged by Melton (1958) suggest that drainage networks are capable of achieving an equilibrium form adjusted to prevailing environmental conditions of climate, vegetation, lithology and soils. Drainage densities attain maximum values in semi-arid areas (Figure 2.5A) where surface runoff rates are high owing to high rainfall intensities over surfaces with sparse vegetation cover and limited soil development. A change in environmental conditions may institute a change in the network through expansion or contraction, the direction of which depends on the existing climatic regime. The peakedness of the drainage density and sediment yield curves (Figure 2.5A) indicates the sensitivity of semi-arid environments where even small changes in precipitation or surface conditions can induce a marked response (Cooke and Reeves, 1976). The problem is to decide what constitutes a lasting change when drainage lines cut during infrequent storms can become persistent (Hack and Goodlett, 1960). However, drainage density cannot increase indefinitely. The position and stability of stream heads are important in determining the magnitude of drainage density in that they reflect the relative dominance of cut and fill processes or a balance between the tractive force of the flow and the strength of the underlying surface. Having examined the structural characteristics of existing networks in terms of their internal composition and density, the logical step is to ask how that structure may have developed.

Channel initiation

Channels originate in a variety of ways related in part to the history of the land surface on which they develop. They may form on a recently exposed surface or during a phase of network expansion resulting from a change in environmental or base-level conditions. They may be influenced in their development by channelways inherited from the past. Channel initiation involves two related problems: to determine the processes whereby water movement becomes sufficiently concentrated to cut a recognizable channel; and to identify the conditions under which the initial cut is maintained and enlarged to form a permanent channel. The latter cannot be entirely divorced from the broader question of drainage network development which is considered later, since permanence implies some level of integration between surface channels.

The way in which water accumulates to generate the conditions necessary for channel initiation involves the study of runoff processes. Water reaching the ground surface can follow several paths on its way downslope (Figure 2.6A). Where the maximum rate of absorption (infiltration capacity) exceeds the rate of receipt (normally expressed by rainfall intensity), water infiltrates the surface and

Fig 2.6 A. Potential routes of water movement: 1 – groundwater flow, 2 – throughflow, 3 – Horton overland flow, 4 – saturation overland flow (comprising return flow and direct precipitation onto saturated areas). The unshaded zone represents more permeable topsoil and the shaded zone less permeable subsoil or bedrock.
B. Schematic diagram of shallow subsurface flow and the generation of saturated conditions in a two-layer soil where a more permeable layer overlies a less permeable one.
C. Relation of moisture content at depths of 0.2 m and 0.4 m 10 days after rain with soil surface curvature in a ploughed field, Beer-Sheba (after Zaslavsky and Sinai, 1981).

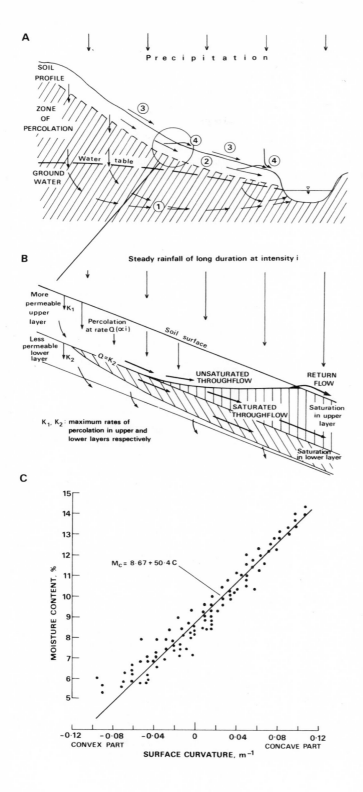

A

Precipitation

SOIL PROFILE

ZONE OF PERCOLATION

③

④

③

②

④

Water table

GROUND WATER

①

B

Steady rainfall of long duration at intensity i

More permeable upper layer K_1

Percolation at rate $Q (\propto i)$

Soil surface

Less permeable lower layer K_2

$Q = K_2$

UNSATURATED THROUGHFLOW

RETURN FLOW

SATURATED THROUGHFLOW

Saturation in upper layer

K_1, K_2 : maximum rates of percolation in upper and lower layers respectively

Saturation in lower layer

C

$M_c = 8 \cdot 67 + 50 \cdot 4 \, C$

MOISTURE CONTENT, %

SURFACE CURVATURE, m^{-1}

CONVEX PART

CONCAVE PART

either moves downward to replenish the *groundwater* reservoirs (route 1) or flows laterally as *throughflow* (route 2), particularly in soils with an impeding horizon of low permeability (Figure 2.6B). Throughflow may be diffuse when water flows through the matrix of the soil or concentrated for example along percolines, zones of greater soil depth and moisture content (Bunting, 1961), or in pipes of variable size and location (Gilman and Newson, 1980; Jones, 1981). This potential for throughflow convergence has important implications for channel initiation. Percolines, for example, often occupy topographic depressions in the headwater area of existing streams and therefore represent preferential zones for channel extension.

Overland flow can be generated in two main ways. *Horton overland flow* (route 3) occurs when rainfall intensity exceeds infiltration capacity, its discharge and depth increasing linearly downslope after sufficient time has elapsed for a steady state to be achieved (rainfall excess = outflow). Horton's (1933, 1945) infiltration theory of runoff predicts that this type of flow will be produced more or less instantaneously and simultaneously over a basin during heavy rain, implying a uniformity of rainfall and infiltration conditions which can only be expected in relatively small basins. Infiltration characteristics in particular are highly variable both spatially and temporally. Also, in humid areas with a dense vegetation cover and well-developed soils, rainfall intensities rarely exceed infiltration capacity. This type of overland flow is therefore much more limited than Horton assumed (Table 2.4) and Zaslavsky and Sinai (1981) have gone so far as to suggest that all rain, be it of high or low intensity, must first enter the soil before part re-emerges on the slope.

Saturation overland flow (route 4) depends on the moisture content of the soil before, during and after rainfall events. Provided rainfall continues long enough for deeper and less permeable soil layers to become saturated, throughflow will be deflected closer and closer to the surface as the level of saturation rises through the soil (Figure 2.6B). If the soil eventually becomes saturated to the surface, saturation overland flow will occur. It consists of two components: *return flow*, comprising that part which emerges at some point on a slope where surface saturation has been attained, and *direct precipitation onto saturated areas*. Being non-Hortonian, this type of flow can occur at rainfall intensities much lower than those required for Horton overland flow. It is also spatially more limited (Table 2.4), being preferentially generated in those localities subject to saturation (Kirkby and Chorley, 1967): at the base of slopes, in hollows, in slope-profile concavities, where soils are locally thin or less permeable. Concavities are particularly important for runoff generation since lateral flow and moisture concentration in those parts will continue after the rain has stopped, keeping them wetter for longer periods and shortening the time period before the onset of runoff when the next rain falls (Figure 2.6C; Zaslavsky and Sinai, 1981). Kirkby and Chorley (1967) have suggested that the two models, the Horton overland flow model and the throughflow model (which includes saturation overland flow as a component), are end-members of a series of runoff and erosion models related to climate, vegetation and soils. Although even this viewpoint may be too restricted (de Vries, 1976) since each of the four flow processes can contribute to channel development, the spectrum is clearly wider than Horton originally envisaged.

Various processes of erosion are associated with these modes of flow. At the surface, erosion takes place by raindrop impact (rainsplash), sheet flow, rill flow in small ephemeral channels, and gully flow. Distinctions are sometimes difficult to

Table 2.4 Principal differences between types of overland flow

Characteristic	Horton overland flow	Saturation overland flow
Rainfall	Strongly related to rainfall intensity	More dependent on rainfall duration
Infiltration	Surface infiltration capacity of critical importance	Transmissibility of lower soil horizons more important
Distribution:		
Temporal	Begins soon after the storm when intensities are high enough	Starts only when the underlying soil layers are saturated
Spatial		
(i) environmental	Semi-arid areas with sparse vegetation and thin soils	Humid areas with dense vegetation and well-developed soils
(ii) local	Widespread over the basin	Limited to zones of saturation
Downslope variation	Linear increase of runoff volume	More complex pattern of change

make, particularly between sheet and rill erosion since the former often includes the effects of rills (Komura, 1976), but the given order appears to represent a sequence of increasing rates of erosion.

Rainsplash is principally a detachment mechanism preparatory to the removal of loosened particles by other surface processes, although there is net transport downslope on inclined surfaces. It is probably most effective in short intense storms which generate little surface runoff or during the early stages of storms that do produce runoff. Once surface flow has attained a certain depth, estimated at 5 mm by Kirkby and Kirkby (1974), rainsplash rapidly declines in importance and entrainment of particles as bed or suspended load takes over as the dominant transport process. Overland flow is a special form of fluvial transport in which thin flows occur over very rough surfaces, so that the applicability of conventional formulae developed for natural streams may be limited. A major problem is to define widely applicable threshold criteria for both runoff generation and erosion by these various surface processes in terms of measurable parameters, given the large range in environmental conditions. Only isolated results tend to exist. Thus, for example, critical rainfall intensities for sheet and rill erosion have been variously defined as 25 mm h^{-1} in Zimbabwe (Hudson, 1971) and 10 mm h^{-1} in England (Morgan, 1977).

Vegetation plays a significant role in determining the efficacy of surface processes by (i) shielding the ground surface from the direct impact of raindrops, (ii) improving soil structure and reducing surface flow velocities, both of which lead to greater infiltration, and (iii) increasing the physical strength of the soil. The distinction usually drawn between semi-arid and humid areas as regards drainage density and sediment yield underlines the importance of vegetation as a control of overland flow runoff and surface sediment loss.

Those factors which reduce surface runoff and increase the importance of subsurface flow are generally the same ones that favour solutional loss from soils. Water moves much more slowly within the soil so that it is better able to come into chemical equilibrium with the soil materials and thereby remove material in solution. Effective transfer of solutes requires a strong downward and lateral flow of water and conditions which favour the chemical reactions necessary for ion mobilization. The high dissolved loads of many rivers (Table 3.6) point to the effectiveness of solution as an agent, although part of the load may come from the deep solution of bedrock. The physical transport of soil material is generally much less important because of the very low flow velocities and the constraints imposed on the size of pore spaces through which particles must pass. Only where large pores, such as soil pipes, develop is subsurface sediment yield likely to be appreciable. In effect piping extends channel processes beyond their obvious domain and provides one important mechanism for the formation and extension of surface channels (Jones, 1981).

Channel initiation by overland flow

A transitional sequence of surface flow types can be recognized: from shallow flows of uniform depth, through irregular flows where the water moves in discontinuous depressions or in definite but shifting channels, to flows in permanent channels. To reach the final stage four requirements must be met:

    (i) surface runoff must be generated with sufficient frequency for effective erosion;

   (ii) the force applied by that runoff must exceed the resistance of the surface;

  (iii) flow convergence must occur in the erosive zone; and

  (iv) incision must occur to a depth sufficient to ensure initially a permanent channel and eventually permanent flow within that channel, although many examples exist of channels which are maintained despite intermittent occupancy.

The critical issues are to determine where on a hillside water becomes erosionally effective and where water flow becomes sufficiently concentrated to cut a recognizable channel.

The Horton (1945) model provides the obvious starting point. Where Horton overland flow is dominant, a thin, irregular sheet of water flows downslope and exerts a shear stress (τ) on the surface given by

$$\tau = \gamma \, d \cos \theta \sin \theta \qquad (2.6)$$

where γ is the specific weight of water, d is the mean depth of flow and θ is the local slope angle. With increasing flow depth downslope and a constant or increasing gradient up to about 40°, shear stress and the potential for erosion will also increase with distance x from the crest of the divide. Horton argued that, at some point on the slope a distance x_c from the divide, applied stress equals the surface resistance to give a 'belt of no erosion' upslope and a zone of potential sheetwash erosion downslope (Figure 2.7), that potential being realized during storms of high enough intensity. Horton regarded the critical distance x_c as the most important factor controlling network development in that it sets a spatial limit on channel initiation. It varies directly with surface resistance, which is determined by soil properties and vegetation, and inversely with slope angle and runoff rate.

Downslope of x_c Horton envisaged the development of a system of sub-parallel rills in which one rill may eventually become dominant (Figure 2.9), the implication being that, once overland flow becomes erosive at x_c, it is unstable and has an inherent tendency to form small channels '. . . due to accidental concentrations of flow' (Horton, 1945, p. 332). There are two related issues: whether overland flow is stable against the tendency to develop rills; and whether small rills tend to grow into more permanent channels.

Overland flow rarely occurs as a uniform sheet. Vegetation and associated

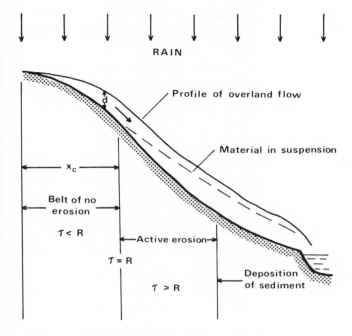

RAIN

Profile of overland flow

Material in suspension

x_c

Belt of no
erosion

$T < R$

Active erosion

$T = R$

Deposition
of sediment

$T > R$

T: eroding stress R: shear resistance of soil surface

Fig 2.7 Hillslope profile showing the critical distance x_c (after Horton, 1945).

microtopography disrupt the flow to give localized concentrations and anastomos-ing runoff patterns. Field measurements are notoriously difficult to make and most work has been carried out on experimental plots of rather limited length (Emmett, 1970; Pearce, 1976; Dunne and Dietrich, 1980). These experiments have shown that overland flow can be erosive without developing rills. Any tendency for flow concentration can be counteracted by either frequent lateral shifting of flow lines or rainsplash erosion on intervening protuberances. Emmett (1970) claimed that the presence or absence of rilling depends on the erosion rate necessary to maintain slopes in dynamic equilibrium. Since rilling is a form of drainage capable of carrying more material, it represents an adjustment to a higher rate of removal.

Natural hillslopes subject to sheetwash erosion can remain unchannelled (Leopold *et al.*, 1966). If Horton's concept of a critical distance is accepted, then the critical length for sheetwash erosion (x_c) is not necessarily the same as that for channel initiation (X_c). Dunne (1980) argued that the point $X_c > x_c$ is reached when the tendency for incision exceeds the counteracting effect of raindrops to level the surface, with downslope areas being most susceptible. The onset of channelization requires another threshold to be attained, related possibly through the erosion rate to critical conditions of slope geometry and flow dynamics. Patton and Schumm (1975) defined such a threshold in western Colorado where gullied and ungullied slopes were differentiated on the basis of slope angle. In his experiments, Emmett (1970) found that depth absorbed more of the downslope increase in discharge than did velocity and this may have been one reason why flow conditions were condu-cive to sheet but not rill erosion. In addition to critical length criteria, a critical area could be defined since channel initiation requires the accumulation of runoff from a minimum area (Schumm, 1956). There is thus a distinction, firstly between whether or not rilling occurs when the flow is erosive, and secondly between x_c and X_c as to where on a slope it is most likely to begin.

The question of overland flow stability has been taken up more formally through deterministic modelling of slope evolution in relation to sediment transport processes (Kirkby, 1971, 1978; Smith and Bretherton, 1972; Luke, 1974). The mathematics show that small-scale irregularities on a surface will tend to grow only where the slope profile is concave. Surfaces which are straight or convex are stable against small perturbations, implying that any channel-like features will tend to disappear. Consequently if, during the long-term evolution of the landscape, profiles develop with convex upper and concave lower parts, the distance from the divide to the onset of wash instability equals the distance to the point of inflection where profile form changes from convex to concave. Indeed a convexo-concave profile would be a necessary condition for the development of a stable channel system. Convergent zones (e.g. contour concavities or hollows) in the concave part of a slope thus form loci for channel initiation. Certainly moisture concentration in concavities is a major element in Zaslavsky and Sinai's (1981) model of surface hydrology. Also, Mosley's (1974) experimental results support this conclusion in showing that erosion tends to be greater on convergent as opposed to planar or divergent slopes.

The criterion for wash instability defines the maximum length a given slope can attain before being subject to channel formation. Assuming a maximum slope of $\tan^{-1}(\frac{1}{2})$, Kirkby (1978) has calculated the maximum stable distances expected under conditions where either overland flow or subsurface flow is dominant (Table 2.5). The values appear to be of the correct order of magnitude but should not be regarded as definitive. These deterministic models provide a rational explanation for Horton's claim of a critical distance but are less successful in accounting for the absence of rilling on certain concave slopes repeatedly subject to Horton overland flow (Dunne, 1980).

Table 2.5   Maximum stable distances and minimum drainage densities predicted for four locations (after Kirkby, 1978)

Location	Annual rainfall, mm	Number of raindays per year	Maximum stable distance, m	Minimum drainage density, km km^{-2}
UK moderate rainfall	700	175	1 500	0.3
UK heavy rainfall	2 500	250	90	5.6
SE Arizona	300	20	2.8	180
Washington DC	1 000	100	360	1.4

The further problem of channel permanency is covered to a certain extent in the models outlined above. Rills are usually small features whose dimensions are controlled by the erodibility of the material into which they are cut. They may be prevented from becoming larger by the short duration of most flows and by the tendency for soil strength to increase with depth. With no net tendency for deepening, rills can be destroyed by rainsplash effects, infilling or lateral shifting of channels during individual storms, or by the action of other slope processes between storms. However, some master rills may grow large enough to maintain their position and escape destruction. Horton's model of network evolution envisages such a development through the process of cross-grading which tends to form a permanent channel (Figure 2.9). Also, infrequent storms of high intensity may have a lasting effect through the cutting of gullies which subsequently influence the location of erosion (Hack and Goodlett, 1960). Channel maintenance depends on the relative rates of incision and infilling, which are in turn dependent on the magnitude and frequency of storms capable of producing surface flow and on the erodibility of the underlying material. Once established, channels provide a locus for surface and subsurface flow convergence, leading to further incision and headcut recession both by surface flows which overtop the channel head and by basal sapping. Although much uncertainty remains, particularly with respect to the process and rate of channel incision, Horton overland flow provides one mechanism whereby hillslope hydrology can be linked to channel initiation.

Channel initiation related to subsurface flow
In addition to the modifications already made, the overland flow model is limited in other more fundamental respects. It remains applicable to semi-arid environments but in more humid areas, where the distribution of surface runoff in the form of saturation overland flow is more restricted, the assumption of uniform overland flow production begins to break down. Distance from divide becomes a less rigid criterion for determining both the occurrence of overland flow and the conditions conducive to channel formation.

The short-term extensions of existing networks observed during suitable storms (Gregory and Walling, 1968; Blyth and Rodda, 1973) help to identify the most likely sites for channel initiation by saturation overland flow. They principally occur in downslope areas and in concavities where moisture content usually remains relatively high and subsurface flow converges. With a lateral flow component proportional in magnitude to the slope, streamline convergence can give rise to very high hydraulic gradients and rapid development of runoff in concave parts, leading to erosion by the outflowing water (Zaslavsky and Sinai, 1981). Morgan (1977) has observed rills developing from a sudden burst of water onto the surface near the base of a slope in mid-Bedfordshire. A small cut was formed which migrated headward as a channel. Channel initiation by saturation overland flow clearly depends on the movement of subsurface water along preferred drainage lines, many of which are highly sensitive to local topography. Thus Kirkby (1978) has argued that hillslope hollows are required to generate saturated conditions and extend the area of wash erosion upslope. Where saturation overland flow is the dominant mechanism, not only is there likely to be a greater distance from divide to channel head than in the Horton model but also a greater variability in that distance even within a given physiographic environment. Nevertheless, channels cannot continue to develop beyond a certain limit and the concept of a critical distance or contributing area remains relevant.

Subsurface pipes also provide a locus for channel development. Flow in natural pipes is now regarded as being more widespread than previously supposed and as having major hydrological and erosional significance (Jones, 1981). The velocity and volume of pipeflow may far exceed those of return flow and saturation overland flow in hollows, with the result that pipeflow can make a significant contribution to flood peaks, especially where pipes are well connected to the existing channel net. Despite attendant problems of measurement and questions as to the continuity and stability of pipe networks, the ability of subsurface flow to follow well-defined and integrated paths suggests a genetic relation between pipe systems and surface channels.

Pipe systems vary considerably in size, location and connectivity. They may exist at more than one level in the soil with each level being activated by storms of different magnitude. Gilman and Newson (1980) identified two principal forms in the upper reaches of the Wye catchment: deep-seated pipes greater than 200 mm in diameter with seasonal or perennial flow, and pipes of about 40 mm in diameter located close to the surface with only ephemeral flow. A basic requirement for pipe initiation is the presence of horizons or surfaces of limited permeability (Jones, 1981). If rates of infiltration exceed the permeability of such interfaces, piping may develop through the selective enlargement of a dense pore network provided the hydraulic gradient or the breakdown of soil resistance passes a critical threshold. The process is particularly likely if cracks or similar lines of weakness can be exploited and pipes associated with percolines appear to have a better chance of developing. Pipe networks having a continuity and form similar to surface channels may subsequently evolve, although this is probably indicative of a more advanced stage of development (Jones, 1981).

Pipe networks can apparently attain a quasi-stable state without necessarily leading to the formation of surface channels (Gilman and Newson, 1980). However, sufficient evidence now exists to establish a link between piping and channel initiation through either roof collapse or concentrated erosion downslope of pipe outlets. Aghassy (1973) identified a process of transition from rilling to gullying in the badlands of the Negev, which passed through a piping phase and continued up to third-order channels. I have observed the development of a second-order system in a semi-arid area of south-east Spain as a direct result of roof collapse, the exposed network providing a locus for further erosion by surface flows. Whether or not channels formed in this way are maintained depends partly on the frequency with which runoff is generated thereafter. Zaslavsky and Sinai (1981) have proposed a positive feedback mechanism in which, once erosion has been initiated, it will progress at an increasing rate because of streamline convergence and greatly increased seepage forces associated with the initial cut. Upslope retreat along the line of buried pipes provides another mode of headward extension, the critical threshold at the channel head being that of roof stability. Hillslope hollows are not the only foci for channel extension (Jones, 1981).

Dunne (1980) has proposed a model for channel formation related to piping, formulated in terms of groundwater rather than throughflow movement. Based upon extensive field observations in Vermont where saturation overland flow produces little surface erosion, he envisaged spring sapping as the dominant mechanism. Because of initial inhomogeneities in the porous medium or differential chemical weathering, more permeable zones develop in the bedrock toward which groundwater movement is concentrated. As the degree of flow convergence and the intensity of chemical weathering increase in a positive feedback, similar in certain respects to that proposed by Zaslavsky and Sinai (1981), the critical conditions for piping erosion are eventually reached, with the subsequent removal of large amounts of weathered material. The excavation of a springhead and local lowering of the ground surface intensify the process, increasing both the probability of further piping and the rate of headward retreat. The further a channel head retreats, the greater is the flow convergence and the rate of chemical weathering. A limit to this self-perpetuating process is set by the minimum catchment area required to supply sufficient water for continued headward growth.

The various mechanisms proposed for channel initiation are not mutually exclusive but vary in their relative effectiveness with environmental conditions in so far as those conditions determine hillslope hydrology and surface/subsurface resistivity. Even though Horton overland flow is regarded as dominant in semi-arid areas, subsurface as well as surface processes are important. Some of the most spectacular examples of piping come from those areas. Also, the distinction commonly drawn between Horton and saturation overland flow tends to obscure an underlying complexity in the relationship between flow mechanisms and the erosion processes which generate channels. All flow routes can contribute to the formative process. In a field dominated for so long by the Horton model, much uncertainty remains, particularly about the conditions necessary for piping and the processes of channel incision. Clearly the initiation, maintenance and growth of surface channels are bound up with the long-term development of stream networks.

Network evolution

The initial question to ask is why networks evolve. Given that a certain land area has to be drained and that surface runoff can be subdivided into unconcentrated and concentrated forms, various levels of drainage efficiency can be imagined (Chorley and Kennedy, 1971, p. 235–6). From the point of view of the slower unconcentrated form, maximum efficiency is achieved when basin slopes are as short as possible, which requires a complex bifurcating network of small channels. Parker's (1977) experimental results confirm that drainage efficiency (expressed by the ratio of discharge output to rainfall input) does improve as drainage density increases up to a maximum. From the point of view of concentrated runoff in channels, water is removed more efficiently by larger channels which offer less resistance and maximum efficiency is achieved when one large channel drains the area. These ideal states are clearly incompatible and in reality a compromise is achieved between the two extremes. In the first place a minimum area is required to accumulate sufficient runoff for channel initiation (Schumm, 1956). Beyond some maximum drainage density, efficiency may in fact decline as channel paths lengthen and become more circuitous (Parker, 1977). At the other end of the scale, a limit is set by the maximum length which a drained slope can attain before being subject to channel formation. Kirkby (1978) has predicted minimum drainage densities for four environments based on his deterministic model of hillslope hydrology (Table 2.5).

The ideal scheme is complicated further: firstly, by the fact that not all water flows off the surface and in some environments subsurface flow is a dominant component; and secondly, by the presence of eroded debris. In Parker's experiments maximum sediment production again represented a compromise between different levels of drainage extension and their relative efficiency in transporting the eroded debris. Thus the extent of the compromise between extremes of drainage density reflects the dominant hydrologic and sediment conditions in a basin, both of which are environmentally constrained and neither of which are independent. The previous analysis of drainage density variation (pp. 16–20) provides a background for deciding on the character and relative significance of environmental controls. Rivers are merely another slope element within drainage basins, which may or may not be adjusted in their network geometry to the most efficient removal of water and sediment for given conditions. Carlston (1963) certainly assumed that drainage density was so adjusted as regards runoff, with the mean annual flood ($Q_{2.33}$) as the major influence.

Evidence of network evolution

A complete specification of network evolution requires information on initial conditions, the physical processes and principles involved, the time scale involved, and the changing character of environmental controls. Such information is rarely, if ever, available. Evidence of network evolution has been assembled from three main sources: direct observation, inference from existing networks, and theoretical modelling. Underlying all is the knowledge gained from the analysis of established networks, which has been used as a basis for comparing networks of supposedly different age or environment and as a basis for constructing and testing evolutionary models.

Direct observation of network development is necessarily restricted to a few suitable sites, such as artifically produced surfaces (Schumm, 1956) or recently exposed areas (Morisawa, 1964; Price and Howarth, 1970). Based on his observations in the clay pits of Perth Amboy, Schumm (1956) proposed a schematic evolution of a third-order basin, which involved headward growth of a dominant channel with branching at the tip once a critical length was reached. Tributaries formed on valley-side slopes of sufficient length and steepness as this process continued up to a limit defined by available area.

Sequences can also be directly observed in laboratory experiments where the developmental process is accelerated (Flint, 1973; Parker, 1977). Parker's results from a test plot measuring 9 m by 15 m are by far the most comprehensive. Two sets of experiments were carried out: one at a slope of 0.43° in which base-level was lowered before each run; and one at a slope of 1.83° with no base-level lowering except after the network had achieved maximum extension. The networks grew primarily by headward extension and bifurcation of first-order streams (exterior links) but different modes of growth were identified in the two sets (Figure 2.8A). In the first the network developed fully as it slowly extended headward (mode 1), while the second was characterized by the rapid growth of long first-order channels with tributaries being added later (mode 2). Thus elongation and elaboration (infilling of the net) were more distinct processes in the second set. Although the mixing of slope and base-level conditions complicates identification of their individual effects, a third set of experiments did suggest that the base-level condition was mainly responsible for the different modes of growth.

Sequences observed in the field or laboratory generally refer to small-scale development and the problem is to apply results to the larger-scale longer-term evolution of natural networks. Similarity of form is no guarantee of similarity of process. With laboratory experimentation there are problems of maintaining appropriate scaling ratios between model and prototype and of isolating the effects of imposed conditions. Parker's experiments included two main initial conditions, either or both of which could have influenced network growth. Despite these drawbacks, such small-scale studies are valuable particularly in suggesting possible details of network evolution.

Fig 2.8   Experimental study of drainage network evolution (after Parker, 1977):
A. Examples of network growth by different modes. Networks are shown at equivalent times during the experiments.
B. Changes in sediment yield during four experiments with base-level lowering between each experiment.
C. Changes in the number of first-order streams during network development to maximum extension. Time is indexed by the volume of water over the system.

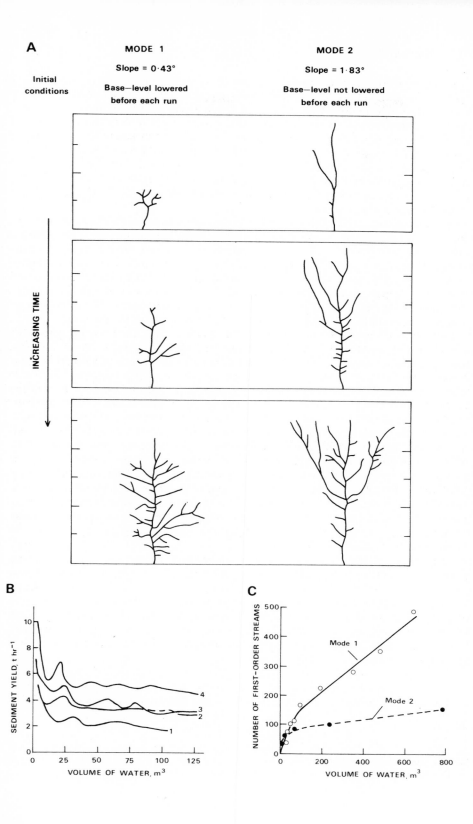

A

MODE 1

Slope = 0·43°

Base—level lowered
before each run

MODE 2

Slope = 1·83°

Base—level not lowered
before each run

Initial
conditions

INCREASING TIME

B

SEDIMENT YIELD, t hr⁻¹

VOLUME OF WATER, m³

C

NUMBER OF FIRST-ORDER STREAMS

Mode 1

Mode 2

VOLUME OF WATER, m³

Patterns of network evolution have been *inferred* either directly or indirectly on the assumption that time and space are interchangeable under certain circumstances (the ergodic hypothesis). Direct applications involve the arrangement of networks at supposedly different stages of development in a temporal sequence. By arranging selected topographic maps in such a way, Glock (1931) postulated several phases of development:

    (i) *initiation* of a skeletal pattern,

    (ii) *elongation* by headward growth of the main streams,

    (iii) *elaboration* through the addition of small tributaries,

    (iv) *maximum extension*, and

    (v) *abstraction* when tributaries are lost as relief is reduced through time.

Ruhe (1952) examined the networks developed on five glacial tills of variable age and, from the different degrees of dissection, inferred how drainage density changed through time (Figure 2.12). Such studies provide only broad indications of change and suffer in particular from their failure to pay adequate attention to the effects of factors other than time which may have produced the differences. Faulkner (1974) has argued that ergodic transforms are only permissible in non-competitive systems with uniform climate, lithology and available relief.

Indirect applications involve relationships between selected network properties and a variable believed to change progressively through time. Relative relief has been a favourite candidate in this surrogate role. On the basis of a direct relation between the proportion of tributary–source (TS) links and relative relief in 39 mature drainage basins, Abrahams (1977) has proposed firstly, that TS links rather than S (source) links develop as relief is increased by stream incision, and secondly, that TS links are preferentially abstracted with declining relief. The abstraction of exterior links tends to increase the mean lengths of both exterior and interior links as relief declines and channel infilling becomes more prevalent (Abrahams, 1976). These results imply that the planimetric properties of mature networks are controlled to a certain extent by evolutionary changes in relief. Although the problem of distinguishing evolutionary changes from spatial variations remains, controlled sampling can reduce the risk of incorporating environmental effects. Without using relative relief as a surrogate for time, other studies have also inferred modes of network growth at the detailed scale from tests of the random topology model (James and Krumbein, 1969; Flint, 1980).

Theoretical models have been developed along both deterministic and probabilistic lines. Horton's (1945) deterministic model is an excellent example of how physical theory (the infiltration theory of runoff) and observed form (the laws of drainage network composition) can be rationalized in an evolutionary context. A system of sub-parallel rills initiated beyond the x_c distance is modified by the processes of micropiracy and cross-grading to form a master rill (*a b* in Figure 2.9), incision by which creates side slopes on which new rill systems develop. This process continues until the available length of overland flow is less than x_c, a constraint on development which is best visualized within a diamond-shaped drainage area. Without such a shape it is difficult to determine which rill becomes dominant at each stage. The model is restricted in other more fundamental respects. It suffers

Fig 2.9   Schematic development of a drainage network (after Horton, 1945):

A. In a diamond-shaped basin.

B. Cross-sectional diagram of the process of cross-grading and the development of a master rill. Arrows indicate the resultant direction of overland flow.

C. Development of a fourth-order network on a newly exposed surface.

A

STAGE 1: development of a master rill

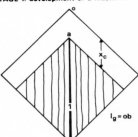

$l_g = ob$

STAGE 2: development of lateral tributaries

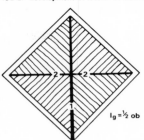

$l_g = \frac{1}{2}\, ob$

STAGE 3: further tributary development

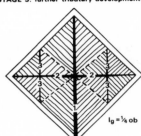

$l_g = \frac{1}{4}\, ob$

STAGE 4: space—filling process complete

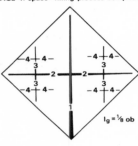

$l_g = \frac{1}{8}\, ob$

l_g = maximum length of overland flow

B

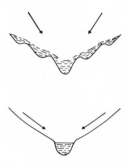

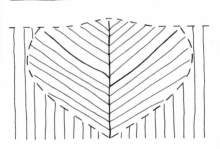

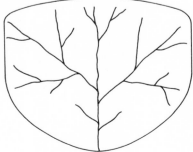

C

STAGE 1

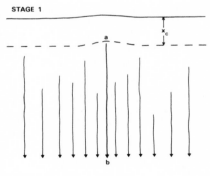

STAGE 2

STAGE 3

STAGE 4

STAGE 1: A single rapid tilt brings a smooth landsurface of permeable rocks above sea-level

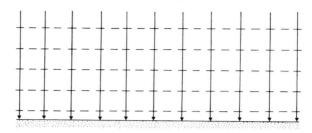

STAGE 2: Perturbation of the flow field leads to flow concentration toward a more permeable zone where piping erosion eventually occurs. A spring head is excavated, leading to further flow concentration, accelerated chemical weathering and repeated piping at the same site

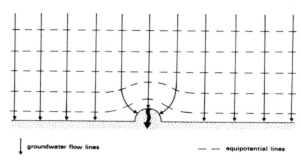

↓ groundwater flow lines   — — equipotential lines

STAGE 3: Spring head retreat increases flow convergence and the potential for future spring sapping. Water emerging along the valley sides exploits a susceptible zone to form a tributary which also undergoes headward retreat

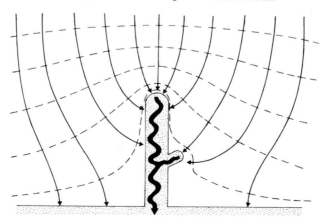

STAGE 4: The process of repeated failure, headward retreat and branching forms a network of valleys. The pattern stabilizes when the declining drainage area of each spring head is no longer large enough to supply enough groundwater to cause piping in the weathered bedrock

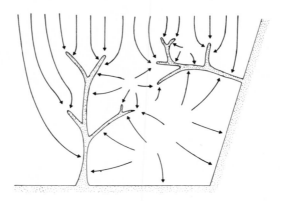

Fig 2.10 A model of drainage network development by spring sapping (after Dunne, 1980).

from the same environmental limitations already ascribed to Horton overland flow and the related concept of the x_c distance. Cross-grading and micropiracy are inconceivable processes of channel integration in large-scale networks. Governed by the principles of competition and the x_c distance, Horton's model is best applied to small-scale networks developed on unvegetated surfaces with low infiltration capacity and limited soil cover (Schumm, 1956).

Dunne's (1980) spring sapping hypothesis deals directly with subsurface flow (Figure 2.10). Headward retreat along an initial channel disrupts the groundwater flow pattern. Water emerging along valley sides exploits some susceptible zone to form a tributary which also migrates headward and may eventually branch. The process of repeated failure, headward sapping and branching continues until the drainage area available at each spring head is too small to supply sufficient water for channel development. A balance is then struck between channelization and hillslope processes. This model, applicable at a larger scale than Horton's, explains why drainage patterns sometimes reflect geologic structure and how stream capture can occur as neighbouring spring heads compete for water. Little is known about what controls channel spacing or the location of tributary development.

Probabilistic tendencies can be incorporated in several ways: through the random generation of complete networks (Leopold and Langbein, 1962), the construction of random growth models (Howard, 1971a), and the simulation of specific processes such as stream capture (Howard, 1971b). An important aspect of growth modelling is the probability of branching in network development.

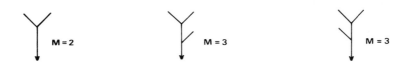

M = 2   M = 3   M = 3

POSSIBLE NETWORKS AT
t = (n + 1)

(i) Headward bifurcation

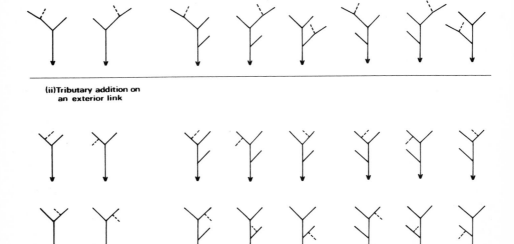

(ii) Tributary addition on
an exterior link

(iii) Tributary addition on
an interior link

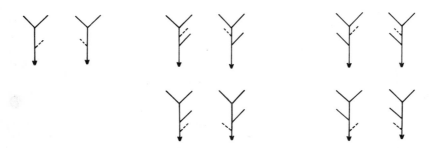

Fig 2.11   Possible branching events in networks having an initial magnitude of 2 or 3.

Table 2.6 Probabilities of branching by addition of an exterior link

Initial network magnitude, n	Number of possible branching events (i)	(ii)	(iii)	Model A (i) P(E)	P(I)	F_n	Model B (ii, iii) P(E)	P(I)	F_n	Model C (i, iii) P(E)	P(I)	F_n
2	2	4	2	1	0	0	$\frac{2}{3}$	$\frac{1}{3}$	$\frac{1}{2}$	$\frac{1}{2}$	$\frac{1}{2}$	1
3	6	12	8	1	0	0	$\frac{3}{5}$	$\frac{2}{5}$	$\frac{2}{3}$	$\frac{3}{7}$	$\frac{4}{7}$	$\frac{4}{3}$
4	20	40	30	1	0	0	$\frac{4}{7}$	$\frac{3}{7}$	$\frac{3}{4}$	$\frac{2}{5}$	$\frac{3}{5}$	$\frac{3}{2}$
5	70	140	112	1	0	0	$\frac{5}{9}$	$\frac{4}{9}$	$\frac{4}{5}$	$\frac{5}{13}$	$\frac{8}{13}$	$\frac{8}{5}$

P(E), probability that an exterior link branches
P(I), probability that an interior link branches
$F_n = P(I)/P(E)$

Assuming that networks grow sequentially by the addition of an exterior link (first-order stream), three branching events are possible (Figure 2.11):
   (i) bifurcation at the head of an exterior link;
   (ii) right or left tributary development on an exterior link; or
   (iii) right or left tributary development on an interior link.
Dacey and Krumbein (1976) considered 3 different combinations of these possibilities: Model A = (i), Model B = (ii) and (iii), Model C = (i) and (iii). If at time n the network has a magnitude of n and at time (n + 1) a magnitude of (n + 1), various branching probabilities can be calculated (Table 2.6). In particular F_n has respective values of 0, $(1 - \frac{1}{n})$ and $2(1 - \frac{1}{n})$ for the three models. For Model B which has the same probability distribution as Shreve's (1966) random topology model, $F_n <$ 1 but approaches 1 as n increases, implying that branching is more likely on exterior links during early stages of growth but that interior and exterior link branching become equally likely in larger networks. Empirical tests revealed that Models B and C fit the data best, suggesting that even during the early stages branching occurs both at the edges and in the interior of networks. This result conflicts with the opinion that growth is headward rather than sideways at least in the initial phases but does conform with both Dunne's (1980) spring-sapping model and Parker's (1977) first set of experiments (mode 1, Figure 2.8A). Despite the danger of arguing from simulated to natural processes, this approach appears to offer interesting possibilities. It links probabilistic-topologic reasoning to the problem of network genesis. Also, if the morphology of first-order basins varies with position in the network (Marcus, 1980), so might the mode of growth and channel extension.

This treatment of theoretical models is by no means exhaustive. Faulkner (1974), for example, has developed a growth model for competitive gullies based on the concept of allometry, a physical statement about proportional change within systems. However, it has underlined the problem of providing definitive statements about network evolution. Even models stated in deterministic terms contain probabilistic elements. As the scale at which network growth is considered decreases, the possibility improves of relating that growth to the physical processes involved. No one model can hope to be entirely satisfactory but there is sufficient evidence to indicate general features of network evolution.

Modes of evolution

The limited data available suggest that drainage density increases relatively rapidly at first as channels invade an unoccupied area and then changes more slowly as a limit or equilibrium value is approached (Figure 2.12). As shown previously, that value is related to environmental conditions. Parker's (1977) data indicate how both the rate of change and maximum value of drainage density can vary with different initial conditions. Indeed inherited characteristics can profoundly influence network development (Hack, 1965). As channels extend and incise themselves, landscape mass is removed and the zone of maximum erosion tends to migrate headward. Sediment is derived from progressively further upstream and downstream parts must continually adjust to this supply. The tendency for sediment yield to decrease exponentially during experiments (Figure 2.8B) reflects not only the headward migration of the zone of maximum sediment production but also the increasing likelihood of sediment storage as the drained area expands. Downstream response may take the form of pseudo-cyclic aggradation and incision (Schumm and Parker, 1973), with associated changes in channel form.

For convenience, network evolution can be subdivided into various phases similar to those proposed by Glock (1931): (i) *initiation*, (ii) *extension* by headward growth (elongation) and tributary addition (elaboration), (iii) *maximum extension*, and (iv) *integration* by abstraction and capture. No historical inevitability should be assumed from this progression since one or more phases may be absent or vary in relative significance during evolution. Parker (1977) could find no clear distinction between initiation and other phases of extension.

Three possible modes of *network growth or extension* have been considered (Table 2.7). Contemporary opinion favours a combination of the second and third modes with headward growth and branching being possibly more important in the initial phases. Assuming that the physical requirements for channel initiation are met, the essential problem is to determine how exterior links (first-order streams) are added to networks. Such additions will clearly affect the topologic and link length properties of evolving networks.

Table 2.7   Modes of network growth

Dominant mode of growth	Source
Downslope growth and coalescence	Horton (1945); Leopold and Langbein (1962)
Headward growth and branching	Schumm (1956); Howard (1971a); Flint (1973); Parker (1977 – mode 2)
Lateral and headward growth	Dacey and Krumbein (1976); Parker (1977 – mode 1); Dunne (1980)

In Parker's (1977) experiments the number of exterior links increased rapidly at first (Figure 2.8C), especially where the network developed fully during headward extension (mode 1). Bifurcation ratios fluctuated considerably, tending to increase to maxima of 7–11 before falling as higher-order streams formed. However, these oscillations were quickly damped out and bifurcation ratios became more stable as

Fig 2.12   Changes in drainage density through time:
A. Inferred from drainage patterns developed on glacial tills of different age in Iowa (after Ruhe, 1952 and Leopold et al., 1964).
B. In small-scale laboratory experiments (data of Flint, 1973).
C. In laboratory experiments with different modes of network growth (after Parker, 1977). Time is indexed by the volume of water over the system.

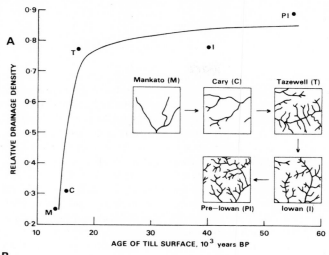

A

RELATIVE DRAINAGE DENSITY (y-axis): 0·2, 0·3, 0·4, 0·5, 0·6, 0·7, 0·8, 0·9

AGE OF TILL SURFACE, 10^3 years BP (x-axis): 10, 20, 30, 40, 50, 60

Mankato (M) → Cary (C) → Tazewell (T) → Iowan (I) → Pre—Iowan (PI)

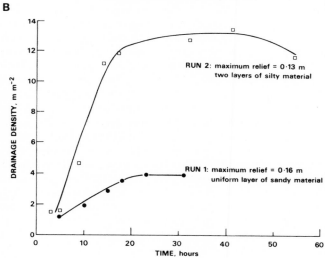

B

DRAINAGE DENSITY, m m^{-2} (y-axis): 0, 2, 4, 6, 8, 10, 12, 14

TIME, hours (x-axis): 0, 10, 20, 30, 40, 50, 60

RUN 2: maximum relief = 0·13 m
two layers of silty material

RUN 1: maximum relief = 0·16 m
uniform layer of sandy material

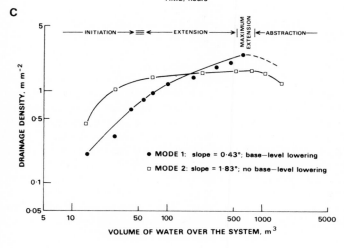

C

DRAINAGE DENSITY, m m^{-2} (y-axis): 0·05, 0·1, 0·5, 1, 5

VOLUME OF WATER OVER THE SYSTEM, m^3 (x-axis): 5, 10, 50, 100, 500, 1000, 5000

INITIATION → ≡ ← EXTENSION → MAXIMUM EXTENSION ← ABSTRACTION —

● MODE 1: slope = 0·43°; base—level lowering
□ MODE 2: slope = 1·83°; no base—level lowering

the network approached maximum extension when values tallied more closely with Shreve's (1966) prediction.

As bifurcation ratios attain more improbable values (Coffman *et al.*, 1972) or the length of an exterior link increases beyond a certain limit, a branching event becomes more likely. The stability of a given length of stream presumably varies with environmental conditions. The length properties of exterior links differed for the two modes of growth in Parker's experiments. In mode 1 the length distributions changed little during evolution, suggesting a degree of regularity where networks develop fully in extending headward. In mode 2, on the other hand, exterior link lengths tended to decrease with time. In particular, the S (source) links which were primarily responsible for the rapid headward growth (Figure 2.8A) became markedly shorter as tributaries developed after the initial phase. TS links, which appear to develop later (Abrahams, 1977) and be less subject to such changes, tended to have more stable length distributions.

The addition of exterior links is likely to be a discontinuous process conditioned partly by location in the network. The preferential development of TS rather than S links as relief increases (Abrahams, 1977) confirms that internal rather than headward growth dominates later phases (*elaboration*) when conditions for headward extension become more critical. Growth within networks cannot take place independently because of competition between adjacent streams for available drainage area (Figure 2.13). Along major tributaries which join master streams at relatively small angles, the more limited area on the acute side may favour stream development on the opposite (obtuse) side (Flint, 1980). The first link at the outlet of such a tributary is therefore more likely to be trans than cis (Figure 2.13B). The effect of this areal asymmetry may persist upstream to give further branching on the obtuse side but becomes less confining beyond the third junction. Also, competition on one side of a stream (Figure 2.13A) may induce successive tributaries to develop on opposite sides, leading to a preponderance of trans links in networks. Although the frequencies of cis and trans links do not always differ (Dunkerley, 1977), the main point is that the constraint of available area can influence tributary arrangements during evolution and produce non-random tendencies in network topology. Indeed any irregularity in basin shape or position of trunk streams may constrain tributary development (Flint, 1980).

Assuming that exterior links grow to a critical length and then become unstable, there should be an absence of short interior links. The fact that link length distributions of all link types at all stages of growth appear to have gamma densities in observed and simulated networks lends support to this argument (Dunkerley, 1977). However, the lengths of interior links are influenced by several factors and not only the branching probability of exterior links. Where growth occurs other than by bifurcation at the headward end, the addition of tributaries in later phases would tend to shorten interior links (Figure 2.11 (iii)), especially where links are bounded by tributaries on opposite sides. In so far as link length increases with the magnitude of the link joined downstream (Smart, 1981), such effects are more likely toward the margins of a network. Abrahams (1980) has found that longer interior links tend to be associated with smaller divide angles (defined as the angle between the two divides meeting at the downstream end of an interior link), presumably because of the more limited area available for tributary development above the junction. In addition, the length of an interior link is not necessarily constant through time because of junction migration (Schumm, 1956). The average spacing between bifurcations, which partly determines link length properties, is

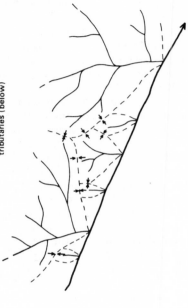

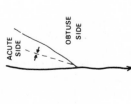

A. SAME-SIDE TRIBUTARIES

POSSIBLE CONSEQUENCES: (1) Dearth of short cis links during development

(2) Capture of proximal stream in post-formational adjustment

(3) A tributary sequence along one side of a main stream characterized by long distances between larger tributaries (below)

B. AT JUNCTIONS

ACUTE SIDE

OBTUSE SIDE

ACUTE SIDE

OBTUSE SIDE

C

C

T

T

POSSIBLE CONSEQUENCES: (1) Tendency for the first link along the tributary to be trans, especially if the junction angle is small. This areal constraint may persist but at a declining level until the third junction along the tributary (Flint, 1980)

(2) Where the main stream and tributary follow sub-parallel courses above the junction, thereby limiting the interfluvial area, the first link upstream is more likely to be trans in both streams, followed by cis links (below)

Fig 2.13 Competitive situations in network development. Double arrows indicate competition at inter-stream divides.

controlled by those environmental factors which determine the density of drainage but the problem remains of defining that average for given conditions. Analyses of existing networks can be used to generate hypotheses but decisions as to the relative merits of alternative hypotheses become rather arbitary when applied in an evolutionary context.

Maximum extension signifies the imposition of limits to further expansion, which are determined by hillslope stability relative to the tendency for channel cutting. Channel-head position reflects an approximate balance between erosive forces on the one hand and the counteracting effects of surface resistance and infilling from side slopes on the other. Nevertheless, intermittent divideward extensions can occur at times of heavy rainfall (Morgan, 1972). Longer-term migration is dependent on the magnitude–frequency characteristics of channel-extending events and the morphology of the headward zone, with slope concavity in profile and plan being of critical importance (Kirkby, 1978; Calver, 1978). Where subsurface flow is dominant, Kirkby (1978) has predicted that, while profile concavity is restricted to a narrow band close to existing streams, contour concavities (hollows) are relatively common in the stream head area which is therefore a zone susceptible to channel extension. Calver (1978) has demonstrated that in the long term concavity can extend upslope into areas of convex slope profile without climatic or associated changes, leading to the preferential lowering of divides along valley axes. Although divideward limits may not be strictly constant through time, the fluvial system can attain an approximately stable drainage density whose maximum value is controlled by environmental conditions (Figure 2.5).

Further changes to network form (*integration*) may take place through capture and abstraction of streams. Competition is a major element in many evolutionary models (e.g. Horton, 1945). Based on an allometric growth model,

$$A_d = A_o e^{Kt} \tag{2.7}$$

where K is the growth rate of a basin with area A_d and t is time, Faulkner (1974) postulated that gully systems will grow at a constant rate until an intermediate stage is reached when they become competitive and either expand ($K > 0$), entrench ($K = 0$) or contract ($K < 0$). Once a critical area is attained, estimated at $35,000 \text{ m}^2$ for gullies in southern Alberta, successful systems return to a constant rate of growth. Based on the relative dearth of short cis links in their networks, James and Krumbein (1969) proposed that post-formational readjustments result in the elimination of proximal and less successful tributaries through the process of lateral erosion or capture (Figure 2.13A). Although an earlier origin has been suggested for the initiation of cis–trans differences (Smart and Wallis, 1971), the reduction of inter-stream divides can through time lead to the diversion of surface waters (Miller, 1975). Capture is a discontinuous process operating over a range of basin scales, which again emphasizes the interdependence of adjacent streams in networks.

Rather than following maximum extension in strict temporal sequence as Glock (1931) assumed, *abstraction* coexists with extension but becomes the dominant process once drainage density has reached a maximum (Parker, 1977). Abstraction begins in the downstream part of a basin and proceeds headward as relative relief is reduced, which explains the tendency for higher drainage densities in headwater areas. The infilling of channels reflects in part a shift in the long-term balance between hillslope and channel processes in favour of the former (Abrahams, 1976). Contraction may be strongly related to geology and topography in so far as they influence the position of the water-table (Anderson and Burt, 1978). TS rather than S links may be preferentially abstracted as relief declines (Abrahams, 1977) but this need not always be so (Parker, 1977). The net effect of abstraction is a decrease in drainage density because of a loss of exterior and, by definition, interior links. Such losses tend to increase the mean length of both types of link (Abrahams, 1976; Parker, 1977). These results underline the changeable character of network properties during evolution.

No explicit time scale has been given for this general picture of network evolution. While small-scale studies over a limited time can suggest the types of process and change which might be involved, extrapolation to large-scale networks is dangerous. Real networks have evolved over millenia and been subject to complex variations in environmental and base-level conditions. Climate in particular has fluctuated considerably over the past 20,000 years (Figure 5.2). Even minor changes in precipitation characteristics can induce a marked network response in sensitive areas (Cooke and Reeves, 1976). Consequently analyses of existing networks, and especially those which use relative relief as a surrogate for time, have the problem of differentiating between time-related and environmentally-related change. Any broad view of network evolution has to be considered against this background of changing external as well as internal conditions.

Nor can network evolution be divorced from hillslope development since drainage patterns and hillslopes show a high degree of adjustment. The channel network provides a fundamental link between hillslopes and rivers in that it determines, largely through its density, the level of interaction between these two systems of water and sediment transfer. On the one hand, streams act as local base-levels for hillslopes, thereby influencing slope stability through their rate of incision and the extent of basal under-cutting. On the other hand, hillslopes influence stream behaviour in so far as they represent source areas for the water and debris to which streams must respond. A major motivation for studying network structure has been the belief that short-term hydrograph characteristics can be predicted from network variables. Larger peak discharges can be hypothesized where drainage density is higher and hillslope distances are shorter. However, although topologic and geometric variables have been variously used in predictive equations (e.g. Newson, 1978), the problem of separating individual effects remains and network properties tend to figure as subsidiary influences on hydrograph response. At some appropriate timespan longer than that considered for short-term stream behaviour, the hillslope and fluvial systems may attain a state of dynamic equilibrium in which they are mutually adjusted to provide a steady removal of debris, although the development of a flood-plain can significantly weaken slope–basal stream relationships.

Not only do hillslope–network links require investigation but also those between networks and channels. Traditionally they have been studied separately. Leopold and Miller (1956) sought to establish a suitable methodology based on Horton's laws and the discharge-area relation, arguing that stream order is related to discharge and thence to hydraulic variables such as width, depth and velocity. However, stream order provides little more than a crude index of discharge or position within the network hierarchy. Similar exercises which include more precise topologic variables (Onesti and Miller, 1978) or which relate specific channel parameters to planimetric properties (Flint, 1974, 1976) may produce better results, but the basic need remains for a fully integrated model which combines the related elements of network and channel morphology.

3
Fluvial processes

The morphology of natural river channels is determined by the interaction of the fluid flow with the erodible materials in the channel boundary. The underlying problem is to understand that interaction given that it involves the distinct processes of entrainment, transport and deposition of sediment. The basic mechanical principles are well established but a complete analytical solution is still a long way off, largely because natural streams represent the movement of a fluid–solid mixture in boundaries that are themselves deformable. Even the motion of a single particle cannot be described adequately and the problem becomes more complex when the boundary material is cohesive. To the extent that a larger flow implies a greater force, a discussion of streamflow fluctuation provides a background to the mechanical work performed by streams.

Streamflow fluctuation

Water reaching a stream channel may have followed any one of the routes identified previously (Figure 2.6A). Each route gives a different response to rainfall or snowmelt in terms of the volume of flow produced and the timing of contributions to the channel. Consequently the character of discharge variation is determined by the relative contribution from each source, which is in turn influenced by climatic factors and the physical characteristics of a basin.

For convenience total flow is traditionally subdivided into two parts: direct or storm runoff, and baseflow (Figure 3.1). The distinction is based on the time of arrival in the stream rather than the route followed, although the two are necessarily related. Direct runoff consists of surface flow (Horton or saturation overland flow) and a substantial part of the subsurface flow, while baseflow is mainly supplied from groundwater sources. Since water flowing at depth beneath the surface moves relatively slowly, its outflow into the stream lags behind the occurrence of rainfall and tends to be very regular. Groundwater flow thus maintains a steady basal flow throughout the year in more humid environments.

Most measurements of stream discharge are made at gauging stations, where discharge (Q) is defined by the continuity equation as the product of cross-sectional area (A = w.d) and mean velocity (v)

$$Q = A.v = w.d.v \tag{3.1}$$

Provided a long enough record exists, measurements can be manipulated to yield a flow-duration curve which shows the frequency with which discharges of different magnitude are equalled or exceeded. Thus a discharge of 7.6 m³ s⁻¹ is equalled or exceeded about 10 per cent of the time at the Bollin gauging station (Figure 3.2A). Mean annual discharge generally has a frequency of about 25 per cent and occupies approximately 40 per cent of the total capacity (bankfull cross-sectional area) of

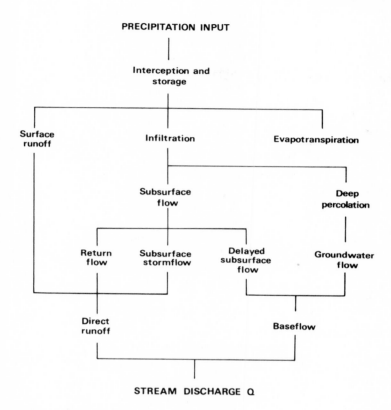

PRECIPITATION INPUT

Interception and storage

Surface runoff   Infiltration   Evapotranspiration

Subsurface flow   Deep percolation

Return flow   Subsurface stormflow   Delayed subsurface flow   Groundwater flow

Direct runoff   Baseflow

STREAM DISCHARGE Q

Fig 3.1 Schematic diagram of the runoff process.

the channel (Dunne and Leopold, 1978). If a sediment rating curve relating transport rate to discharge is also available, the flow-duration curve can be converted into a cumulative sediment transport curve to show the contributions made by various discharges to the total load transported.

Various procedures exist for computing flood frequencies. One of the simplest is based on discharge maxima in a series of years, from which the recurrence interval or return period (T in years) of flood events can be calculated:

$$T = (n + 1)/N \qquad (3.2)$$

where n is the number of years of record and N is the rank of a particular event. The resultant flood-frequency curve shows the average time interval within which a flood of given size will occur as an annual maximum (Figure 3.2B). Thus in any one year the probability of the annual maximum exceeding a flood with a recurrence interval of 10 years is $\frac{1}{10}$. The mean annual flood with a return period of about 2.33 years ($Q_{2.33}$) has occasionally been used in relating channel form variables to discharge (e.g. Ferguson, 1973). Another flow with assumed morphologic significance is bankfull discharge (Q_b), defined as that discharge at which the channel is completely full, with a reported recurrence interval of 1.5 years in the United States (Leopold *et al.*, 1964). These kinds of data are useful for regional analyses of flow characteristics and for classifying the river regimes of moderately sized basins. The

A

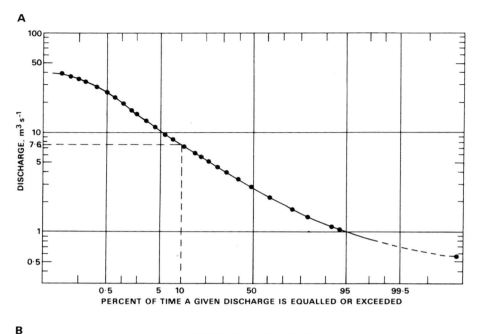

PERCENT OF TIME A GIVEN DISCHARGE IS EQUALLED OR EXCEEDED

B

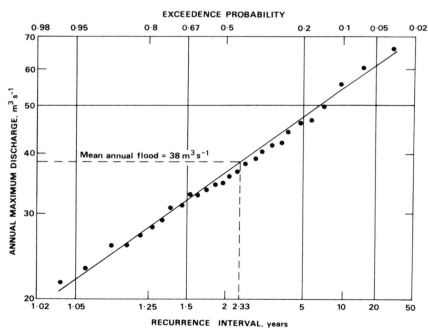

Fig 3.2   Flow-duration (A) and flood-frequency (B) curves for the River Bollin, Cheshire. The top scale of the flood-frequency curve gives the probability that the corresponding discharge is equalled or exceeded in any one year, while the bottom scale gives the average number of years in which the annual peak equals or exceeds the corresponding discharge.

regime of a river may have an important influence on channel form adjustment (Harvey, 1969; Stevens *et al.*, 1975).

Not surprisingly discharge is highly correlated with drainage area (Figure 1.2A). In many basins discharge of a given frequency (f) increases less rapidly than drainage area (A_d) to give an exponent n in

$$Q_f = cA_d^n \tag{3.3}$$

which is less than 1. The value of n is not independent of the frequency of flow considered or drainage area, tending to increase with more frequent flows and decrease with increasing basin size because of storage effects. Since drainage area is easier to measure, it has often been used as a surrogate for discharge in empirical studies of channel morphology.

The shape of the discharge hydrograph at any point depends on the way in which water is added to the stream and on the storage characteristics of the basin. Runoff supplied to a channel moves downstream as a wave of increasing and then decreasing discharge. The transmission of a flood wave is subject to two main effects which alter its character:

  (i) translation, in which the wave moves downstream without any significant change in shape; and

  (ii) reservoir action, whereby the time base of the wave is lengthened through temporary storage in the channel and valley bottom.

In upstream parts where drainage area is small and slopes are steep, runoff responds rapidly to rainfall and the translation effect is dominant. With increasing drainage area and lower basin slopes, temporary storage becomes more important to give a decreasing discharge per unit area and a smaller value of n in equation (3.3). Thus, the shape of the channel and network geometry influence stream behaviour in the short term. Attempts to evaluate the effects of the latter on hydrograph characteristics have suffered from the lack of an adequate theoretical basis which would help to separate individual influences.

Natural river flow is highly variable in time and space. Partly because of the increasing availability of flow records, discharge has become a primary independent variable in geomorphological approaches to the description and analysis of river channel form (Figures 1.2B, 4.7). The importance of discharge can perhaps be best appreciated from the dominant-discharge concept and the hydraulic geometry approach pioneered by Leopold and Maddock (1953). However, discharge is a summary variable which does not express directly the forces involved in shaping channels. To that extent the role of discharge has possibly been overemphasized. A closer link is needed between channel form adjustment and the mechanical work performed by streams, for which background theory is available.

Mechanics of flow

Water flowing in an open channel is subject to two principal forces: gravity, which acts in the downslope direction to move water at an acceleration of $g\sin\beta$ where g is gravitational acceleration ($= 9.81$ m s^{-2}) and β the angle of slope; and friction, which opposes downslope motion. The relationship between these two forces ultimately determines the ability of flowing water to erode and transport debris.

Open channel flow can be classified into various types based on four criteria (Table 3.1). Simple mathematical models can be constructed only if the flow is

Table 3.1   Types of flow in open channels

Type of flow	Criterion
Uniform/Non-uniform (varied)	Velocity is constant/variable with position
Steady/Unsteady	Velocity is constant/variable with time
Laminar/Turbulent	Reynolds' Number (R_e = $vR\rho/\mu$) is < 500/ > 2 500, with a transitional type when $500 \le R_e < 2\,500$
Tranquil/Rapid	Froude Number (F = $v/\sqrt{gd}$) is < 1/ > 1, with critical flow when F = 1

Symbols: v, velocity; R(= w.d/2d + w), hydraulic radius;
w, width; d, depth of flow; ρ, density;
μ, viscosity; g, gravity constant

assumed to be uniform and steady but flow in natural rivers is characteristically non-uniform and unsteady. The important distinction lies between laminar and turbulent flow.

Water is a viscous fluid that cannot resist stress, however small. In *laminar flow* each fluid element moves along a specific path with uniform velocity and no significant mixing between adjacent layers. A very thin layer of fluid in contact with the boundary is slowed so completely that it has no forward velocity but resistance to motion along internal boundaries is less than at the bed and each successive layer of fluid away from the bed can slip past the one below to give a velocity profile which is parabolic in shape (Figure 3.3A). In this way is shear stress,

$$\tau = \mu \, \frac{dv}{dy} \tag{3.4}$$

distributed throughout the flow, where dv/dy is the velocity gradient at depth y.

When velocity or depth exceeds a critical value, laminar flow becomes unstable and the parallel streamlines are destroyed. In *turbulent flow* the fluid elements follow irregular paths and mixing is no longer confined to molecular interactions between adjacent layers but involves the transfer of momentum by large-scale eddies. Accordingly the equation for shear stress must be modified to include an eddy viscosity (η) term,

$$\tau = (\mu + \eta) \, \frac{dv}{dy} \tag{3.5}$$

Because $\eta \gg \mu$ turbulent flow exerts larger shear stresses than does laminar flow for the same velocity gradient (dv/dy). Also, velocity tends to be more evenly distributed with depth because of the larger-scale mixing which slows faster bodies of water up the profile and speeds up slower ones below (Figure 3.3A).

The mathematical analysis of laminar flow is well advanced but this type of flow rarely occurs in nature except as a very thin layer (the laminar sublayer) close to the channel boundary or as shallow overland flow (Emmett, 1970). At first sight the equation for the velocity profile (3.5) appears to offer a means of evaluating in theory the shear stress acting at the bed (τ_o), an important force in grain movement. However, turbulent flow is so complex and irregular that a suitable physical model has yet to be formulated and analysis relies heavily on experimentation. Representative values of eddy viscosity and the velocity gradient at the bed are difficult if not impossible to obtain. Consequently the possibility of applying relatively simple models to the problem of fluid transport is denied.

Velocity and resistance

Velocity is a vector quantity having both magnitude and direction. It is one of the most sensitive and variable properties because of its dependence on most of the factors which characterize open channel flow.

Velocity varies in four dimensions (Figure 3.3):

(i) With distance from the stream bed – Aside from its variation with the type of flow (laminar or turbulent), the shape of the velocity profile is strongly influenced by the size of roughness elements on the stream bed and the depth of flow (d). If the former is expressed in terms of bed material size (D), the two variables can be incorporated in a single index, the relative roughness ratio d/D. For a given depth of flow, the larger the roughness elements the steeper is the velocity gradient toward the bed. Since stream beds generally contain a range of grain sizes, the problem is to select a grain diameter which best expresses this component of resistance.

(ii) Across the stream – Velocity increases toward the centre of a stream as the frictional effects of the channel banks decline but the degree of symmetry in cross-channel velocity can be highly variable, changing with the shape and alignment of the channel. In particular the velocity distribution in channel bends is characteristically asymmetric with the main current moving toward the outer bank. The close relationship between velocity distribution, cross-sectional shape and erosive tendency is emphasized by the basic distinction between wide, shallow channels where the velocity gradient is steepest and the boundary shear stress therefore greatest (equation 3.5) against the bed, and narrow, deep sections where the velocity gradient is steepest against the banks, producing a greater tendency for bank erosion (Figure 3.3B).

(iii) Downstream – In addition to local fluctuations, change in velocity at the longitudinal scale has been a major interest of geomorphologists concerned in particular with the development of an equilibrium stream profile. Despite a declining slope along most rivers, velocity tends to remain constant or increase slightly (Carlston, 1969) as the channel becomes hydraulically more efficient and resistance decreases in the downstream direction. Variations in the rate of change of velocity do occur both along and between rivers, since velocity is merely one variable that can be adjusted to accommodate the downstream increase in discharge.

(iv) With time – Over time periods measured in seconds point velocities may reach values of 60–70 per cent or more of the time average velocity because of the inherent variability of turbulent flow, thus making it difficult to define the initiation of particle motion in terms of velocity. At the larger time scale of days, weeks or months, velocity responds to fluctuations in discharge. The increase in depth with discharge tends to drown out roughness elements in the bed and thereby produce an increase in velocity. However, the effect is not uniform and the exponent m (the rate of change of velocity) in

$$v = kQ^m \tag{3.6}$$

can vary considerably from section to section (Park, 1977).

Velocity is thus a highly variable quantity in time and space. The character of that variation is important since velocity influences the processes of erosion, transportation and deposition (Figure 3.5D). Velocity is usually measured by current

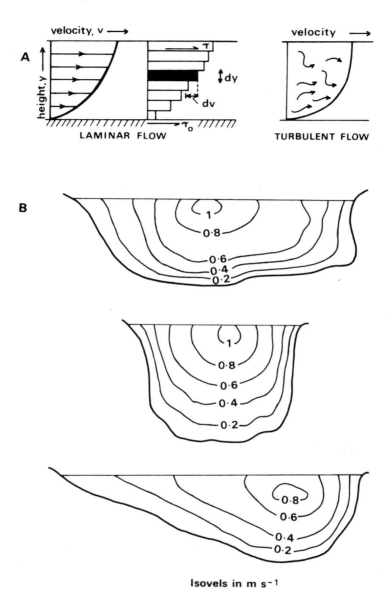

Isovels in m s⁻¹

Fig 3.3 Variations in streamflow velocity:
A. With depth – typical velocity profiles for laminar and turbulent flow are shown.
B. At natural channel cross-sections.
C. Downstream – relationship of velocity to discharge, Brandywine Creek (after Wolman, 1955).
D. With time – (i) velocity fluctuations at a point over a short time period, (ii) at-a-station changes in velocity with discharge measured over two years, River Bollin.

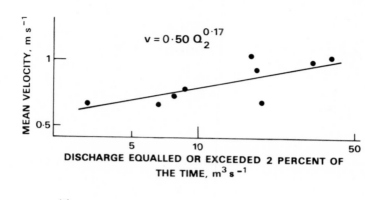

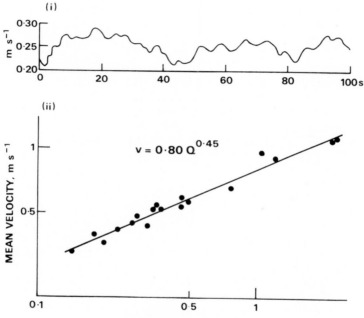

meter at selected points in the flow cross-section and expressed as an average value. However, mean velocity at a cross-section is not the most relevant measure for defining the initiation of erosion but it remains the most widely used parameter, partly because of measurement difficulties close to the stream bed.

Velocity is strongly related to *flow resistance*, one of the most important elements in the interaction between the fluid flow and the channel boundary. Several resistance equations have been developed (Table 3.2), of which the Darcy–Weisbach is recommended for its dimensional correctness and sounder theoretical basis (Task Force, 1963). All of the equations assume that resistance approximates that of a steady, uniform flow but in natural channels with erodible boundaries the resistance problem is much more involved.

Table 3.2   Flow resistance equations

Chezy equation (1769)	$v = C \sqrt{Rs}$	
Manning equation (1889)	$v = \dfrac{KR^{\frac{2}{3}} s^{\frac{1}{2}}}{n}$	where K = 1 (SI units),
		K = 1.49 (imperial units)
Darcy–Weisbach equation	$ff = \dfrac{8gRs}{v^2}$	

Symbols: C, n, ff are the respective resistance coefficients;
v, mean velocity; R, hydraulic radius;
s, slope of the energy gradient; g, gravity constant

Resistance in a flow carrying sediment comprises several components: grain or surface roughness, form roughness, channel irregularities, and suspended material in the flow. *Grain roughness* is a function of relative roughness (d/D or R/D) and in rough channels with fixed boundaries is often expressed in the form

$$\frac{1}{\sqrt{ff}} = c \log \left(a \, \frac{R}{D_x} \right) \tag{3.7}$$

where c and a are constants and D_x is a measure of the size of roughness elements (Figure 3.4A). While the roughness height of uniform material is simply taken as the grain diameter, the problem with non-uniform material where the effective size exceeds the mean is to choose a representative grain diameter. No one diameter has been generally accepted as suitable for this role, although D_{84} is commonly used as a roughness height. D_{90}, the diameter which equals or exceeds 90 per cent of the material, has been suggested for British gravel rivers (Charlton *et al.*, 1978). A single figure may not be representative of grain roughness at cross-sections where the grain size distribution varies markedly across the bed; nor are the effects of bank friction explicitly included in equation (3.7) (Hey, 1979).

Grain roughness is probably the dominant component of resistance where stream beds consist of gravel (2–64 mm) or cobbles (64–256 mm). Equation (3.7) predicts that, as depth increases with discharge at a cross-section, the effect of grain roughness is drowned out and flow resistance decreases, although possibly at a declining rate with higher discharge (Figure 3.4B). Consequently velocity may also tend to change more slowly at higher flows, producing non-linearities in hydraulic geometry (Richards, 1973, 1977; Figure 4.7B).

Form roughness stems from features developed in the bed material and often exceeds grain roughness in importance. It presents a particular problem in that, once grains are set in motion, the shape of the bed can be modified to give a variable form roughness dependent on flow conditions. In sand-bed streams where the bed is most readily moulded into different shapes, a sequence of bed forms correlated with increasing velocity has been defined (Figure 3.4C), each form offering different levels of resistance (Simons and Richardson, 1966). However, understanding of the relationship between bed form geometry and hydraulic roughness remains incomplete and attempts to predict the occurrence of different bed forms in terms of selected flow, fluid and sediment properties have met with only qualified success (Lawson and O'Neill, 1975). Nevertheless, changes in bed configuration represent an important self-regulating mechanism available to streams at the interface of the fluid flow with the erodible bed. As discharge and sediment load increase with the passage of a flood wave, a transition from ripples to dunes

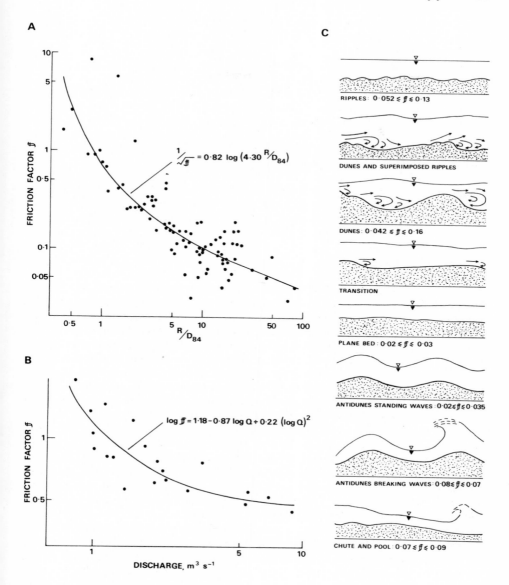

Fig 3.4 A. Relationship between friction factor and relative roughness (data of Leopold and Wolman, 1957; Limerinos, 1970; Charlton et al., 1978; Hey, 1979).
B. Relationship between friction factor and discharge at a sandy-bed cross-section, River Bollin.
C. The sequence of bed forms related to increasing flow intensity, with corresponding values of the Darcy-Weisbach friction factor in flume experiments (after Simons and Richardson, 1966).

may so increase the flow resistance as to offset the improved hydraulic efficiency associated with a larger depth, and thereby slow the rate of change of velocity (Richards, 1973, 1977).

Dunes are rarely found in gravel-bed streams where bed mobility is more restricted. There, the roughness due to bars becomes increasingly important at lower flows with grain roughness dominant at higher ones (Parker and Peterson, 1980). However, in streams with very coarse beds the form drag exerted by individual particles can be considerable. Bathurst (1978) distinguished two roughness regimes based on whether relative roughness (d/D) is less than or greater than about 3; form roughness is dominant in the first and grain roughness in the second. Resistance to flow under such conditions remains rather poorly defined.

The remaining components of resistance due to *channel irregularity* and *suspended matter* have received comparatively little attention. Natural channels are characteristically irregular and considerable energy loss can occur because of local bank irregularities and changes in channel alignment. Indeed channel curvature may introduce an energy loss greater than that associated with grain roughness (Leopold *et al.*, 1960).

Material suspended in the flow tends to damp down turbulence and thereby reduce resistance. For a fixed dune bed, Vanoni and Nomicos (1960) showed experimentally that suspended sediment concentrations of 3.64 and 8.08 kg m^{-3} decreased friction by 5 and 28 per cent respectively relative to clear-water flow. However, data are rather sparse and the general opinion is that suspended material has a relatively small influence on flow resistance (Raudkivi, 1976).

All treatments of the resistance problem tend to be oversimplified. Neither the flow, form nor roughness of individual cross-sections is uniform. Resistance is invariably computed from one of the equations (Table 3.2) using hydraulic data rather than by direct measurement, so that computed values include the effects of all types of roughness. Attempts to separate total resistance into its component parts (e.g. Einstein and Barbarossa, 1952) have achieved only qualified success. Much of the empirical work on resistance has been carried out under controlled conditions in laboratory flumes and it is not entirely clear how applicable are the results to the field situation where energy loss can be highly localized. In short, knowledge of the resistance mechanism remains far from complete, particularly in natural streams. And yet flow resistance is a primary concern through its link with sediment transport and the way in which a stream consumes its energy. Indeed Davies and Sutherland (1980) have proposed that stream behaviour and channel development are governed by a principle of maximum resistance in which boundary deformation continues until flow resistance has attained local maxima, a hypothesis that remains to be tested.

Stream energy
Energy is a quantity expressed as
force (mass x acceleration) x distance through which the force acts
and having the dimensions of $ML^2 T^{-2}$. In the fluvial system three types of energy are relevant – potential, kinetic and thermal (heat) – only the first two of which can perform mechanical work. That work takes various forms:
(i)   work done against viscous shear and turbulence (internal friction);
(ii) work done against friction at the channel boundary;
(iii) work done in eroding the channel boundary;
(iv) work done in transporting the sediment load.

Since energy must first be used to maintain the flow against internal and boundary friction ((i) and (ii)), a critical energy level must be reached before a stream can perform erosional and transportational work. The concept of an erosion threshold is fundamental and needs to be incorporated in sediment transport equations (e.g. Bagnold, 1977).

Water with a mass m entering a river at a height h above a given datum (baselevel or the next tributary junction) has a potential energy

$$PE = mgh \qquad (3.8)$$

As water moves downslope that potential or position energy is gradually converted into kinetic energy

$$KE = \tfrac{1}{2} mv^2 \qquad (3.9)$$

In conservative systems the principle of energy conservation

$$PE + KE = constant \qquad (3.10)$$

applies and relatively simple models can be developed for describing system behaviour. Between any two points, a loss in potential energy is matched by an equivalent gain in kinetic energy. However, rivers are non-conservative systems. Friction causes much of the available mechanical energy to be dissipated in the form of heat which can perform no mechanical work. Consequently the well established principles of mechanics cannot readily be used to solve flow problems without making far-reaching assumptions.

Nevertheless, it is relevant to ask how potential energy could be distributed in the fluvial system since different distributions may be associated with different network topologies (Knighton, 1980a). A precise formulation has yet to be achieved but could provide a basis for modelling stream behaviour and establishing network–channel links.

The importance of energy distribution has been recognized in the development of theoretical models concerned with the search for a general principle governing stream behaviour and channel form adjustment. Arguing by analogy between fluvial and thermodynamic systems, Langbein and Leopold (1964) postulated that the most probable or modal state represents a compromise between a uniform distribution of energy expenditure and minimum total work. Yang (1971a) argued that, in moving toward a state of dynamic equilibrium, a natural stream chooses its course in order to minimize the time rate of potential energy expenditure, manifest in the development of meanders (Yang, 1971b) and riffle–pool sequences (Yang, 1971c).

However, direct considerations of energy expenditure in natural streams are very few. Nor has the amount of work required to move from one channel state to another been directly calculated despite its relevance to models of channel form adjustment. There is a need to relate more closely the activity of fluvial processes and the forms they develop to the physical concept of work. Bagnold (1966, 1977) has led the way in relating sediment transport rate to available stream power, where the power (or rate of doing work) per unit length of stream is

$$\Omega = \gamma Q s \qquad (3.11)$$

where γ ($= \rho g$) is the specific weight of water, Q is discharge and s is slope. Power so defined is the rate of potential energy expenditure per unit length of channel.

Thresholds of erosion

The movement of particles depends on their physical properties, notably size, shape and density. Grain size has a direct influence on mobility and a typical classification is shown in Table 3.3. A base distinction exists between non-cohesive and cohesive (including solid rock) materials. In cohesive sediments, which generally consist of particles in the silt–clay range, resistance to erosion depends more on the strength of cohesive bonds between particles than on the physical properties of particles themselves, making the erosion problem much more complex.

Table 3.3   Grain-size classification

| Class name | Size range | |
	mm	phi units
Boulders	$\geqslant 256$	$\leqslant -9$
Cobbles	64–256	-6 to -9
Gravel	2–64	-1 to -6
Sand	0.064–2	4 to -1
Silt	0.004–0.064	8 to 4
Clay	$\leqslant 0.004$	$\geqslant 8$

Bed erosion

The characteristics of stream bed material depend on the initial supply conditions and the subsequent action of such processes as sorting and abrasion. Most stream beds consist of cohesionless grains. As the flow over a surface of loose grains gradually increases, a condition is reached when the forces tending to move a particle are in balance with those resisting motion. The problem is to define this threshold state. Three related approaches have been used, initial movement being specified in terms of either a critical shear stress (τ_{cr}), a critical velocity (v_{cr}) or the lift force.

A reasonable estimate of the boundary shear stress (τ_o) exerted by the fluid on the bed can be obtained from

$$\tau_o = \gamma R s \qquad (3.12)$$

where γ is the specific weight of water, R is hydraulic radius and s is slope. Derived from a consideration of the balance of forces in a steady non-accelerating flow (see Leopold *et al.*, 1964, p. 156–7), this quantity is a spatial average which does not necessarily provide a good estimate of bed shear at a point. Recognizing this limitation, the critical shear stress (τ_{cr}) can then be defined by equating the two sets of forces involved:

applied forces – fluid forces and the downslope component of the particle's submerged weight

resisting forces – the component of the particle's submerged weight acting normal to the bed and any constraining forces due to neighbouring grains.

For spherical grains of diameter D on a flat bed, equating the moments of forces acting about a downstream contact point (A in Figure 3.5A) gives

$$\tau_{cr} = \eta\, g\, (\rho_s - \rho)\; \frac{\pi}{6}\; D \tan \phi \qquad\qquad (3.13a)$$

This elementary deterministic model predicts that the shear stress needed to initiate movement increases with particle size, grain shape and the degree of packing (η) also being influential.

Equation (3.13a) has been expressed in many ways, most notably by Shields (1936) who recognized that critical shear stress depends not only on particle size but also on bed roughness. The resultant plot (Figure 3.5C) relates a dimensionless critical shear stress (θ) to a particle Reynolds number ($\propto D/\delta_o$, where δ_o is the thickness of the laminar sublayer) which defines the bed roughness condition. The plot not only separates zones of no motion and motion but reveals that the relationship between threshold stress and particle size is not as straightforward as a simple resolution of forces would at first suggest. On hydraulically rough beds (the common condition in natural streams), θ rapidly attains a constant value of 0.06 to give thereafter

$$\tau_{cr} = 0.06\, g\, (\rho_s - \rho)\, D \qquad\qquad (3.13b)$$

However, at lower stresses the thickness of the laminar sublayer increases and, for particles less than about 0.7 mm, the relationship becomes inverse so that the threshold stress needed for entrainment must increase as particles get smaller. Particles in that size range are submerged in the laminar sublayer and therefore not subject to the greater stresses in the overlying turbulent layer.

An alternative approach defines the critical condition in terms of velocity rather than shear stress, but the same basic trends are revealed (Figure 3.5D). Hjulström's empirical curve predicts that medium sand (0.25–0.5 mm) is the most easily eroded fraction, higher velocities being required to set both coarser and finer grains in motion. Mean velocity is not the most relevant parameter in this context but the problem is to define and measure a bottom velocity representative of the threshold condition.

These approaches have important limitations. They fail to cope adequately with the variability of either flow conditions near the stream bed (Figure 3.3D(i)) or bed material characteristics. Short-term pulsations in the flow can give rise to instantaneous stresses of at least three times the average, so that particles may be entrained at stresses much lower than predicted. Sediment entrainment is a function not only of the average shear stress on the bed but also of the intensity of turbulence above it, which can exert an impulse force on grains. Since eddy size and hence the energy available for moving grains are related to the size of the system, the size of the channel can influence the entrainment process (Raudkivi, 1976). Natural bed material is neither spherical nor of uniform size. Larger particles may shield smaller ones from direct impact so that the latter fail to move until higher stresses are attained. Characteristics other than size influence particle mobility, notably the degree of grain exposure (Fenton and Abbott, 1977), bed relief and sediment fabric (Laronne and Carson, 1976). Thus for a given grain size > 8 mm, the Shields' threshold criterion may vary by nearly an order of magnitude depending on whether the bed is loosely or tightly packed (Church, 1978). Consequently empirical and theoretical attempts to define the threshold for grain entrainment

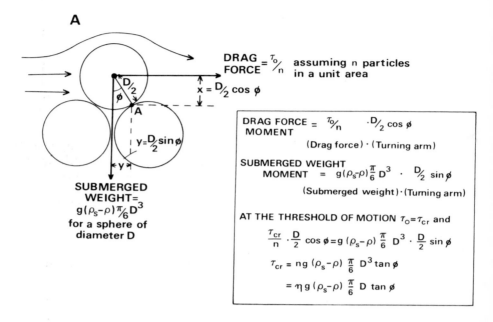

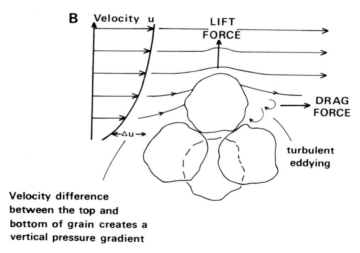

Fig 3.5   A. The critical shear stress (τ_{cr}) defined for a grain resting on a horizontal bed, where ρ is fluid density, ρ_s sediment density, g gravity constant, D grain diameter, and $\eta = nD^2$ a measure of grain packing.
B. Lift and drag forces acting on a submerged particle.
C. The Shields' entrainment function.
D. Erosion and deposition criteria defined in terms of threshold velocities (after Hjulström, 1935).

can at best predict an average state. The inherent variability of natural flow and bed material conditions gives a statistical character to the problem and this has led to the development of probabilistic models of particle motion (e.g. Hung and Shen, 1976).

C

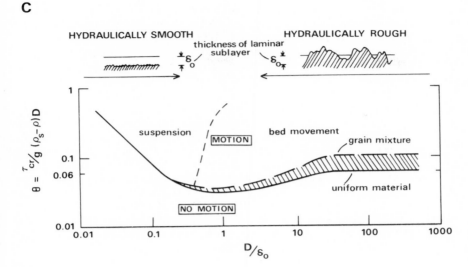

D

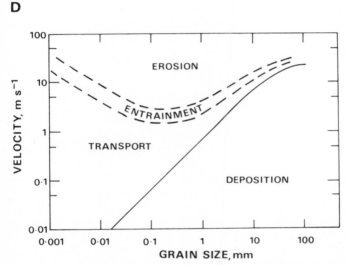

In addition to the drag forces acting roughly parallel to the bed, there is a force (the *lift force*) normal to the bed which may be able to entrain particles irrespective of the magnitude of the drag forces (Figure 3.5B). This force arises in at least two ways:

   (i) the difference in flow velocity between the top and bottom of a grain sets up a pressure gradient which tends to move the particle vertically upwards;

   (ii) turbulent eddying may produce local velocity components which act directly upwards close to the bed.

The lift force decreases rapidly in magnitude away from the bed as the velocity and pressure gradients become less. There is no generally accepted theory applicable to the lift force and little experimental data available for its estimation. The relative contributions of the lift and drag components are also difficult to determine because of their interrelationship but the lift force may be a crucial mechanism for initiating grain movement, at least in sand-bed streams. The combination of lift and drag provides one explanation for the commonly-observed process of saltation (Figure 3.8A) in which particles of sand size move along the bed in a series of hops.

Much of the work on the threshold condition has been carried out in laboratory flumes with relatively fine material. Helley's (1969) work on the movement of large particles (> 150 mm in diameter) is one of the few field studies and, perhaps surprisingly in view of previous comments, the bed velocities required for entrainment agreed quite closely with those predicted by a deterministic model which included the effects of particle size, shape and orientation. Threshold velocities existed for at least 5 per cent of the time in this coarse bed stream and, although the sample was small, the results support Hjulström's curve (Figure 3.5D). However, it appears that in general both the Hjulström and Shields curves require adjustment when predicting the erosion threshold in natural streams with bed material coarser than sand (Novak, 1973; Baker and Ritter, 1975).

The erosion of cohesive sediment presents a different and more complex problem. The forces resisting motion include not only those associated with particle weight but also the electro-chemical forces which bind the material. Such forces cannot be uniquely expressed as a function of particle size or similar variables. The limited data available suggest that there is no critical shear stress for the erosion of cohesive material in the sense that one exists for cohesionless grains. Erosion takes place in aggregates rather than particle by particle.

Similar remarks apply to bedrock channels as regards the erosion threshold. Several processes have been identified in general terms:

(i) corrosion, or the chemical action of water;
(ii) corrasion, or the mechanical (hydraulic and abrasive) action of water which can be effective when the flow is armed with particles, leading to surface abrasion and pothole development;
(iii) cavitation, a process associated with the effects of shock waves generated through the collapse of vapour pockets in a flow with marked pressure changes.

Cavitation can cause severe erosion (Brown, 1963) but is of limited occurrence because of the high velocities required. These processes remain little more than descriptive terms. However, Foley (1980) has attempted to model abrasion using engineering sandblast theory, distinguishing between low- and high-angle impacts which respectively cause abrasion through cutting and fracturing.

The concept of a critical shear stress or velocity necessary for erosion is appealing, at least in theory. Theory and observation indicate that material in the size range 0.25–1 mm is the most susceptible to movement and, other conditions being equal, will be the first to be entrained. However, the many factors involved are difficult to accommodate theoretically. The heterogeneity of natural stream beds and the variability of flow conditions in the bed region limit the applicability of deterministic models and results obtained from laboratory studies, but field tests remain very difficult to make. A further dimension to the problem is provided by the cohesivity of some stream beds where threshold criteria appear to be less relevant.

Bank erosion

The bank material of natural channels is even more variable than the bed material but does tend to become finer and more uniform downstream with combinations of sands, silts and clays dominant, especially where the flood-plain is well developed. Most channel banks possess some degree of cohesion because of finer material, so that the analysis of bank erosion is not a simple extension of the non-cohesive bed case with a downslope gravity component added. A further complication is provided by the effects of vegetation whose root system can reinforce bank material and thereby increase resistance to erosion. Smith (1976) found that bank sediment with a root volume of 16–18 per cent and a 5 cm root mat afforded 20,000 times more protection from erosion than comparable sediment without vegetation. This effect may be more limited in large rivers with high banks where root systems do not protect lower bank areas.

Bank erosion is one of the principal means of sediment supply to streams. Klimek (1974) estimated that about 2000 m^3 of sediment were supplied each year from a 100 m section of the River Wisloka in Poland. Adjustments to the form and course of river channels and the development of flood-plains depend on bank erosion, which also threatens man-made structures and destroys valuable agricultural land. However, despite its overall importance, relatively few field or laboratory studies have been undertaken.

The main processes involved can be grouped under four headings: direct action of water, slumping, rotational slipping and frost action. The shearing of bank material by *hydraulic action* at high discharges is a most effective process, especially on non-cohesive banks and against bank projections. Large-scale eddying induced by bank irregularities can enlarge existing embayments and increase the amplitude of projections which become more susceptible to subsequent attack. In cohesive banks the exploitation of pre-existing cracks can lead to the removal of joint-bounded blocks which may accumulate at the bank foot and afford temporary protection. These several effects underline the importance of shear stress distribution and local turbulence characteristics in erosion by hydraulic action. In many instances it is the dominant process (Knighton, 1973; Hooke, 1979) and Simons *et al.* (1979) estimated that flow forces were at least 6 times more effective than any other process in their study of the Connecticut River. Those forces can be subdivided into:

   (i) those which act near the surface of the flow, such as water waves induced by wind or passing boats; and

   (ii) those which act near the base of banks and lead to undercutting.

Significantly, velocity and boundary shear stress appear to be at a maximum in the lower bank region even when the flow is near bankfull (Bathurst *et al.*, 1979; Simons *et al.*, 1979).

The collapse or *slumping* of large blocks of material is more closely related to soil moisture than to flow conditions, although oscillations in river stage can influence the degree of bank wetting. Cohesive banks are particularly susceptible to seepage forces and piping mechanisms that may so lower the internal resistance of the material as to induce failure. Wet bank slumping sometimes takes place after the main flow has receded when the bank is thoroughly wetted (Twidale, 1964) and can be a major contributor to bank retreat (e.g. Klimek, 1974). The process is influenced by bank stratigraphy, for example where cohesive materials overlie non-cohesive ones, a relatively common condition in rivers flowing through alluvial deposits. In the River Wisloka, water percolating through the basal region loosens the sandy-gravel and liquifies the lower parts of the overlying silty-clay, thereby inducing slumping over the entire bank face (Klimek, 1974). Analysing the stability of composite banks, Thorne and Tovey (1981) argued that, whereas the lower bank is eroded by hydraulic action, the upper bank is less affected by flow forces but fails

Table 3.4   Factors influencing bank erosion

Factor	Relevant characteristics
Flow properties	Magnitude, frequency and variability of stream discharge Magnitude and distribution of velocity and shear stress Degree of turbulence
Bank material composition	Size, gradation, cohesivity and stratification of bank sediments
Climate	Amount, intensity and duration of rainfall Frequency and duration of freezing
Subsurface conditions	Seepage forces, piping Soil moisture levels
Channel geometry	Width and depth of channel Height and angle of bank Bend curvature
Biology	Type, density and root system of vegetation Animal burrows
Man-induced factors	Urbanization, land drainage, reservoir development, boating

because of undercutting which produces different types of cantilever action in the cohesive material. The slumped blocks may break on impact or remain intact to await removal by subsequent flows, in the meanwhile protecting the underlying gravel from further erosion. This pseudo-cyclic process (undercutting, upper bank failure, and removal of failed blocks) has been observed elsewhere (Stanley *et al.*, 1966) and emphasizes the interrelationship of different processes.

The remaining processes are probably less significant. *Rotational slipping* produces multi-stepped bank profiles through repeated failure along surfaces roughly concave to the slope, a process whose effectiveness is again strongly related to moisture levels in the bank. Where and when climatic conditions allow, the growth of ice crystals or ice wedges may affect bank retreat (Walker and Arnborg, 1966). However, *frost action* is more important as a preconditioning than an erosive process in that it widens pre-existing cracks and disaggregates surface material to leave the bank more susceptible to subsequent attack. This effect again emphasizes that, although hydraulic action and slumping may be dominant, the several processes are not mutually exclusive but frequently act in combination.

The amount and periodicity of river bank erosion are highly variable because of the large number of factors involved (Table 3.4), and average rates (Table 3.5) tend to mask that variability. Little erosion is likely to occur without high discharges but similar flows need not be equally effective because they may not be attacking against a bank in the same condition. Consequently correlations between flow volume and amount of erosion tend to be rather weak. Wolman (1959) found that a large summer flood attacking dry banks produced little erosion but that lesser winter flows acting against thoroughly wetted banks caused considerable bank retreat. Bank wetting and frost action are important preconditioning processes which reduce the strength of bank material and make it more susceptible to erosion. Therefore, multi-peaked flows may be more effective than single flows of comparable or greater magnitude because of the increased incidence of bank wetting (Knighton, 1973). The main point is that the amount of bank erosion is not solely a function of discharge magnitude or even flow conditions, so that a threshold flow cannot reasonably be defined, although at some of her sites Hooke

Table 3.5 Measured rates of bank erosion

River and location	Drainage area, km²	Average rate of bank retreat, m yr⁻¹	Period of measurement	Source
Axe, Devon	288	0.15–0.46	1974–76	Hooke (1980)
Bollin-Dean, Cheshire	12–120	0–0.9	1967–69	Knighton (1973)
Cound, Shropshire	100	0.64	1972–74	Hughes (1977)
Crawfordsburn, N. Ireland	3	0–0.05	1966–68	Hill (1973)
Exe, Devon	620	0.62–1.18	1974–76	Hooke (1980)
Mississippi, Louisiana	–	4.5	1945–62	Stanley *et al.* (1966)
Torrens, S. Australia	78	0.58	1960–63	Twidale (1964)
Watts Branch, Maryland	10	0.5–0.6	1955–57	Wolman (1959)
Wisloka, Poland	–	8–11	1970–72	Klimek (1974)

(1979) found little or no erosion at discharges with a frequency greater than 5 per cent.

Sites experiencing the same flow and meteorological conditions can show considerable variation in the amount of bank erosion (Knighton, 1973; Hooke, 1979). Flow volume and bank moisture levels may provide the conditions necessary for erosion but by themselves they are not sufficient. The local site characteristics which appear to have a major influence on the spatial distribution of erosion are bank material composition, the degree of flow asymmetry and channel geometry. Coarser, sandy materials are more liable to erosion than are those with a high silt–clay content. In composite banks, stability is governed by the strength of the weakest material since its removal will eventually produce failure in the rest of the bank (Krinitzsky, 1965; Thorne and Tovey, 1981). Flow asymmetry was necessary for erosion along the Bollin-Dean as only then were velocities sufficiently high close to the bank face (Knighton, 1973). Not only may the distribution of velocity or shear stress change with discharge but also between reaches of different curvature to give locally varied rates of bank retreat (Hickin and Nanson, 1975).

With so many factors involved (Table 3.4), it is hardly surprising that their individual effects cannot be separated or an erosional threshold defined. Field work has identified some of the relevant variables but measurement periods tend to be rather short (Table 3.5). The need remains for detailed research into the mechanics of bank erosion with increasing emphasis on the distribution of forces against river banks and the changeable quality of bank resistance.

Sediment transport

The transport of material from the land surface to the sea can be rationalized in terms of three process regimes (Statham, 1977):
   (i) a *weathering regime* which includes those processes involved in the physical and chemical breakdown of rocks;

(ii) a *slope regime* in which the products of weathering are moved down the gravity gradient in mass movements and by slope wash processes; and

(iii) a set of *fluid-transfer regimes*, water, air and ice, of which the first is by far the most important.

All material entering a river system must cross the boundary between the slope and fluvial regimes provided by the channel banks and the channel head.

An important distinction is between supply-limited and capacity-limited transport. Much of the material supplied to streams is so fine that, provided it can be carried in suspension, almost any flow will transport it. Although an upper limit must exist in theory, the transport of this fine fraction is largely controlled by the rate of supply rather than the transport capacity of the flow. In contrast, the transport of coarser material (> 0.064 mm) is capacity-limited and therefore intermittent, otherwise channels would show a greater tendency to have beds of solid rock rather than cohesionless grains. The intermittency of bed-material transport and the possibility of temporary deposition mean that the residence times of material moving through even small drainage basins are likely to be large, of the order of 100s or 1000s of years.

Figure 3.6 illustrates the main elements in the movement of material through the fluvial system. The load carried by natural streams can be separated into three components:

(i) the *dissolved load*, consisting of material transported in solution;

(ii) the *wash load*, comprising particles finer (< 0.064 mm) than those usually found in the bed and moving readily in suspension; and

(iii) the *bed-material load*, including all sizes of material (> 0.064 mm) found in appreciable quantity in the bed.

The bed-material load may be transported as *bed load*, when particles move by rolling, sliding or saltation at velocities less than those of the surrounding flow, or as *suspended load*, when particles are transported and maintained in the main body of the flow by turbulent mixing processes (Figure 3.8A). This distinction is somewhat arbitrary because there is an interchange of particles between the two modes of transport. Details of the exchange process are not well understood. The bed-material load is the principal concern because of its influence on the adjustment and development of river channel form.

The dissolved load

Solutes in rivers are derived from rock and soil weathering, from the atmosphere, and from the effects of man's activity, the last of which is becoming increasingly important as the discharge of industrial effluent and the use of agricultural fertilizers increase. Much of the dissolved load is supplied by some form of subsurface flow because contact times between water and soluble materials are longer. Consequently basins where subsurface flow is a major contributor to stream discharge and where materials are readily soluble tend to have higher dissolved loads.

Unlike suspended sediment, solute concentration (C) declines with increasing discharge (Q) at a cross-section to give an n value in

$$C = kQ^n \qquad (3.14)$$

which is usually less than 0. This reflects a dilution effect as the contribution from near-surface flows with lower solute levels increases at higher discharges. However, since n usually exceeds $- 1$, the total dissolved load ($Q_{diss} = C.Q$) continues to increase with discharge. Indeed the dilution effect may become progressively less

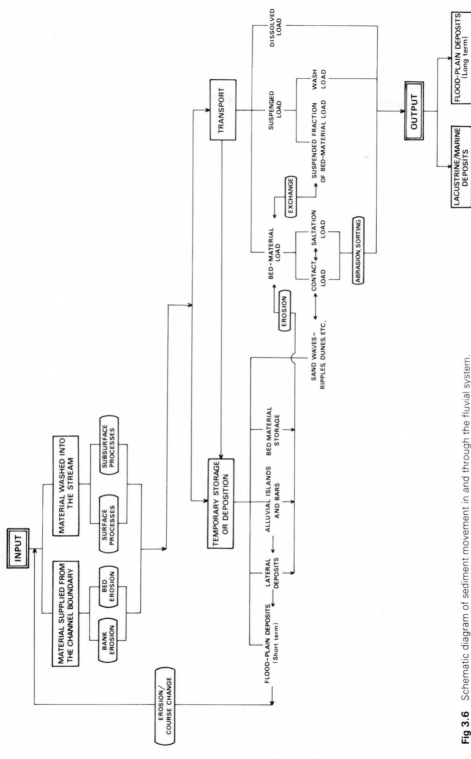

Fig 3.6 Schematic diagram of sediment movement in and through the fluvial system.

Table 3.6   Sediment and dissolved loads of major rivers

River	Mean discharge (10^3 m^3 s^{-1})	Drainage area (10^3 km^2)	Mean sediment load (10^6 tonnes yr^{-1})	Mean dissolved load (10^6 tonnes yr^{-1})	Per cent of total load carried in solution
Africa					
Congo	39.2	4 000	53	47	48
Zambezi	7.1	1 340	100	15	13
Niger	6.1	1 125	68	10	13
Orange	2.9	1 000	150	12	7
Nile	2.8	3 000	111	17	14
Asia					
Brahmaputra	19.3	580	795	75	12
Mekong	18.3	795	346	59	14
Yenisei	17.2	2 600	13	73	83
Lena	16.3	2 430	15	85	83
Ganges	11.6	975	524	76	13
Huang Ho	1.5	752	1 600	–	–
Australia					
Murray-Darling	0.7	1 070	32	9	22
Europe					
Volga	8.4	1 350	26	77	77
Danube	6.4	805	68	60	48
Dnieper	1.6	500	1	11	91
North America					
Mississippi	18.4	3 267	350	131	27
St Lawrence	10.7	1 025	5	54	91
Mackenzie	9.6	1 800	117	70	37
Columbia	8.0	670	29	35	56
Yukon	6.2	770	79	34	30
South America					
Amazon	175	6 300	498	290	37
Orinoco	30	950	86	50	37
Parana	18	2 800	112	56	33
Magdalena	7.5	240	240	28	10

Sources: Holeman (1968), Inman and Nordstrom (1971), Meybeck (1976)

significant at very high discharges when the concentration is dominated by the near-constant solute content of the storm runoff component (Gregory and Walling, 1973). The variation of solute concentration both within and between storms tends to produce a wide scatter of points on concentration–discharge graphs.

A large part of the dissolved load is carried by relatively frequent flows. In the Mississippi about 90 per cent is transported by flow events occurring monthly (Sedimentation Seminar, 1977). Dissolved load makes a significant contribution to the total load, implying that solution is an effective denudational process, although measured values may include the effects of man's activities. Accurate data are rather sparse but it has been estimated that about 41 tonnes km^{-2} of dissolved material are carried each year to the oceans (Meybeck, 1976), comprising roughly 38 per cent of the total load of the world's major rivers. However, the proportion of the total load carried in solution and the actual amounts vary considerably (Table 3.6). Also, non-denudational sources such as rainfall inputs and pollution can significantly affect the figures. Those factors which influence the relative contributions of surface and subsurface flow to total stream discharge largely control the sediment–solute balance. Dissolved load is less dependent than sediment load on the quantity of flow and, since it has little effect on stream behaviour relative to channel form adjustment, it is largely ignored in the subsequent discussion.

The wash load
The wash load moves in suspension at approximately the same speed as the flow and only settles out where flow velocities are much reduced. Some very large volumes are involved (Table 3.6), particularly along the Huang Ho where most of the silty load is derived from erosion of the loess lands in central China (Stoddart, 1978).

The rate of wash load transport is principally determined by its rate of supply from the drainage basin rather than the transport capacity of the stream. Most of the material is supplied from the erosion of cohesive river banks, with fine sediment being sheared off by the flow or thrown into suspension after bank collapse, and from surface and subsurface erosion in the catchment area by such processes as rainsplash and surface wash. While bank erosion is partly dependent on flow characteristics, the second source is independent of conditions in the stream.

The relative contributions from channel and non-channel sources vary with basin size. Although difficult, their assessment can be approached by: direct measurement of source area erosion, which is feasible only in small basins; comparison of measured sediment loads with yields estimated from a soil loss equation and a delivery term; or measurement of selected suspended sediment properties. Grimshaw and Lewin (1980) distinguished channel from non-channel sources on the basis of sediment colour in the River Ystwyth of central Wales. In this small basin (A_d = 170 km^2), just over half of the suspended sediment came from the channel itself but the proportion of non-channel sediment increased at very high discharges. In general, the upper parts of catchments which have steeper and shorter slopes tend to supply sediment from non-channel sources. Further downstream where slopes are longer and less steep, the potential for temporary storage of eroded material increases and the contribution from channel erosion becomes relatively more important. At least 65 per cent of the material carried by the lower Waimakariri River in New Zealand is supplied locally from the bed and banks of the channel (Griffiths, 1979).

Being supply- rather than capacity-limited, the rate of wash load transport is not directly a function of stream discharge. Because of the highly variable character of sediment supply, plots of wash load concentration against discharge often show a very wide scatter of points and no well-defined relation (e.g. Colby, 1963). Part of that scatter may be the result of hysteresis in which larger loads occur on the rising rather than the falling stage at the same discharge. Sediment yields from the catchment are usually highest soon after the start of rainfall when sediment is more readily available for transport, so that most of the sediment supplied by surface wash reaches the stream when discharge is rising. However, hysteresis relationships are not independent of basin size. In small basins the sediment peak tends to precede the discharge peak but may lag behind the discharge peak by a considerable time in large basins where upstream sources continue to supply the bulk of the load.

Despite the attendant problems, sediment-rating curves relating suspended sediment load (Q_{susp}) to discharge (Q) in the form

$$Q_{susp} = rQ^j \tag{3.15}$$

are often used in analysing sediment transport characteristics (Figure 3.9A). Values of j typically lie in the range of 1.5 to 3. However, a clear distinction is not always drawn between the wash load and the suspended fraction of the bed-material load in constructing such curves. The first is largely controlled by the availability of sediment in the catchment, while the latter is strongly related to flow conditions. Consequently estimates of catchment erosion from such equations are liable to error unless account is taken of different supply sources and basin size.

Sediment yield, or the total sediment outflow from a watershed, includes wash load as the dominant component. It is controlled by four main groups of factors: precipitation and runoff characteristics; soil resistance; basin topography; and the nature of the plant cover. Its overall variation with climate is commonly defined by curves which relate sediment yield to mean annual precipitation or mean annual runoff (Figure 3.7). The Langbein and Schumm (1958) curve based on group-averaged data reaches a peak at an effective precipitation of about 300 mm, trailing off at lower values because of lower runoff totals and at higher values because an increasingly abundant vegetation cover affords better protection against erosion.

The broad pattern indicated by that curve needs qualifying in several respects. Dendy and Bolton (1976), again using United States data, produced a curve in which the sediment yield peak occurs at a slightly higher precipitation of 450–500 mm. However, tropical areas are not represented in either data set and it seems that sediment yield may again begin to increase for precipitation amounts over 1100 mm, reaching a second maximum at 1200–1500 mm in humid climates with highly seasonal rainfall (Figure 3.7B and C). Indeed sediment yield may be more a function of the seasonal variability of precipitation than of the annual amount (Wilson, 1973). A comprehensive reanalysis of available data by Walling and Kleo (1979) has revealed not only considerable variability in annual sediment yields but also a more complex average relationship with three peaks (Figure 3.7D). The first could reflect the simple relationship proposed by Langbein and Schumm (1958), while the remaining two may indicate the effects of seasonal precipitation regimes associated with areas of high rainfall mediterranean climate (1250–1350 mm) and tropical monsoon conditions (> 2500 mm). In effect the Langbein and Schumm curve incorporates the interacting factors of precipitation/runoff magnitude and vegetation cover, but the former may be more significant than those authors indicated since the increasing vegetation cover in more humid areas

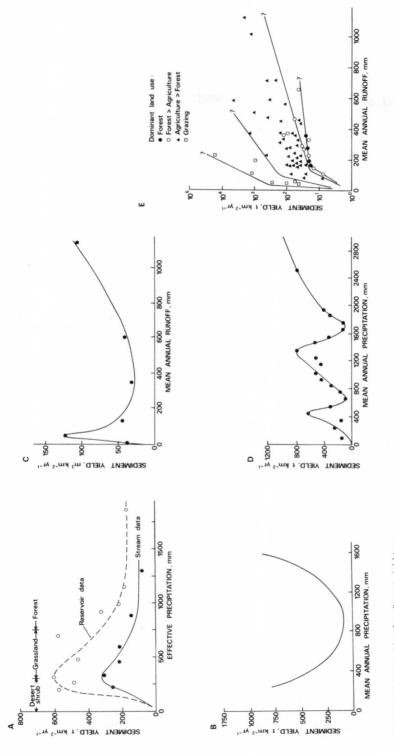

Fig 3.7 Relationship of sediment yield to:

A. Effective precipitation (after Langbein and Schumm, 1958);
B. Mean annual precipitation (after Fournier, 1960);
C. Mean annual runoff (after Douglas, 1967);
D. Mean annual precipitation (after Walling and Kleo, 1979);
E. Mean annual runoff for four land use types (after Dunne, 1979).

does not reduce erosion to the extent originally supposed. Also, it should be recognized that the influence of relief (which may be predominant according to some authors) and the widespread impact of human activity serve to distort any global pattern and especially one which is based on precipitation magnitude alone.

Although implicitly included in Langbein and Schumm's curve, the effect of vegetation or ground cover cannot be expressed by any single relationship between sediment yield and a simple climatic index in view of land use variability even within relatively uniform climatic areas. A 9-year study in small Colorado catchments showed that the conversion from sagebrush to grass cover reduced sediment yield by 80 per cent without significantly affecting annual runoff totals (Lusby, 1979). Dunne (1979) has analysed the sediment yields of 61 Kenyan catchments classified according to the land-use types:

    (i) Forest (F),
    (ii) Forest cover > 50 per cent of the basin with the remainder under cultivation (FA),
    (iii) Agricultural land > 50 per cent with the remainder forested (AF),
    (iv) Grazing land (G).

Within each type sediment yield increases with mean annual runoff (related to mean annual precipitation by $Q = 0.000033P_m^{2.27}$), but major differences exist in the rate of that increase (Figure 3.7E). As the average cover density decreases from (i) to (iv), sediment loss becomes increasingly sensitive to runoff and there appears to be a progressive increase in the rate at which sediment yield varies. Dunne concluded that sediment yield, which varied considerably from 8–20,000 t km^{-2} yr^{-1}, was largely controlled by land use, with climatic and topographic factors having subsidiary effects. These results emphasize the potential variability of sediment yield even within relatively small areas and the need for caution when using global syntheses, particularly in palaeohydrologic reconstructions (chapter 5).

Although suspended sediment transport is more erratic than dissolved load transport and is mainly associated with higher discharges, most of the material is still carried by relatively frequent events of moderate magnitude. For various rivers Wolman and Miller (1960) calculated that about 99 per cent of the total suspended load is transported by flows recurring more frequently than once every 10 years, and that 80–90 per cent of the load is carried by flows recurring more frequently than once a year. Despite subsequent modifications (e.g. Baker, 1977), evidence points to the validity of these conclusions for a wide range of conditions (Sedimentation Seminar, 1977; Webb and Walling, 1982). Catastrophic events may individually carry larger amounts of sediment but their contribution to suspended sediment transport over the entire range of discharges is less significant because they recur so infrequently.

Catchment erosion represents not only a loss of assets to agriculture and forestry but also a potential liability further downstream. Reservoir siltation reduces storage capacity and the life expectancy of reservoirs, while the silting-up of rivers may affect navigation and increase the risk of flooding in lower reaches. The silt concentration in the Huang Ho is so high that a reduction of 10–40 per cent could decrease peak discharge by about 20 per cent without any change in the actual volume of water (Stoddart, 1978).

Wash load transport has effects of more immediate relevance to stream behaviour and channel form adjustment. Very high concentrations damp down turbulence and alter the apparent viscosity of the flow, enabling the transport of a slightly larger bed-material load than would otherwise be the case (Simons *et al.*,

1963). Where there is strong infiltration from the stream into the bed and banks, as in ephemeral streams, part of the wash load may be deposited as a caked layer which stabilizes the boundary and improves its resistance to erosion (Harrison and Clayton, 1970). Large suspended loads can also contribute to rapid changes in stream course, and influence the style of flood-plain development.

On the whole, the dissolved and wash load components have little direct influence on channel geometry. However, rivers with a large wash load may be morphologically different from those with a relatively large bed-material load because of the long-term effect of transport characteristics on the boundary composition of alluvial channels. A large wash load is in part diagnostic of a high silt–clay content in the channel banks. Using the percentage silt–clay in the channel perimeter as an index (M) of the type of sediment load, Schumm (1960) has argued that streams carrying predominantly wash load should have channels which are relatively narrow and deep. A larger bed-material load requires wider and shallower cross-sections in which greater shear stresses are directed against the bed, enabling the stream to transport the coarser load.

The bed-material load

Unlike dissolved and wash load transport, the rate of bed-material transport is almost entirely a function of the transporting capacity of the flow. Field measurements are notoriously difficult to make and much work has been carried out in laboratory flumes where conditions can be simplified. Many variables are involved (Table 3.7), whose independence/dependence cannot always be determined as simple cause and effect because of intercorrelation. Indeed, the independence or dependence of variables alters with the system of interest, be it flumes, natural streams in the short term or natural streams in the long term. The basic problems are twofold: to understand the dynamics of bed-material movement; and to establish a relationship between sediment transport rate and relevant properties of the flow, fluid and sediment, thereby enabling the prediction of transporting capacity for given conditions.

Table 3.7   Variables pertinent to bed-material transport

Flow properties	Fluid properties	Sediment properties	Other properties
Discharge (Q)	Kinematic viscosity (ν)	Density (ρ_s)	Gravity (g)
Velocity (v)	Density (ρ)	Size (D)	Plan-form geometry
Flow depth (d)	Temperature (T)	Sorting (σ)	
Width (w)	Wash load concentration (C)	Fall velocity (v_s)	
Slope (s)			
Resistance (ff)			

As regards the **dynamics of movement**, particles roll, slide or saltate along the bed in a shallow zone only a few grain diameters thick once sediment motion begins ($\tau_o > \tau_{cr}$). Material transported in this way constitutes the *bed load*. Rolling is the primary mode of transport in gravel-bed streams, while saltation is largely restricted to grains of sand size (Table 3.3). With further increases in the strength of the flow, the less massive particles may be carried upwards into the main body of the flow to be transported as *suspended load*, possibly once a second threshold ($\tau_o > \tau'_{cr}$ where $\tau'_{cr} > \tau_{cr}$) has been reached (Yalin, 1972). Movement in suspension is maintained against gravity by turbulent eddies which are random in strength and

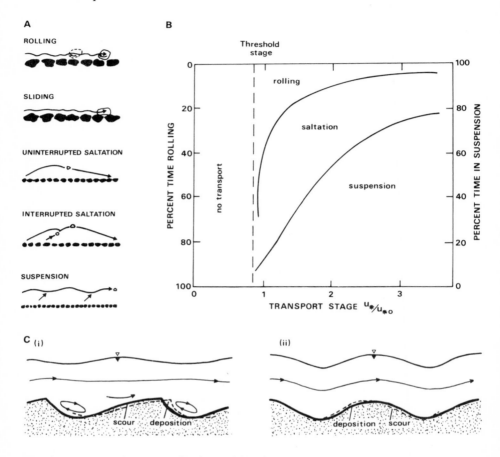

Fig 3.8   A. Modes of transport of bed-material load.
B. Percent of time single particles in a water stream experience rolling, saltation and suspension as a function of transport stage. Percent of time in saltation is represented by the distance between the curves (after Abbott and Francis, 1977).
C. Schematic diagram of the pattern of erosion and deposition over a dune (i) and antidune (ii) bed.

direction, so that grains do not follow predictable paths. The conventional separation of bed-material load into these two components is an idealization. A distinct value of τ'_{cr} corresponding to the initiation of suspended transport does not exist in nature; nor is there a sharp boundary separating regions of bed load from suspended load transport.

The theoretical formulation of a transport function requires a set of criteria with which to distinguish the several modes of transport (rolling, saltation and suspension; Figure 3.8A). Based on flume experiments in which the movement of single grains was traced photographically, Abbott and Francis (1977) attempted to define such a criterion in terms of transport stage, u_*/u_{*_o}, where u_* ($= \sqrt{\tau_0/\rho}$) is the shear velocity of an observed flow and u_{*_o} is the threshold shear velocity at which motion begins. The development of suspension from saltation (regarded as an intermediate step) occurred much less rapidly than that of saltation from rolling (Figure 3.8B). Rolling soon gave way to saltation, the time spent in the rolling mode decreasing very rapidly from about 60 per cent close to the threshold stage (u_*/u_{*_0} = 1) to 20 per cent at $u_*/u_{*_0} \sim 1.4$. Saltation was a persistent mode of transport even above $u_*/u_{*_0} = 1.9$ when suspension became dominant. Figure 3.8B suggests that all modes of bed-material transport can occur simultaneously over a wide range of flow conditions, even though one may predominate at any given stage. Although higher stresses are probably required for full suspension in natural rivers, this work demonstrates how the transport modes in sandy beds can be distinguished. It does, however, exclude the effects of grain – grain interactions which become important when $u_*/u_{*_0} > 2$ (Leeder, 1979).

Grain movement is characteristically intermittent, especially in gravel-bed streams when the flow is just above the erosion threshold. In sand-bed streams where ripples and dunes develop, grains tend to move in groups as the bed form migrates downstream (Figure 3.8C). Grains on the lee side may be temporarily buried and not re-exposed until the bed form has progressed. The development of such forms emphasizes the strong links between sediment transport, bed configuration, resistance and flow conditions close to the bed. The irregularity of movement in which individual particles travel short distances before temporarily coming to rest has led to the formulation of stochastic models, with appropriate probability distributions being defined for the step lengths and intervening rest periods.

Sediment transport equations give the maximum amount of material (capacity) that can be carried for given conditions of the flow, fluid and sediment. In parallel with the subdivision of bed-material load, separate equations have been developed for bed load, suspended load and total load using both deterministic and probabilistic approaches.

Many *bed load formulae* can be classified according to whether they relate the sediment transport rate per unit width (q_{sb}) to either excess shear stress ($\tau_o - \tau_{cr}$) or excess discharge per unit width ($q - q_{cr}$):

$$q_{sb} = X' \, \tau_o \, (\tau_o - \tau_{cr}) \qquad \text{Du Boys type} \qquad (3.16)$$

$$q_{sb} = X'' \, s^k \, (q - q_{cr}) \qquad \text{Schoklitsch type} \qquad (3.17)$$

where X' and X'' are sediment coefficients (Graf, 1971). Based on his view of the stream as a transporting machine which expends power to perform work, Bagnold (1977) has developed a semi-theoretic bed load function,

$$q_{sb} \simeq (\omega - \omega_o) \, [(\omega - \omega_o)/\omega_o]^{\frac{1}{2}} \, (d/D)^{-\frac{2}{3}} \qquad (3.18a)$$

which is essentially of the second type (3.17) with an added relative roughness term (d/D) and stream power per unit width ($\omega = \gamma Qs/w$) replacing discharge. Although the function has subsequently been modified in two main respects to give (Bagnold, 1980)

$$q_{sb} \simeq (\omega - \omega_o)^{\frac{3}{2}} \, d^{-\frac{2}{3}} \, D^{-\frac{1}{2}} \qquad (3.18b)$$

it still implies a greater transport rate not only at a higher excess power $\omega - \omega_o$ (constant depth and grain size) but also at a lower flow depth d (constant excess power and grain size) (Figure 3.9B). The problem remains, however, of determining the threshold stream power ω_o which is not directly measurable in natural rivers.

Einstein's (1950) approach represented a break with traditional methods in that explicit recognition was given to the stochastic nature of bed particle movement

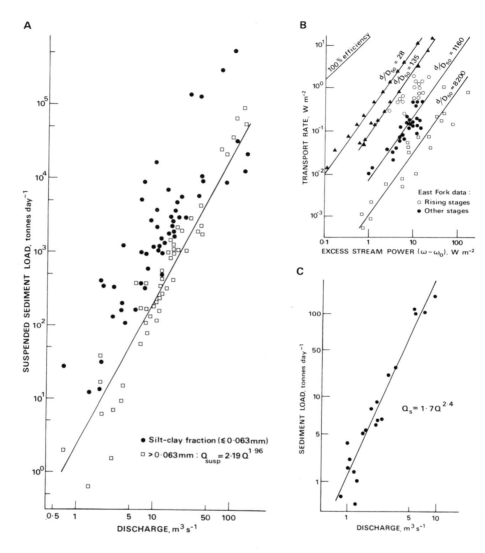

Fig 3.9   A. Variation of suspended sediment load with discharge for grain sizes less than and greater than 0.063 mm, Rio Grande at Albuquerque (data of Nordin and Beverage, 1965). The plotted line applies only to the coarser fraction.

B. Bed-load transport rate as a function of excess stream power per unit bed area $(\omega - \omega_o)$ for different relative depths (d/D_{50}) (after Bagnold, 1977). The data include measurements made in a laboratory flume (▲) and natural rivers (○, ●: East Fork River; □: Clearwater River).

C. Sediment load as a simple power function of discharge, River Bollin.

and to the different rates at which individual size fractions in the load may be transported. The transport rate

$$q_{sb} = NW \qquad (3.19)$$

is the product of the weight of each particle (W) and the number of particles (N) eroded from an area of the bed (A), where

$$N = \frac{Ap}{a} \qquad (3.20)$$

p is the probability of any particle being eroded per unit time and *a* the bed area occupied by each particle. Clearly the problem lies in determining *p*.

Many bed load equations rely on the empirical determination of coefficients, which limits their overall applicability. The equations predict the maximum load that a stream can theoretically carry but capacity transport requires an unrestricted supply of material. In heterogeneous beds the flow may be closer to capacity for one size of material than for another, since transport efficiency declines with increasing grain size (Leopold and Emmett, 1976). If only part of the material is moved over a wide range of flows, the coarser fraction may accumulate at the surface to form a protective armour coat which hinders or prevents further transport. Such time-based elements of the transport process are geomorphologically relevant but are not incorporated in conventional equations.

The *suspended load* (q_{ss}) can be calculated from

$$q_{ss} = \int_{o}^{y} cv \qquad dy \qquad (3.21)$$

provided the vertical variation of velocity (v) and suspended sediment concentration (c) with depth (y) is known. Most analytical treatments of suspension are based on the concept of diffusion whereby particles are dispersed in the flow through the action of turbulent mixing. In general, diffusion models describe a vertical distribution of suspended sediment in which both the concentration and grain size decrease exponentially with distance from the bed. Although the suspension process is not completely understood, agreement between predicted and observed values seems to be much better for suspended than for bed load transport.

At low transport rates most material moves close to the bed and the *total bed-material load* can be estimated from bed load equations. At other times the total load ($Q_s = q_s.w$) can be obtained in one of two ways: indirectly, by simple addition of the two components estimated separately,

$$Q_s = Q_{sb} + Q_{ss} \qquad (3.22)$$

or directly, from a total load formula in which the need to distinguish between the bed (Q_{sb}) and suspended (Q_{ss}) loads is avoided. Some procedures include wash load while others do not, depending on whether or not they rely on field measurements of suspended sediment.

The accuracy of transport equations is difficult to check because reliable measurements of bed-material discharge are relatively scarce. Considerable errors can be introduced if corrections are not made for the wash load component in suspended sediment samples which are often used as the basis for estimates (Graf, 1971). Despite the problem of evaluating equations developed initially for different ranges of flow and sediment conditions, extensive tests have been carried out (Task Committee, 1971a; White *et al.*, 1973). The large variation in results between different formulae and the wide divergence between predicted and measured loads point to the general inadequacy of sediment transport theory. There is no general agreement on a suitable list of independent variables for predicting sediment discharge. Indeed such is the range of factors involved (Table 3.7) that a widely acceptable theory will be slowly if ever achieved (Vanoni, 1975). Simple relationships of the form,

$$Q_s = kQ^n \tag{3.23}$$

may suffice as first-order approximations to observed data (Figure 3.9C; Task Committee, 1971a).

The bed-material transport rate can be highly variable both within and between cross-sections in a reach, and with time. Fluctuations may be random or quasi-periodic, and of different time scales. Over intervals measured in minutes, fluctuations occur as dunes pass a given point, maximum amounts of transport being associated with the passage of dune peaks and smaller amounts with that of intervening troughs (Leopold and Emmett, 1976). In gravel-bed streams, large bars may take a full season to move through a cross-section. These fluctuations emphasize the need for sampling over long enough time periods in order to obtain reliable time-averaged estimates of sediment discharge.

The transport rate may vary during the hours, days or months that a flood wave takes to move through a channel reach, leading to short-term changes in stream bed elevation as a result of *scour and fill*. It has been observed that in sand-bed streams particularly the channel bed is scoured at high discharges on the rising stage and filled to approximately the pre-flood level on the falling stage (Leopold *et al.*, 1964), and that scour occurs more or less continuously along a reach (Emmett and Leopold, 1965). However, the spatial and temporal pattern of the scour-and-fill process is more variable than these statements would suggest. Specific loci of scour exist, in channel bends, at tributary junctions and around obstructions. Scour and fill may alternate locally several times during a flood, with only a small part of a reach experiencing simultaneous scour or fill at any one time, implying that the process may be related to bed-form migration (Foley, 1978). Andrews's (1979) observations along a short reach (430 m) of the East Fork River revealed two distinct types of cross-section:

(i) 'scouring' sections which scoured at discharges (Q) above bankfull (Q_b) and filled at $Q < Q_b$, when the sediment-transport rates were respectively relatively large and small; and

(ii) 'filling' sections which filled at $Q > Q_b$ and scoured at $Q < Q_b$, when the respective transport rates were relatively small and large.

At any discharge except bankfull, some sections were accumulating bed material (fill), while others were losing bed material (scour). The sequence of scour and fill was related to the distinctive hydraulic geometries of the two types of section (Table 3.8), in which significant reversals occurred at about bankfull in the relative magnitude of variables (notably velocity) because of their different rates of change in scouring and filling sections. Interestingly the channel had returned to its pre-flood elevation within one year. Thus the scour-and-fill process may be regarded as a short-term mechanism for smoothing out irregularities in the transport rate and thereby maintaining a channel reach in quasi-equilibrium.

In the short span of engineering time, the sediment transport rate can be

Table 3.8 Hydraulic characteristics of scour and fill sections, East Fork River (after Andrews, 1979)

Characteristic	Scour sections	Fill sections
b	$< \bar{b}$	$> \bar{b}$
f	$\sim \bar{f}$	$\sim \bar{f}$
m	$> \bar{m}$	$< \bar{m}$
p	$< \bar{p}$	$> \bar{p}$
j	$> \bar{j}$	$< \bar{j}$
Channel shape	Relatively narrow and deep	Relatively wide and shallow
Velocity	Larger velocity at higher discharges	Larger velocity at lower discharges

Symbols: b, f, m, p and j are respectively the rates of change of width, depth, velocity, resistance (ff) and bed-material transport with discharge; $\bar{b}$, $\bar{f}$, $\bar{m}$, $\bar{p}$ and $\bar{j}$ are the corresponding reach averages obtained from 11 cross-sections.

regarded as a variable dependent on flow, fluid and sediment properties (Figure 1.1), provided any differences in the input and output of sediment along a reach are temporarily accommodated by scour or fill. In the longer term a stream adjusts its geometry to the water and sediment discharges supplied. Equation (3.18) implies that, if over a period of time a stream is neither aggrading nor degrading its channel, the width/depth ratio must have become adjusted to maintain a continuity of sediment transport in which input and output are equal. The bed is then protected from downcutting by a constant sediment layer. Any increase or decrease in the mean supply rate of mobile sediment would result in aggradation or degradation in an attempt to restore a balance by respectively decreasing or increasing relative roughness d/D, which would have the reverse effect on the mean transport rate (Bagnold, 1977).

Most rivers have had hundreds of years in which to make this adjustment. However, sediment continuity can be upset by man's activities. Reservoirs are very efficient sediment traps and a stream may degrade its bed below a dam in order to adjust to the larger discharge/load ratio. Channel improvements such as straightening and bank strengthening may so increase flood heights that downstream transport is severely disrupted. The important point is that a close relationship exists between channel form and the input–output conditions of sediment load in a channel reach. The absence of a general bed-material transport theory is a drawback in modelling that relationship adequately.

One significant aspect of the relationship is the relative effectiveness of events having different magnitude–frequency characteristics. Although based initially on suspended load measurements, the view that relatively frequent events of moderate magnitude perform most of the work (Wolman and Miller, 1960) is supported by evidence from streams which carry predominantly bed load (Pickup and Warner, 1976; Andrews, 1980). In the Yampa River of Wyoming, Colorado, the most effective discharges in terms of bed-material transport recur on average between 1.5 and 11 days each year (Figure 4.3D; Andrews, 1980). However, only about 25 per cent of the bed material is then in motion, so that coarser fractions tend to accumulate and form a stabilizing layer. Catastrophic events, particularly in small basins, may redistribute larger material to such an extent that channel form is more or less permanently affected because that material remains immobile under subsequent flow conditions (Stewart and La Marche, 1967).

Downstream changes in bed material characteristics represent an element of the transport process which is of immediate geomorphological relevance. Since several of the factors, notably slope and discharge, which influence the rate of particle movement change systematically in the downstream direction, both the size and size distribution (sorting) of bed material may be expected to vary similarly. Two sets of processes are involved: abrasion and sorting.

Abrasion is a summary term covering such mechanical processes as grinding, impact and rubbing, which chip and fracture particles not only during transport but also in place when the combined effects of lift and drag forces cause particles to vibrate (Schumm and Stevens, 1973). Sorting reflects the action of:

(i) selective entrainment, in which only that fraction of the bed material smaller than the threshold size is transported by a given flow event (Figure 3.5C and D); and

(ii) differential transport, in which smaller particles are transported faster and further than are larger ones.

Clearly sorting is influenced by all the variables involved in sediment transport. Chemical breakdown may also contribute to downstream changes under certain conditions.

Historically, abrasion was regarded as the dominant process responsible for the size reduction of bed material commonly observed along alluvial rivers. However, largely as a result of abrasion tank experiments (e.g. Kuenen, 1956), it was realized that observed rates of reduction were much larger than could be attributed to abrasion effects. Bradley *et al.* (1972) concluded that about 90 per cent of the downstream size reduction in Knik River gravels is caused by sorting, with the balance attributable to abrasion. However, recent work has re-established the status of abrasion (in conjunction with in situ weathering) as an effective process of particle wear (Schumm and Stevens, 1973), with maximum effectiveness possibly in upper reaches where slopes are steeper and particles larger.

Several models have been developed to describe the two processes. If, as a result of abrasion, it is assumed that the decrease in particle size (D) per unit distance downstream (L) is proportional to particle size,

$$\frac{dD}{dL} = -\alpha D \tag{3.24}$$

then the solution describes an exponential decrease of particle size with distance,

$$D = D_o e^{-\alpha L} \tag{3.25}$$

where α is a coefficient of abrasion and D_o is the initial grain size at $L = 0$. Models of the sorting process based on standard sediment transport equations (Rana *et al.*, 1973; Deigaard and Fredsøe, 1978) or stochastic particle motion (Troutman, 1980) yield a similar result. In essence α can be thought of as including the undifferentiated effects of both abrasion and sorting. The rate of change (α) may vary over large river distances to give at least two segments, where the upper and lower segments have respectively larger and smaller rates of particle size decrease (Rana *et*

Fig 3.10 Downstream changes in bed material characteristics, River Noe, Derbyshire:
A. Exponential decrease of mean grain size;
B. Discontinuous exponential decrease of mean grain size to show the effect of tributary inflow;
C. Increase in mean particle roundness;
D. The effect of tributary inflow on sediment sorting represented as discontinuous exponential change (solid lines) or pseudo-periodic variation (dashed line).

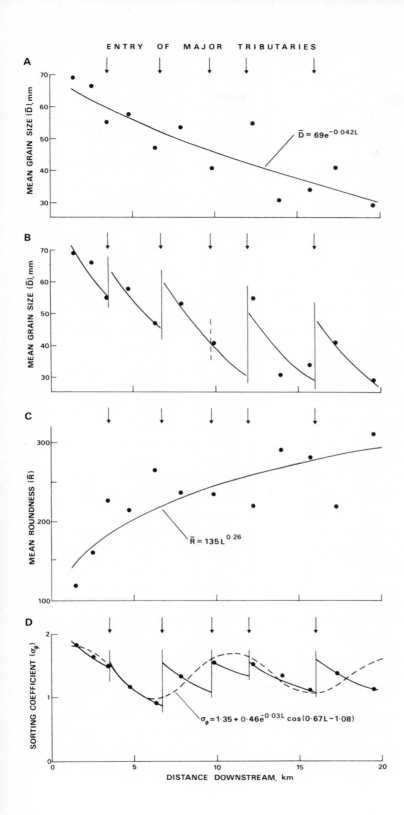

ENTRY OF MAJOR TRIBUTARIES

A

$\bar{D} = 69e^{-0.042L}$

B

C

$\bar{R} = 135L^{0.26}$

D

$\sigma_\phi = 1.35 + 0.46e^{-0.03L}\cos(0.67L - 1.08)$

DISTANCE DOWNSTREAM, km

al., 1973). Such a discontinuity has been observed in Japanese rivers corresponding to a deficiency of grains in the size range of 1–4 mm (Yatsu, 1955), which may reflect a threshold between gravel-bed and sand-bed sections of a river.

Equation (3.25) is usually calculated for the mean ($\overline{D}$) or median (D_{50}) grain size obtained from samples collected along a river by discrete or bulk sampling methods. It predicts a rapid decrease in grain size in headwater reaches where the initial material is usually coarse, and a much lower rate of change further downstream, both of which are largely borne out by observation. Grain size decreased from 330 mm to 44 mm in the first 42 km of the Knik River in Alaska (Bradley *et al.*, 1972). Only a slight reduction was observed along 3200 km of the lower Amazon where cross-channel variations in particle size at several sections were at least as great as downstream ones (Nordin *et al.*, 1980). Even in relatively short streams a downstream decrease is not always observed (Hack, 1957; Brush, 1961).

Plots of grain size against distance downstream also tend to show large amounts of scatter about regression lines (Figure 3.10A), which can be attributed to several causes. Sampling errors and the natural variability of bed material size within local reaches can introduce considerable noise into the data sufficient to mask any systematic downstream trend (Church and Kellerhals, 1978). Particle lithology is not always considered but, because lithology influences the size of material supplied initially and the subsequent rate of wear, different lithologies may be expected to behave in different ways. Finally, the introduction of fresh material from bank and tributary sources complicates the overall pattern to produce, in the case of the latter, increases in grain size below junctions (Figure 3.10B). Where a sequence of tributaries enters a main stream, grain size may vary discontinuously in such a way that an exponential decrease below each junction is followed by a stepped increase at the next junction (Troutman, 1980), the magnitude of that increase being possibly related to the relative sizes of the main stream and tributary at each confluence (Knighton, 1980b). Thus, underlying the main downstream trend are random and systematic variations not explicitly catered for by equation (3.25).

Properties other than size change through downstream transport. Particles tend to become rounder as a result of abrasion (Figure 3.10C; Mills, 1979). Bed material is generally better sorted with distance downstream, although tributary inflow can again disrupt the picture (Figure 3.10D) to produce either discontinuous change similar to that proposed for particle size (Troutman, 1980) or a pseudo-periodic variation if tributary entry follows some regular pattern (Knighton, 1980b). The main point is that sediment properties are not unchanging and their observed state reflects a wide range of influences in the long-continued action of the sediment-transport system.

Particles are reduced in size by abrasion processes and assigned their position along a stream by sorting processes. Even without the complications caused by sediment inflow from different sources, the modelling of downstream transport conditions is hindered by the unknown efficiency with which sediment transport equations developed originally for cross-sectional variations can be applied three-dimensionally to the downstream case. Strict equilibrium cannot be maintained for very long where sorting processes operate alone and a downstream decrease in particle size is to be achieved, because equality of sediment input and output would require a progressive coarsening of bed material with time at a cross-section, leading to stream bed aggradation and the development of a new slope. However, although any overall reduction in particle size must be due to abrasion and breakage, the time scale for sorting processes to change bed material size may be much shorter than the time scale for bed slope adjustment (Deigaard and Fredsøe, 1978). Downstream changes are an important element of the transport process because of the relationship between sediment properties and those aspects of stream behaviour and channel form which also vary longitudinally.

Sediment deposition

The final element of the process triumvirate, deposition, has received comparatively less attention from geomorphologists and yet alluvial rivers build a wide range of depositional forms (Table 3.9). In addition to the progressive sorting which contributes to the downstream reduction in particle size, local sorting occurs over much shorter distances, related to the local distribution of stream forces. Deposition begins once the flow velocity falls below the settling velocity of a particle, which for a given particle size is less than that required for entrainment (Figure 3.5D). Settling velocity is closely related to particle size, so that the coarsest fraction in motion should be deposited first with progressively finer grains settling out as the flow velocity continues to fall. The net effect is a vertical and horizontal (downstream and transverse) gradation of sediment sizes.

The most common depositional feature is the *flood-plain* formed from a combination of within-channel and overbank deposition, although many sedimentary forms are involved (Lewin, 1978). During lateral channel migration, erosion of one bank is approximately compensated by deposition against the other, principally but not exclusively in the form of point-bars. With continuing migration, a point-bar is built streamward and also increases in height through the deposition of sediment carried onto the bar surface by inundating flows (Figure 3.11). Since the innermost parts of a point-bar are occupied by progressively less frequent flows during construction, the final stages may take considerable time, although Hickin and Nanson (1975) estimated that point-bar ridges along the Beatton River are produced gradually over a period of 27 years. Also, progressively finer sediment is carried onto the bar as it grows surfaceward to give a vertical gradation of sizes from coarsest to finest. Over a long period of lateral and downvalley shifting, the channel may occupy all positions on the valley floor, continually building the flood-plain from within-channel deposits. From measured rates of bank erosion and historical map information, Hooke (1980) estimated the time period required for a complete traverse of the 1.2 km wide flood-plain of the River Exe in Devon to be about 1300 years.

The term flood-plain implicitly includes the idea of flooding as a natural attribute of rivers. Although bankfull discharge has a variable recurrence interval its relative frequency suggests that vertical accretion could be a major process of flood-plain construction, with natural vegetation aiding the depositional process. Schumm and Lichty (1963) and Burkham (1972) have described how new flood-plains were built after destruction by major floods in as little as 20 and 50 years respectively. Vertical accretion took several forms: (i) formation of natural levées; (ii) direct deposition in the extra-channel areas; and (iii) development of channel islands which subsequently became attached to one bank (Figure 3.11), a process which has been observed elsewhere (Knighton, 1972). The sediment deposited by overbank floodwaters comes from material carried in suspension, either as wash load (silts and clays) or the finer fractions of the bed-material load (fine and medium sands). Since the transporting ability of the flow tends to decrease away

Table 3.9 Characteristic river deposits (partly after Task Committee, 1971b)

Place of deposition	Name	Characteristics
Channel	Transitory channel deposits	Largely bed load temporarily at rest; part may be preserved in more durable channel fills or lateral accretions
	Alluvial islands	Formed initially from the lag deposition of coarser sediment with finer deposits above; a dominant feature of braided reaches
	Channel fills	Accumulations in abandoned or aggrading channel reaches
Channel margin	Lateral deposits	Point-bars on the convex bank of meanders and marginal bars which may form an alternating sequence along straight reaches; added to by vertical accretion; may be preserved through channel shifting
Flood-plain	Vertical accretion deposits	Usually fine-grained material deposited from the suspended load of overbank floodwaters; includes natural levée and backswamp deposits
	Splays	Local accumulations of predominantly sandy material, formed when water escapes from channels onto adjacent flood-plains through breaks in natural levées
Piedmont	Alluvial fans	Formed by ephemeral or perennial streams emerging from steeply dissected terrain onto a lowland; sediments rapidly decrease in size with distance from the fan apex; several fans may coalesce to form an alluvial plain (bajada)
River mouth	Deltas	Formed where a stream deposits its load upon entering the sea or any body of standing water; three sets of sedimentary structures are characteristic

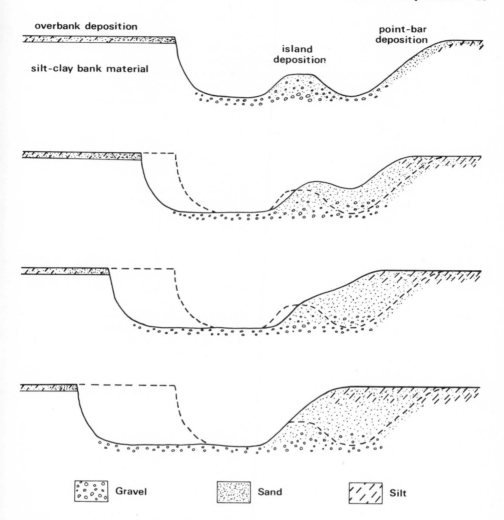

overbank deposition

silt-clay bank material

island deposition

point-bar deposition

| | Gravel | | Sand | | Silt |

Fig 3.11 Diagrammatic representation of the progressive construction of a flood-plain as a stream migrates laterally, based partly on observations along the River Bollin-Dean. As the stream erodes the left bank a point-bar is gradually constructed against the right bank and eventually incorporates alluvial island deposits. Deposits show both vertical and horizontal gradation of sediment size.

from the channel margins, both the amount and mean size of deposited sediment should similarly vary. Also, as the flood recedes and flow velocities over the flood-plain decline, an upward fining of sediment may develop. The rate of vertical accretion depends on the frequency of inundating flows and their sediment load. When major floods have a low sediment content, extensive erosion rather than deposition may occur (Burkham, 1972).

Wolman and Leopold (1957) concluded that lateral accretion and within-channel deposition are the dominant processes in flood-plain formation, accounting for up to 90 per cent of the deposits. If overbank deposition was the main process, then the channel would appear to become gradually depressed within its own alluvium. However, the relative importance of lateral and vertical accretion is not constant and overbank deposition may assume greater significance where flooding is more frequent and fine-grained material more readily available for transport. Not only may the time scales of the two processes be different (compare Hooke, 1980 with Burkham, 1972), but the reworking of flood-plain alluvium during lateral channel migration tends to destroy the stratigraphic evidence for vertical accretion, leading possibly to misinterpretation as to the original mode of formation. In the valley of the River Delaware, a thick sequence of flood-plain sediments deposited over 6000 years contains no point-bar deposits and is largely the result of overbank deposition (Ritter *et al.*, 1973).

Flood-plains provide storage space for sediment as it moves through a drainage basin (Figure 3.6), the potential for which increases as they become wider with distance downstream. The channel–hillslope relationship therefore becomes more disjunct. For a hypothetical river 16 km in length, Statham (1977) has calculated that the residence time of material ranges from 48 years in the main channel itself to 4000 years if a flood-plain is included. Although very approximate, these figures emphasize the importance of flood-plains in the discontinuous transport of basin sediment. Much of the soil eroded from the Piedmont uplands since European farming began about 1700 is still stored on hillslopes and in flood-plains (Trimble, 1975). In that and other senses (e.g. pollutants), the flood-plain reflects environmental conditions. It is also important to environmental planners concerned with reducing the risk due to floods, for many densely populated areas are concentrated on flood-plains. The flood-plain is an integral part of the fluvial system, whose deposits influence channel form through the composition of the channel boundary and therefore the type of material supplied to a stream.

4

The adjustment of channel form

Classification is a basic scientific procedure designed to impose some sort of rational order on the diversity of the real world. Based on different criteria, various classifications of natural rivers have been proposed, although none is particularly quantitative. Rivers have been classified as youthful, mature and old according to their stage of development in the cycle of erosion (Davis, 1899), and as consequent, subsequent and obsequent according to their hierarchical position in the evolutionary sequence of drainage networks. Both classifications use time as the basic criterion but neither considers directly the main variables which influence river channel form.

Both the magnitude of discharge and the character of the flow regime have a large effect on channel form adjustment (Harvey, 1969; Stevens *et al.*, 1975). Although characteristic river regimes have been identified (Beckinsale, 1969), they have not been successfully related to channel form and discharge has not proved to be an effective basis for classification except where size is a primary consideration. Nevertheless, ephemeral streams are recognized as separate from perennial ones in terms of response to fluvial processes (Alexander, 1979).

Schumm (1963a) has subdivided channels into three types on the basis of the dominant mode of sediment transport, using the percentage silt–clay in the channel boundary (M) as his criterion:

  (i) bed-load channels (M $\leqslant$ 5),
  (ii) mixed-load channels (5 < M < 20),
  (iii) suspended-load (or wash-load) channels (M $\geqslant$ 20).

The classification is based on data from a restricted range of sand-bed streams, which may limit its overall applicability, and rests on the assumption that M adequately reflects transport mode. A more precise classification in terms of sediment load would require a data base which is simply not available. A further dimension to Schumm's scheme is provided by the tripartite categorization of river channels into:

  (i) eroding – progressive degradation of the stream bed and/or channel widening, due to a deficiency of total sediment load;
  (ii) stable – no progressive change in channel form, although short-term variations may occur during floods;
  (iii) depositing – progressive aggradation and/or bank deposition due to an excessive load delivered to the stream.

Channel stability is a relative term defined here in terms of the balance or otherwise between sediment supply and transportability. Natural channels cannot usually be defined in the field as falling readily into one of these three categories.

From a practical viewpoint, a more satisfactory classification is based on boundary composition, a factor which influences the type of sediment transport, resistance to erosion and therefore the adjustability of channel form to discharge

(Figure 1.1). In effect Schumm's classification is based on it. Without specifying distinct boundaries, an initial subdivision into *cohesive* and *non-cohesive* channels can be followed by further categorization (Table 4.1). Other categories can be added to cope with special conditions, such as supra-glacial streams. The distinctions are not new but Howard (1980) has argued that abrupt thresholds exist between bedrock, sand-bed and gravel-bed channels in particular, each type having a distinct hydraulic geometry. Most natural channels can be assigned to one of these three classes. Frequently the bed and banks of a channel are composed of different material, a common contrast being between cohesive banks and a non-cohesive bed, and the classification can be extended to cover this eventuality. One implication of such a classification is that empirical results obtained for one type of channel may not apply to another.

Table 4.1   A classification of river channels

Primary type	Secondary type	Characteristics
A. Cohesive	A1. Bedrock channels	No coherent cover of unconsolidated material; generally short segments, concentrated in steep headwater reaches
	A2. Silt-clay channels	Boundaries have a high silt-clay content, giving varying degrees of cohesion; resistance controlled by inter-particular forces
B. Non-cohesive	B1. Sand-bed channels	'Live-bed' channels composed of largely sandy material which is transported at a wide range of discharges
	B2. Gravel-bed channels	'Threshold' channels of coarse gravel or cobbles which are transported only at higher discharges
	B3. Boulder-bed channels	Composed of very large particles (>256 mm) which are moved infrequently; grades into A1

Whatever classification is used, it is apparent that a wide range of channel types exists. Classifications generally apply to segments of channel rather than entire river systems because a stream of sufficient length will tend to have a range of types, indicating differential behaviour in the longitudinal direction. Transitions may be gradual or abrupt, as for example where a stream changes rapidly from gravel-bed to sand-bed status at the discontinuity in the downstream decrease of bed material size (Yatsu, 1955). The application of a suitable classificatory scheme to the world's rivers could provide an important basis for studying the distributional characteristics of channel types.

Characteristics of adjustment

A natural river can be thought of as an open system with inflows and outflows of energy and matter (Leopold and Langbein, 1962). Such a viewpoint emphasizes the important characteristics of stream behaviour: the external constraints or controls imposed on the system; the adjustments to the internal geometry of the system in response to those controls; and the nature of that adjustment, especially as regards system equilibrium.

The dominant **controls** of channel form adjustment are discharge and sediment load, independent variables which integrate the effects of climate, vegetation, soils, geology and basin physiography (Figure 1.1). Given an adequate supply of data it should be possible to show how the internal geometry of the system is related to these controls, at least in theory. Discharge data are relatively plentiful even though gauging stations are rarely close enough to ensure an adequate downstream sample. However, information on sediment load is particularly meagre and there is the additional problem of determining the relative significance of different aspects of the load, be it the type, amount or some other characteristic. Both controls vary considerably through space (along and between rivers) and with time. Along many rivers the addition of water and sediment from tributary sources of variable size produces discontinuous change in the controls, with parallel discontinuities in channel morphology. Yet many empirical relationships are presented as if change was continuous.

The choice of a suitable time scale within which to study physical relationships has been a recurring theme among geomorphologists (Schumm and Lichty, 1965; Cullingford *et al.*, 1980). Time is a continuous variable but representative time periods can be defined:

   (i) Instantaneous time ($< 10^{-1}$ years);
   (ii) Short time scale (10^1–10^2 years);
   (iii) Medium time scale (10^3–10^4 years);
   (iv) Long time scale ($> 10^5$ years).

In instantaneous time, stream properties can possess single values but they are not representative in that channel form is not simply the product of instantaneous conditions. Indeed reversals of cause and effect can occur when channel and related hydraulic properties influence the passage of flood waves and sediment discharge.

Over the short time scale, the stream transports its load selectively and the temporal pattern of discharge may be thought of as a single entity, although no one parameter can adequately express all the relevant details of discharge variation. This time period is most significant from an observational standpoint and reasonably well-defined relationships can be expected between the independent variables and certain elements of channel form. At the medium time scale, the stream adjusts its internal geometry in such a way that the sediment supplied can be transported with the discharge available, so that material does not accumulate indefinitely. These two time periods are the most relevant as regards channel form adjustment, since mean water and sediment discharge are independent variables to which an average channel geometry is related. Over longer time periods in which landscape mass is removed and large climatic fluctuations occur (Figure 5.2), discharge and load conditions are no longer constant in the mean and adjustment becomes both more complex and less definable.

Discharge and sediment load are not the only independent controls. Valley slope is an inherited characteristic which determines the rate of energy loss along rivers and therefore modifies the relation between channel form and the primary variables, although at longer time periods it too becomes part of the adjustable system. Aside from its effect on the type and rate of sediment supplied, geology acts as a constraint on channel adjustment through its influence on bed and bank material composition, most notably in bedrock channels. Like geology, vegetation plays several roles; as a stabilizing influence on bed and bank materials, and as a constraint, particularly in forested environments where local adjustments are frequently required to accommodate the effects of downed timber (Heede, 1981). Finally, the long history of human activity makes it unlikely that rivers have remained unaffected by man-induced modifications, reservoir construction being the most conspicuous modern example. Underlying the primary controls of discharge and sediment load are many constraints operating at a variety of scales.

Adjustments to the internal geometry of the fluvial sytem involve a large number of variables whose interdependence is not always clear because the role of a single variable cannot easily be isolated. As before (Table 3.7) those variables can be grouped into flow properties, fluid properties and sediment-related characteristics (including sediment load), with the significant addition of channel form. A distinction can be drawn between:

(i) flow geometry, which includes the interactions among a set of dependent and semi-independent variables during temporal changes in discharge, with emphasis on the cross-sectional and reach scales; and

(ii) channel geometry, which refers to the three-dimensional form of the channel fashioned over a period of time to accommodate the mean condition of discharge and sediment load.

Clearly the two are related but not necessarily in a simple way. Although flow geometry is more concerned with short-term response which the channel itself can influence, average patterns of behaviour are still sought which may have longer-term implications.

A stream must satisfy at least three physical relations in adjusting its *flow geometry*: continuity (equation 3.1), flow resistance (Table 3.2), and a sediment transport equation. In a system with n variables, n independent equations are required for a unique solution to a given problem. With discharge and sediment load as the independent variables, resistance and debris size as semi-independent, and water-surface width, flow depth, velocity, slope and the pattern of flow as dependent, the requisite number of equations is not available and probably never will be (Maddock, 1969). There is therefore an element of indeterminacy in the behaviour of streams with mobile beds. Hey (1978), however, has argued that the problem is determinate, although his equations amount to little more than formal statements.

Certain aspects of adjustment can be approached through the technique known as 'hydraulic geometry' (Leopold and Maddock, 1953), which assumes that discharge (Q) is the dominant independent variable and that dependent variables are related to it in the form of simple power functions:

$$w = aQ^b \tag{4.1}$$
$$d = cQ^f \tag{4.2}$$
$$v = kQ^m \tag{4.3}$$
$$s = gQ^z \tag{4.4}$$
$$n = tQ^y \tag{4.5}$$
$$ff = \ell Q^p \tag{4.6}$$
$$Q_{susp} = rQ^j \tag{4.7}$$

where w, d, v, s, n, ff and Q_{susp} are respectively width, mean depth, mean velocity, slope, resistance (Manning's n or the Darcy–Weisbach ff) and suspended sediment load. From the continuity equation,

$$Q = w.d.v = aQ^b.cQ^f.kQ^m \qquad (4.8)$$

it follows that

$$a.c.k = 1 \qquad (4.9)$$
$$b + f + m = 1 \qquad (4.10)$$

The technique can be applied to both at-a-station and downstream adjustment. It suffers from the lack of direct consideration given to sediment transport and from the assumption of linearity in the relations (Richards, 1973), but has provided valuable information on stream behaviour. It represents one methodology for breaking into a system with more unknowns than independent equations.

Channel geometry is the three-dimensional entity which, as 'regime theory' assumes, can be largely characterized in terms of the adjustable variables, width, depth and slope, with meander form added as a fourth. Alternatively, the adjustment of channel geometry to external controls can be considered in terms of four degrees of freedom:

   (i) Cross-sectional form – the size and shape of a channel in cross-profile either at a point or as a reach average;

   (ii) Bed configuration – the distinct forms moulded in the bed of particularly sand- and gravel-bed streams (the sequence of bed forms associated with the former (Figure 3.4C) may also be regarded as part of the flow geometry);

   (iii) Planimetric geometry or channel pattern – the two-dimensional form of the channel when viewed from above, the commonest subdivision being into straight, meandering and braided (Leopold and Wolman, 1957);

   (iv) Channel bed slope – the gradient of a stream at the reach and longitudinal scales, where the latter also refers to the overall shape of the longitudinal profile.

These degrees of freedom provide the framework for the discussion which follows but, although considered separately, they should not be thought of as independent of one another. To these could be added channel position and the form of the drainage network (chapter 2).

The four components are rather broad and each needs to be expressed in terms of a representative set of parameters suitable for model building and obtaining relations. They are adjustable over a range of spatial and temporal scales (Figure 4.1), implying a differential ability to absorb change and assume an equilibrium form for given constraints of stream size and boundary resistance. The longitudinal profile has historically been a primary interest of geomorphologists but it is the least changeable component and can properly be regarded as an additional constraint on more adjustable ones. As the time scale increases, so does the potential influence of past conditions on present form, with the attendant problem of assessing the extent to which present channel geometry is adjusted to prevailing levels of the control variables. Such a problem has implications not only for the reliability of empirical relationships, between form and control variables on the one hand and between different form variables on the other, but also for the question of whether a general physical principle is governing channel form adjustment, the search for which has been a major concern over the past two decades (e.g. Langbein and Leopold, 1964; Yang, 1971a).

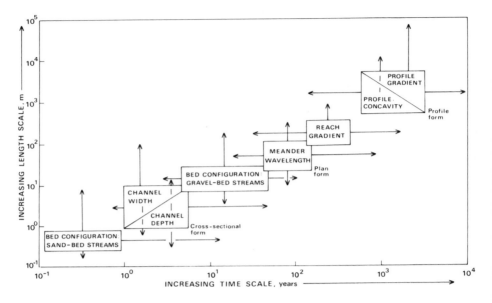

Fig 4.1   Schematic diagram of the time scales of adjustment of various channel form components with given length dimensions in a hypothetical basin of intermediate size.

The concept of equilibrium

An important characteristic of open systems is their ability for self-regulation. Negative feedback mechanisms moderate the effects of external factors in such a way that a system can maintain a state of equilibrium in which some degree of stability is established. True stability never exists in natural rivers which frequently change their position and which must continue to pass a range of discharges and sediment loads. However, they can become relatively stable in the sense that, if disturbed, they will tend to return approximately to their previous state and the perturbation is damped down (Figure 4.2). For relatively constant conditions of the controlling variables, a natural river may develop characteristic forms, recognizable as statistical averages about which fluctuations occur.

Various types of equilibrium can be defined (Chorley and Kennedy, 1971), of which three are particularly relevant (Figure 4.2A):

(i) *Static equilibrium* – a balance between opposing forces brings about a static condition in certain system properties. Although widely used in the design of stable structures, it has little apparent relevance to the fluctuating condition of natural rivers. However, it has been applied by means of tractive force theory to the problem of specifying the shape of the 'threshold' channel (Figure 4.4), defined as that channel (usually in coarse bed streams) whose boundary has sediment everywhere at the threshold of movement (Lane, 1953). Although idealized, such a channel represents one end of a spectrum of channels at different stages of sediment mobility.

(ii) *Steady-state equilibrium* – the condition of an open system in which the macro-properties at least are invariable with respect to a given time scale, implying an absence of trends, cycles or any other time-related pattern of change. However,

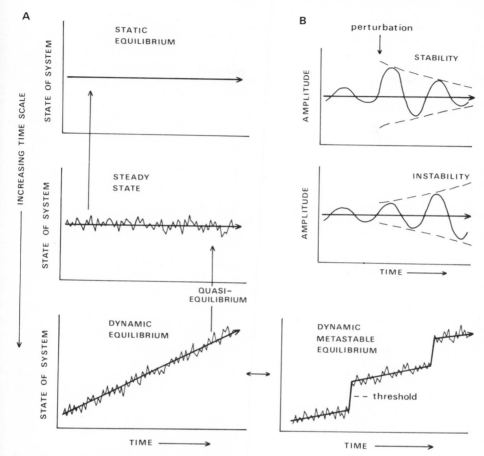

Fig 4.2 A. Diagrammatic representation of types of equilibrium.
B. Definition sketches of stability and instability in an oscillating mechanical system subject to a perturbation.

the instantaneous state of the system may oscillate about that condition to give the concept the character of a statistical average, making it more applicable to the behaviour of natural rivers. The equilibrium of 'regime theory' with a timespan of 10^1–10^2 years may be classified as this type. Basically regime theory amounts to a set of empirical equations developed originally by Anglo-Indian engineers for the purpose of designing stable canals, an approach from which Leopold and Maddock (1953) derived considerable inspiration in formulating hydraulic geometry. Although natural rivers experience a wider range of flows than do irrigation canals, the implication is that a stream can adjust its non-fluid boundaries to imposed conditions in order to obtain and maintain a steady-state equilibrium over at least the short time scale.

(iii) *Dynamic equilibrium* – a balanced state maintained by dynamic adjustments as fluctuations occur in the energy flow over the short term or as the system continuously changes its condition over the longer term, the simplest case of the latter being a linear trend in the average condition of the system (Figure 4.2A).

Oscillations about any trend may be so much greater than changes in the trend itself that, when a system is observed over a short time period, the former override the latter to give an impression of steady-state equilibrium. This tendency toward a steady state is termed *quasi-equilibrium*. Although termed steady-state equilibrium, Schumm's (1977) condition of grade applicable at a time scale of 10^2–10^3 years is essentially this type. These three types of equilibrium have different connotations but can be arranged in order of increasing time scale to give some unity to the equilibrium concept as it applies to rivers (Schumm, 1977). Other types can be defined, such as *dynamic metastable equilibrium* (Figure 4.2A), in order to cope with situations in which abrupt episodes of stream adjustment occur as significant thresholds are crossed.

The concept of equilibrium has a long history in the engineering and geomorphological literature. Hydraulic engineers have been mainly concerned with stable channel design, whereas geomorphologists have been more interested in the behaviour of natural rivers as they approach and attain equilibrium, usually over long time periods. Prior to 1950 the geomorphological approach was largely qualitative. Davis (1899) borrowed Gilbert's (1877) concept of grade (or equilibrium) in which erosion and deposition are approximately balanced and set it in the temporal framework of his cycle of erosion. However, Gilbert's equilibrium is an equilibrium of action which emphasizes dynamic adjustment without reference to time as a controlling variable and as such is more in tune with contemporary opinion. Mackin's (1948, p. 471) definition of a graded stream as one '. . . in which, over a period of years, slope is delicately adjusted to provide, with available discharge and prevailing channel characteristics, just the velocity required for the transportation of the load supplied from the drainage basin' represents a watershed between traditional and modern ideas. It distinguishes between a long-term balance and short-term adjustments but remains qualitative and retains the previous emphasis on channel slope as the principal means of adjustment.

The modern approach is more quantitative and stems directly from the empirical work on hydraulic geometry (Leopold and Maddock, 1953; Wolman, 1955). No exact equilibrium is implied but rather a quasi-equilibrium manifest in the tendency of many rivers to develop an average behaviour, although the empirical mean may not be as well defined as originally supposed (Knighton, 1975; Park, 1977). Adjustments to cross-sectional form (Wolman, 1955) and channel pattern (Leopold and Wolman, 1957) receive greater emphasis as means of achieving equilibrium and attention focuses more on the dynamics of the adjustment process than on the stability of a particular channel shape or profile.

Extensions of these ideas into the realms of theory development have involved analogies between thermodynamic and fluvial systems, with application in particular of the entropy principle. Using the concept of minimum entropy production which is one criterion for equilibrium in thermodynamic open systems, one approach proposes that rivers tend toward a state in which the energy distribution is most probable (*the most probable state*), attained through a compromise between two opposing tendencies – a uniform distribution of energy expenditure and minimum total work (Langbein and Leopold, 1964). The most probable state is characterized by a minimum variance of the system components. The variance-minimization principle has been presented in two main forms: (i) minimization of the variance of selected variables measured at different sections along a reach (Langbein and Leopold, 1966; Dozier, 1976); (ii) minimization of the sum of squares of exponents in hydraulic geometry relations (Langbein, 1964a; Maddock,

1969). Variance minimization is thus regarded as a constraint on stream adjustment additional to the physical requirements of continuity, flow resistance and sediment transport.

Minimum variance theory has been much criticized and direct tests of its validity as a criterion for stream equilibrium are certainly difficult to achieve. However, it does provide one rationale for river channel adjustment which combines deductive methodology with the probabilistic viewpoint that only average or most probable states can be predicted. It has been applied to various problems, ranging from meanders (Langbein and Leopold, 1966) to the behaviour of straight channels with mobile beds (Maddock, 1969) and to the development of hillslopes subject to overland flow (Emmett, 1970). As regards the context for which the theory was originally derived, it appears to predict reasonably well average exponent values in at-a-station hydraulic relations (Williams, 1978a).

Yang (1971a, 1976) has used the entropy principle in a slightly different way to develop the thesis that, subject to given conditions of discharge, sediment load and valley slope, rivers adjust their flow and channel geometry in order to minimize the rate of doing work or unit stream power, which is equivalent to minimization of the velocity–slope (*vs*) product. The hypothesis has been used to derive equilibrium stream profiles (1971a), to explain the formation of meanders (1971b) and riffle–pool sequences (1971c), and to show that unit stream power (*vs*) is the dominant factor governing the rate of sediment transport (1976), an important element of stream equilibrium not specifically catered for in minimum variance theory. A later development (Song and Yang, 1980) claims that minimization of *vs* is a special case of the more general tendency for rivers to minimize their stream power (γQs). In that respect it parallels Chang's (1980, p. 1445) proposition:

> The necessary and sufficient condition of equilibrium occurs when the stream power per unit length γQs is a minimum subject to given constraints. Hence, an alluvial channel with water discharge Q and sediment load Q_s as independent variables, tends to establish its width, depth and slope such that γQs is a minimum.

With Q given, minimum γQs implies minimum channel slope (s). However, given the constraint imposed on stream adjustment by valley slope, the potential for channel slope minimization may be limited over the short and medium time scales.

In common with many scientific ideas, all these hypotheses employ some minimization principle as a basis for theory development. They are not the only hypotheses which could be or have been formulated regarding the equilibrium behaviour of rivers. Kirkby (1977) has suggested that a principle of maximum efficiency may be operating such that a channel is adjusted over a period of years to carry the sediment load supplied as efficiently as possible. However, there is as yet no universally accepted set of criteria for determining whether all or part of a river system is in equilibrium. A definition, for example, in terms of a balance between the input and output of sediment load is beyond the wherewithal of direct testing. Indeed it has been argued that external controls rarely remain constant for long enough to enable the attainment of equilibrium and that relatively minor fluctuations in external variables can trigger major changes to internal geometry. Also, recent work has suggested that greater emphasis should be placed on the transient rather than equilibrium behaviour of natural streams (Thornes, 1974; Stevens *et al.*, 1975), a view which, considering the non-uniform and unsteady character of streamflow, has much to recommend it.

Rivers can at best attain an approximate equilibrium, manifest at some suitable time scale intermediate between short-term fluctuations and long-term evolutionary tendencies in a regularity of channel geometry adjusted to external controls. In order to assess the ability of the fluvial system to make the necessary adjustments, there is a need to know the time period required for a stream to develop characteristic forms and the time period over which such forms are likely to persist. Different components of channel geometry adjust at different rates (Figure 4.1) so that both time periods may be expected to vary from one component to another. The potential for adjustment also depends on the scale and resistance of the system so that any tendency toward equilibrium may vary not only between river systems but also between different parts of the same system. As yet there is no suitable theory which can cope with all ramifications to the equilibrium concept.

The concept of dominant discharge

The frequent reference made above to a mean state which reflects the adjustment of channel geometry to imposed conditions suggests that a dominant or channel-forming discharge may be largely responsible for that geometry. Introduced originally to extend the application of regime theory from canals to natural rivers which have a more variable flow regime, the concept of dominant discharge fulfils such a role. The concept is at least a useful analytical device in that the replacement of the frequency distribution of flows by a single discharge simplifies modelling strategies.

Dominant discharge can be defined in various ways: as the flow which determines particular channel parameters, such as meander wavelength (Ackers and Charlton (1970a) defined dominant discharge as the steady flow that would yield the same meander wavelength as the observed range of varying flows within which the steady flow lies); or as the flow which performs most work, where work is defined in terms of sediment transport (Wolman and Miller, 1960; Figure 4.3A). Since it seems reasonable to suppose that river channels are adjusted on average to a flow which just fills the available cross-section, dominant discharge has been equated with bankfull flow, thereby giving it additional morphogenetic significance. This assertion was based on an apparent consistency in the frequency with which bankfull discharge occurs along streams (Wolman and Leopold, 1957), and on an approximate correspondence between the frequency of bankfull discharge and the frequency of that flow which cumulatively transports most sediment (Wolman and Miller, 1960). Flood flows may individually transport greater loads but recur too infrequently to have a greater cumulative effect. A link is thus established between dominant discharge, most effective discharge and bankfull discharge with an approximate recurrence interval of 1–2 years.

This link is limited in several respects:

(i) The bankfull channel cannot always be defined in the field, especially where the valley bottom is too narrow for an active flood-plain or where several benches exist (Woodyer, 1968). There is no consistent method for specifying the bankfull channel, although many have been devised (Figure 4.3B; Williams, 1978b).

(ii) Bankfull discharge is not necessarily of constant frequency even within a single basin (Pickup and Warner, 1976). From data for 36 stations, Williams (1978b) found that the recurrence interval of bankfull discharge averaged 1.5 years as Leopold *et al.* (1964) maintained but the range was very wide, from 1.01 to 32 years (Figure 4.3C).

A

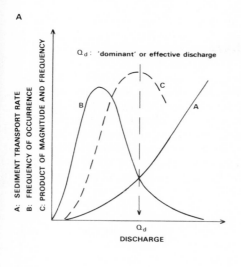

B

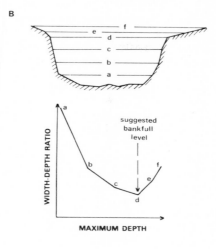

C

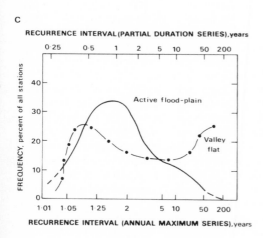

D

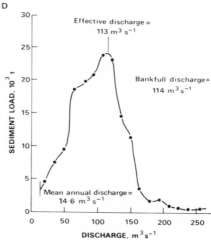

Fig 4.3 A. Dominant discharge defined in terms of the magnitude and frequency of sediment transport by a given range of discharges (after Wolman and Miller, 1960).
B. Identification of the bankfull channel as the height at which the width-depth ratio becomes a minimum.
C. Frequency distributions of the recurrence interval of bankfull discharge where the bankfull channel was defined in terms of either an active flood-plain (36 stations) or a valley flat (28 stations) (after Williams, 1978b). The modal recurrence interval for the former is about 1.5 years on the annual maximum series.
D. Mean annual sediment load transported by discharge increments, Snake River, Wyoming (after Andrews, 1980).

(iii) Channel form parameters do not necessarily correlate best with bankfull discharge. Meander wavelength, for example, may be better related to more frequent sub-bankfull flows (Carlston, 1965). Also, different parameters may be adjusted to different discharge values.

(iv) Bankfull discharge may not be the most effective flow as regards sediment transport. On the one hand Baker (1977) has argued that rarer flows are more effective agents in streams with a high proportion of large discharges and relatively resistant boundaries, while on the other Pickup and Warner (1976) found that the most effective discharge was more frequent than bankfull, recurring on average about 3–5 times each year. However, other results (Andrews, 1980) have confirmed Wolman and Miller's (1960) conclusion. Andrews's study of bed-load transport in the Yampa River is particularly instructive in that it covers a wide range of bed material sizes (median grain size varied from 0.4 to 86 mm). Despite the variable frequency of bankfull discharge, it corresponded very well with the most effective transporting flow (Figure 4.3D) which had a recurrence interval of 1.18–3.26 years. As drainage area decreased, the relative proportion of high discharges increased and the most effective flow became less frequent.

This final point can be pursued further. In those rivers or segments of river where the flow regime is very variable (that is, the ratio of individual flood peaks to the mean annual flood is large) or where the channel boundary is very resistant, the concept of dominant discharge and the related concept of channel equilibrium may become less applicable (Stevens *et al.*, 1975; Baker, 1977). There, channel characteristics may exhibit non-equilibrium tendencies rather than fluctuations about some mean condition, since the fluvial system has a memory for past events.

Bankfull discharge is not necessarily of constant frequency or the most effective flow. Channel form is the product not of a single formative discharge but of a range of discharges which may include bankfull and of the temporal sequence of flow events. However, the bankfull channel is the one reference level which can reasonably be defined and it remains intuitively appealing to attach morphologic significance to bankfull flow. Hey (1978) still advocates its use for design purposes.

The limitations of the dominant discharge concept imply that regression models which express a particular channel parameter (y) as a function of a particular discharge (Q) in the form $y = f(Q)$ should apply only to rivers which are in regime or a steady state. Such models should not be used to describe mean behaviour where large fluctuations in discharge are common (Pickup and Rieger, 1979). Nevertheless, linear regression models of this kind have provided the major basis for empirical studies of river channel form.

Cross-sectional form

The cross-sectional form of natural channels is characteristically irregular in outline and locally variable. Table 4.2 lists the parameters commonly used to describe that form, measurements for which are usually obtained by stretching a tape or cable across the stream and measuring down to the channel boundary at set distances. Width and mean depth give the gross dimensions of the channel but do not uniquely define cross-sectional shape (Hey, 1978). Nevertheless, width–depth ratio remains the most commonly used index of channel shape even though it is not always the most appropriate (Pickup, 1976a). In particular it provides no indication of cross-sectional asymmetry, a characteristic which is often associated with

Table 4.2   Cross-sectional parameters

Channel size	Channel shape
Width, w	Width–depth ratio, w/d
Mean depth, d	d_{max}/d (Fahnestock, 1963)
Cross-sectional area, A = w.d	Asymmetry (Figure 4.6A(i); Knighton, 1981a):
Wetted perimeter, P	$A^* = A_r - A_l/A$
Hydraulic radius, R = A/P ~ d	$A_2 = 2x(d_{max} - d)/A$
Maximum depth, d_{max}	
Bed width, w_b	

Definitions: A_r, A_l are respectively the cross-sectional areas to the right and left of the channel centreline; x is the horizontal distance from the channel centreline to the point or centroid of maximum depth

meanders but which, until recently (Knighton, 1981a), has not been specified in terms of measurable parameters.

The parameters usually refer to the bankfull channel or, when flow geometry is the specific concern, to the cross-section at a particular frequency of flow. Both present problems of definition. In the case of the latter, some standard discharge index needs to be defined in order to compare upstream and downstream sections but a single index may not be equally representative of the flow distribution at each section. The choice is often arbitrary and may have limited channel-forming significance (Richards, 1977). Aside from bankfull discharge itself (Q_b), the choice has included mean anual discharge (Q_m) (Leopold and Maddock, 1953) and the flows which are equalled or exceeded 2 per cent, 15 per cent and 50 per cent of the time (Wolman, 1955).

The equilibrium cross-section

Rivers that erode their boundaries flow in self-formed channels which, when subject to relatively uniform controlling conditions, are expected to show some consistency of form at least on average. No general theory exists for predicting the equilibrium channel under any conditions but, for sufficiently simple ones, a deterministic solution can be obtained. The *threshold channel* formed in coarse material is such a case (Lane, 1953).

Based on the fundamental assumption that all particles on the channel boundary are on the verge of movement at the threshold discharge, a resolution of the forces involved yields a cross-section which is roughly parabolic in shape and similar to some natural channel forms (Figure 4.4). Out of the infinite number of cross-sections which can satisfy the tractive force criteria, the type B channel is the minimum cross-section having the threshold property. The angle of repose of the material forming the boundary of the threshold channel is the major factor governing its shape. In terms of bed material size (D in mm) and discharge (Q in m³ s⁻¹), Henderson (1963) defined a limiting slope (s) at which the type B channel remains stable from

$$s = 0.00012 \ D^{1.15} Q^{-0.46} \tag{4.11}$$

If the slope is greater than this value, the type A channel with less scouring capacity is needed for stability, while at lower slopes the type C channel is most stable.

The theory has limited applicability to real channels which not only transport sediment but also migrate laterally. In effect it defines a lower limit for cross-sectional form, suitable for design purposes. A more realistic approach is to

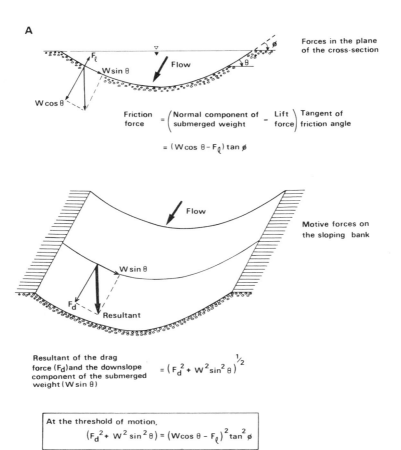
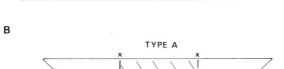
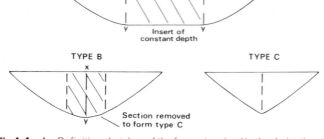

Fig 4.4 A. Definition sketches of the forces involved in the derivation of the threshold channel cross section, where W is the submerged weight of a grain, F_l is the lift force, F_d is the drag force (assumed to be proportional to the local bed shear stress τ), and ϕ is the friction angle (or angle of repose of non cohesive material).
B. Types of threshold channel, the basic one being Type B from which the others can be derived by insertion (Type A) or removal (Type C) of a central section.

consider the 'live-bed' case but then simple deterministic solutions are no longer possible and we run into the 'stable channel paradox' that stable banks are incompatible with a mobile bed (Parker, 1979).

The regime 'theory' of the Anglo-Indian school of engineers offers a more practical approach in which the channel bed is assumed to be live. Derived initially for canals with a steady flow and fine sediment, the 'theory' consists of a set of empirical equations which can be manipulated to give the width, depth and slope of an approximately stable channel whose cross-sectional form is maintained by a local balance between erosion and deposition. The more significant equations are:

$$P = 4.83 \ Q^{\frac{1}{2}} \tag{4.12}$$

$$R = 0.40 \ Q^{\frac{1}{3}} D^{-\frac{1}{6}} \tag{4.13}$$

$$v = 0.51 \ Q^{\frac{1}{6}} D^{\frac{1}{6}} \tag{4.14}$$

where $P \sim w$ and $R \sim d$ for large channels (Lacey, 1929). The equations were based on a narrow range of sediment sizes, which, together with the limited account taken of sediment discharge, restricts their application to natural streams. Indeed large discrepancies have been observed between calculated and field data when the equations have been applied to conditions beyond those for which they were originally intended. In addition, the assumption of a single type of cross-sectional shape, such as Lacey's semi-ellipse, has not been substantiated (Raudkivi, 1976).

Apart from the complementary methods of threshold and regime theory, attempts have been made to define a stable channel geometry by means of minimum variance theory (Langbein, 1964a), the concept of minimum stream power (Chang, 1979a, 1980), a principle of maximum transport efficiency (Kirkby, 1977) and a principle of lateral diffusion of turbulent momentum (Parker, 1979), formulated often in terms of hydraulic geometry relations. Indeed threshold theory has also been extended to derive exponent values in such relations (Li *et al.*, 1976). As if to underline the important effect of sediment character on cross-sectional form, a clearer distinction is now being drawn between sand-bed and gravel-bed streams (e.g. Chang, 1979a, 1980). As yet no satisfactory solution has been obtained for the problem of specifying the equilibrium geometry of channels with mobile beds, which, considering the complex behaviour of natural channels, is hardly surprising.

Spatial variation – downstream
Cross-sectional form adjusts to accommodate the discharge and sediment load supplied from the drainage basin, within the additional constraints of boundary composition and valley slope. Channel dimensions are not arbitrary but are adjusted, through the processes of erosion and deposition, to the quantity of water moving through the cross-section so that the channel can contain all but the highest flows. Since discharge increases downstream with drainage area (Figure 1.2A), width and mean depth should similarly vary (Figure 4.5A). The downstream hydraulic relations of Leopold and Maddock (1953), given as averages for selected rivers in the midwestern United States,

$$w = aQ_m^{0.5} \tag{4.15}$$

$$d = cQ_m^{0.4} \tag{4.16}$$

Table 4.3 Downstream hydraulic geometry relations

Source	Location/Applicable conditions	Discharge	b	f	m	z	y
(i) *Empirical*							
Leopold and Maddock (1953)	Mid-west USA	Q_m	0.50	0.40	0.10		
Wolman (1955)	Brandywine Creek, Pennsylvania	Q_{50}	0.34	0.45	0.32	-0.80	-0.40
		Q_{15}	0.38	0.42	0.32	-0.92	-0.51
		Q_2	0.45	0.43	0.17	-0.97	-0.32
		Q_b	0.42	0.45	0.05	-1.07	-0.28
Brush (1961)	Appalachians	$Q_{2.33}$	0.55	0.36	0.09		
Carlston (1969)	Mid-west USA	Q_m	0.46	0.38	0.16		
Knighton (1974)	Bollin-Dean, Cheshire	Q_{50}	0.46	0.16	0.38		
		Q_{15}	0.54	0.23	0.23		
		Q_2	0.61	0.31	0.08		
Emmett (1975)	Upper Salmon River, Idaho	Q_b	0.54	0.34	0.12		
Charlton et al. (1978)	British gravel-bed rivers	Q_b	0.45	0.40	0.15		
(ii) *Theoretical*							
Langbein (1965)	Minimum variance theory		0.50	0.37	0.13	-0.55	
Smith (1974)	Principle of mass conservation		0.60	0.30	0.10	-0.20	
Li et al. (1976)	Threshold theory		0.46	0.46	0.08	-0.46	
*Parker (1979)	Momentum diffusion, gravel rivers		0.50	0.42	0.08	-0.41	
Chang (1980)	Minimum stream power, gravel rivers		0.47	0.42	0.11		

Discharge (Q) defined as the mean annual flood ($Q_{2.33}$), bankfull (Q_b), mean annual (Q_m), and the one equalled or exceeded 50 per cent (Q_{50}), 15 per cent (Q_{15}) and 2 per cent (Q_2) of the time.
Symbols: $w = aQ^b$, $d = cQ^f$, $v = kQ^m$, $s = gQ^z$, $n = tQ^y$
*Parker's analysis is made in terms of dimensionless variables with the width relation based on empirical data

demonstrate a progressive increase in width (w) and depth (d) with mean annual discharge (Q_m), which in the case of the former is similar to Lacey's regime equation (4.12).

Despite variation in coefficient (a, c) and exponent (b, f) values between streams (Park, 1977), empirical and theoretical evidence (Table 4.3) suggests some consistency in the rates of width and depth adjustment. Certainly width seems to vary approximately as the square root of discharge. This argument is limited in several respects. Firstly, exponent values are not independent of the selected discharge index as the relations obtained by Wolman (1955) and Knighton (1974) illustrate (Table 4.3). Secondly, the relations are usually presented as continuous functions but discharge changes discontinuously downstream largely because of tributary inflow. Consequently adjustments to cross-sectional form may occur abruptly at tributary junctions, particularly in ephemeral streams where the transient rather than steady-state behaviour of channel form may be dominant (Thornes, 1974; Rendell and Alexander, 1979). Thirdly, the exponents are conservative quantities, constrained by the continuity requirement (equation 4.10), and may be rather insensitive in a similar way to the parameters in Horton's (1945) 'laws' of drainage network composition (Table 2.1). Well-defined downstream relations may be expected only along lengths of stream where the main controlling variables of discharge and sediment load vary regularly (Church, 1980).

Channel size is not only influenced by the magnitude of discharge but also by the hydrologic regime. A river with a flashier regime and relatively high peak flows tends to develop wider channels (Osterkamp, 1980). Although based on limited data, a comparison of two rivers in Venezuela reveals major differences in channel width and sinuosity that appear to be the result of different flood characteristics (Table 4.4). Ratios such as Q_p/Q_m provide one means of demonstrating the sensitivity of channel form to flow events and of assessing whether or not a river is likely to develop an equilibrium geometry. Such a tendency is less probable where the ratio is high.

Factors other than hydrologic ones control cross-sectional morphology and in particular the shape of the channel. Pickup (1976b) has argued that an optimal width–depth ratio exists for bed-load transport, suggesting that streams adjust channel shape in order to maximize transport efficiency (Kirkby, 1977). Bagnold's (1977) transport function (equation 3.18) indeed implies that the ratio becomes adjusted to the mean sediment transport rate. Parker (1979) has predicted that, for a given discharge, a 30 per cent increase in gravel load leads to a 25 per cent reduction in centre depth but a 40 per cent increase in width. Certainly a coarser load and therefore a higher proportion of bed-load transport are generally associated with

Table 4.4 Characteristics of Rios Guanipa and Tonoro immediately upstream of their confluence (after Stevens *et al.*, 1975)

River	Drainage area, km²	Valley slope, m m⁻¹	Median bed material size, mm	Channel width, w	Sinuosity	Mean annual discharge (Q_m), m³ s⁻¹	Peak discharge (Q_p), m³ s⁻¹	Q_p/Q_m
Guanipa	2 800	0.0013	0.35	15	2.3	17	105	6
Tonoro	1 300	0.0015	0.35	183	1.1	11	535	47

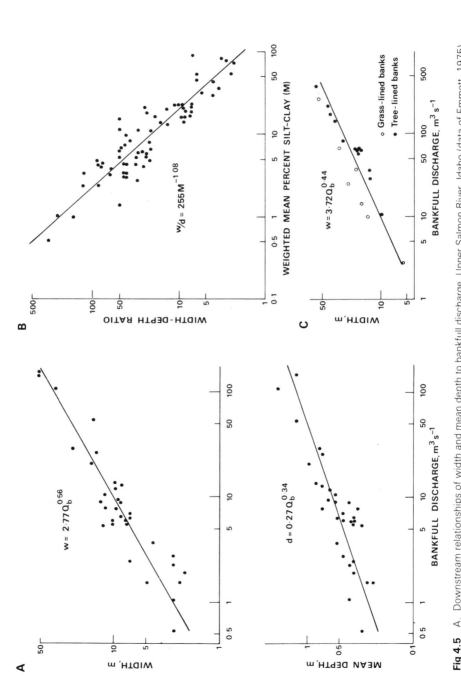

Fig 4.5 A. Downstream relationships of width and mean depth to bankfull discharge, Upper Salmon River, Idaho (data of Emmett, 1975).
B. Relationship of width-depth ratio to the weighted mean percent silt-clay in the channel boundary (after Schumm, 1960).
C. Relationship of width to bankfull discharge along British gravel rivers with grass-lined or tree-lined banks (after Charlton et al., 1978).

wider, shallower channels in which shear stresses are directed more against the bed than the banks. Whether or not the size composition and type of sediment load are more important in controlling channel form than the total amount of sediment being transported is a matter of debate which cannot easily be resolved given the lack of suitable data. It is possible that channel size is adjusted to the total sediment discharge, especially where the stream transports a large bed load, while channel shape is more closely related to the type of load.

In an attempt to circumvent the data problem, Schumm (1960, 1971) has used the percentage silt–clay in the channel boundary (M) as an index of the type of load (p. 85). From the relation (Figure 4.5B)

$$w/d = 255 \ M^{-1.08} \tag{4.17}$$

obtained however for channels containing only small amounts of gravel, he concluded that type of load is the main control on channel shape and that suspended-load and bed-load channels are respectively narrow and deep, wide and shallow. Ferguson (1973) reanalysed Schumm's data relating to the *bank* silt–clay percentage (B) to obtained the relation

$$w = 33.1 \ Q_{2.33}{}^{0.58} \ B^{-0.66} \tag{4.18}$$

which shows that, for a given discharge, channels with cohesive banks (high B) will be relatively narrow. In this sense M(or B) is an index of bank stability since greater cohesiveness increases resistance to erosion. Where banks are of unequal resistance, the strength of the weaker one controls the width.

Combining sediment and discharge data, Schumm (1971) obtained the multiple regression equations

$$w = 44 \ Q_m{}^{0.38} \ M^{-0.39} \tag{4.19}$$

$$d = 0.51 \ Q_m{}^{0.29} \ M^{0.34} \tag{4.20}$$

The implications for downstream hydraulic geometry are:
  (i) well-defined width and depth-discharge relationships are expected if bank material remains constant;
 (ii) if banks become more cohesive (M or B increases), width will increase more slowly and depth more rapidly downstream to give a more box-like cross-section.

Table 4.5 Downstream width–discharge relations for Missouri channels with different sediment characteristics (after Osterkamp, 1980)

Type of channel	Width–discharge equation
(1) High silt-clay bed	$w = 5.1 \ Q_m{}^{0.47}$
(2) Medium silt-clay bed	$w = 7.0 \ Q_m{}^{0.57}$
(3) Low silt-clay bed	$w = 7.5 \ Q_m{}^{0.58}$
(4) Sand-bed, silt-banks	$w = 8.4 \ Q_m{}^{0.59}$
(5) Sand-bed, sand-banks	$w = 9.0 \ Q_m{}^{0.62}$
(6) Gravel-bed	$w = 8.0 \ Q_m{}^{0.55}$
(7) Cobble-bed	$w = 7.5 \ Q_m{}^{0.54}$
(8) Boulder-bed	$w = 7.7 \ Q_m{}^{0.51}$

However, the effects of boundary composition on downstream channel adjustment may not be so simple, as Osterkamp's (1980) results suggest (Table 4.5). As the bed and banks become increasingly sandy and channel stability decreases (1 to 5), channel width not only increases in size at a given discharge but also changes more rapidly with discharge. For increases in bed material size beyond the sand range (5 to 8), the opposite effects occur. There the coarsest fraction of the bed material produces bed armouring which improves channel stability.

Bed material size generally decreases downstream in conjunction with channel gradient. To the extent that channel gradient is constrained by valley slope and a long time scale of adjustment (Figure 4.1), it can be regarded as an imposed variable which might influence cross-sectional form. The relative effects of bed material size and gradient are difficult to separate but steeper slopes tend to give rise to wider, shallower channels. At steep slopes which generate high transport rates and encourage channel migration (Schumm and Khan, 1972), Chang (1979a, 1980) has predicted a rapid increase in width and decrease in depth with increasing slope which may indicate a tendency for braiding, for braiding is usually associated with steeper gradients (Leopold and Wolman, 1957). This example illustrates the strong relationships between the various degrees of freedom, in this case between channel gradient, channel pattern and cross-sectional form.

One final effect, that of bank vegetation, needs to be noted. Vegetation increases bank resistance which leads to channel narrowing. Charlton *et al.* (1978) found that channels with grassy banks were on average 30 per cent wider but tree-lined ones up to 30 per cent narrower than the overall width–discharge relation would suggest (Figure 4.5C). Although real, the protective effect of vegetation is very variable and difficult to quantify.

The dominant controls on cross-sectional form are discharge, the absolute and relative amounts of bed-load transport, and the composition of the channel boundary particularly as it relates to bank stability. The multivariate character of these controls emphasizes that the downstream hydraulic geometry approach can provide only a general indication of trends. Nevertheless, discharge does vary systematically downstream and is the major control of channel size. Although it is recognized that sediment characteristics have a large influence on channel shape, the effects of sediment load have yet to be properly assessed in a downstream context. The extent to which downstream changes in cross-sectional geometry are consistent depends on the regularity with which discharge and load vary in that direction. Orderly changes are unlikely to persist across major geologic or physiographic boundaries that substantially influence the behaviour of the river (Church, 1980; Nanson and Young, 1981).

Spatial variation – local
Wolman (1955) recognized local variations in cross-sectional form as a possible source of scatter in downstream hydraulic geometry relations. In particular, such variations can be related systematically to channel pattern and bed topography.

Divided or braided sections, which are often associated with coarse bed-load transport, tend to have higher width–depth ratios than do comparable sections in meander or straight reaches. Within the latter, cross-sectional asymmetry may oscillate in a pseudo-periodic way, dependent on the degree of riffle–pool or meander development (Figure 4.6A), with maximal asymmetry close to bend apices (Knighton, 1982). If channel pattern is locally variable therefore, considerable fluctuations in cross-sectional shape can occur.

Similar to the contrast between braids and meanders is that between riffles and pools where the former are characterized by coarser bed material and higher width–depth ratios (Richards, 1976a). Provided the contrast is consistent throughout a basin, downstream trends will be affected. On the River Fowey, riffle widths exceeded pool widths by about 12 per cent, leading to downstream width–discharge relations with significantly different coefficient but similar exponent values (Richards, 1976a):

Riffles: $w = 4.54 \ Q^{0.33}$ (4.21)

Pools: $w = 3.85 \ Q^{0.35}$ (4.22)

Compared to the downstream change in riffle depth, depth differences between adjacent riffles and pools were equivalent to a 350 per cent increase in drainage area.

The riffle–pool sequence is an oscillatory bed form (Keller and Melhorn, 1978), which raises the question of lag correlation in channel geometry series at the local scale where a given form variable (y) at some point s may be related to previous (upstream) values at s–1, s–2, . . . of either another form variable (x)

$$y_s = a_o + a_1 x_{s-1} + a_2 x_{s-2} + \ldots + a_p x_{s-p} + \text{(other terms)} \tag{4.23}$$

or itself (autocorrelation)

$$y_s = a_o + a_1 y_{s-1} + a_2 y_{s-2} + \ldots + a_p y_{s-p} + \text{(other terms)} \tag{4.24}$$

As regards the first (4.23), Richards (1976a) found that width was related to bed height (H) lagged by one increment

$$\overset{\bullet}{w_s} = 2.21 \ H_{s-1} \tag{4.25}$$

which suggests that width fluctuations are a product of flow characteristics induced by upstream changes in bed topography. It provides one explanation for the tendency of riffle widths to exceed pool widths since bed height increases over a riffle, deflects the flow toward one or both banks and thus promotes undercutting. Models of the second type (4.24) have been fitted to width, depth and width–depth ratio series measured along 4 lengths of a small gravel-bed stream, and show significant differences between the lengths as regards the degree of structured behaviour in the variation of cross-sectional form (Knighton, 1981b). The width and mean depth series of two of the lengths, together with the appropriate models, are shown in Figure 4.6B.

Underlying the main downstream trends are local fluctuations in cross-sectional form of both a random and systematic nature. Those fluctuations are difficult to quantify and incorporate within downstream hydraulic geometry relations but they do emphasize the need for consistent sampling (at standardized locations) if errors are to be kept to a minimum and the relations interpretable in terms of channel equilibrium.

At-a-station hydraulic geometry

Unlike downstream hydraulic geometry which deals with spatial variations in channel properties at some reference discharge, at-a-station hydraulic geometry deals with temporal variations in flow variables as discharge fluctuates at a cross-section, usually for a range of discharges up to bankfull (Figure 4.7). The relations retain the same basic form (equations 4.1–4.7) but greater emphasis is placed on the adjustment of flow geometry.

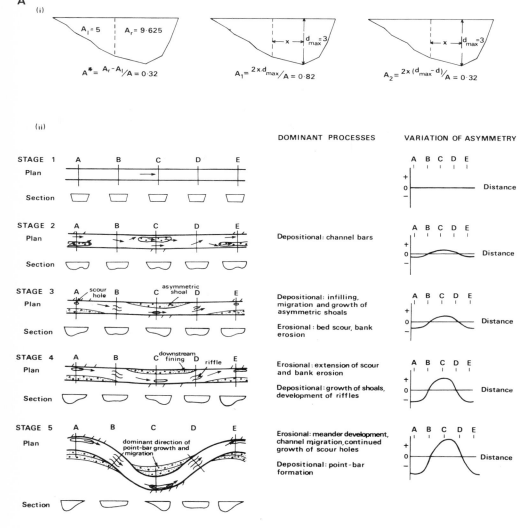

Fig 4.6   Local variations in cross-sectional form:
A.   Cross-sectional asymmetry – definition of asymmetry indices (i) and suggested mode of development and variation (ii).
B.   Mean depth and width series of the bankfull channel along two lengths of a gravel-bed stream. The auto-regressive models for the detrended series are given, where b_s is a random term.

Only two theoretical developments deal explicitly with the at-a-station case: Li *et al.*'s (1976) threshold theory which is restricted to small gravel streams, and Langbein's (1964a, 1965) minimum variance theory. The latter is more flexible in that hydraulic exponents can be predicted for a wide range of channel types. It adopts a probabilistic standpoint in maintaining that only average or most probable relations can be defined. The basic postulate is that, as well as satisfying the

B

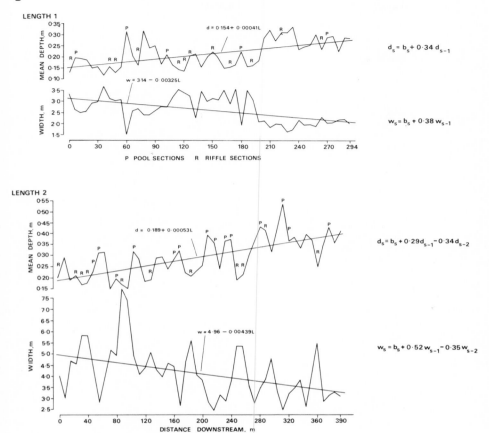

LENGTH 1

$d = 0.154 + 0.00041L$

$w = 3.14 - 0.00325L$

$d_s = b_s + 0.34\,d_{s-1}$

$w_s = b_s + 0.38\,w_{s-1}$

P POOL SECTIONS   R RIFFLE SECTIONS

LENGTH 2

$d = 0.189 + 0.00053L$

$d_s = b_s + 0.29\,d_{s-1} - 0.34\,d_{s-2}$

$w = 4.96 - 0.00439L$

$w_s = b_s + 0.52\,w_{s-1} - 0.35\,w_{s-2}$

DISTANCE DOWNSTREAM, m

physical requirements of continuity (equation 4.8), sediment transport and flow resistance, a stream adjusts to increasing discharge by minimizing the total variance of its dependent variables, where the relevant variances are the squares of the hydraulic exponents. Thus if width, depth and velocity are the only adjustable variables, the variance sum to be minimized is

$$b^2 + f^2 + m^2 \qquad\qquad (4.26)$$

Table 4.6 illustrates a minimum variance calculation where width adjustment is constrained by $b = 0.19f$, an example applicable to a section with cohesive but non-vertical banks (Williams, 1978a).

The theory has been criticized for its lack of direct consideration of sediment transport and for the mathematical liberties in the original derivation, although alternative derivations are possible (Knighton, 1977; Williams, 1978a). It depends on the log-linear form of hydraulic geometry which may not apply under all conditions (Richards, 1973). A further problem is the selection of variables to be included in a minimum variance adjustment. Williams (1978a) has considered various combinations of dependent variables and shown that Langbein's

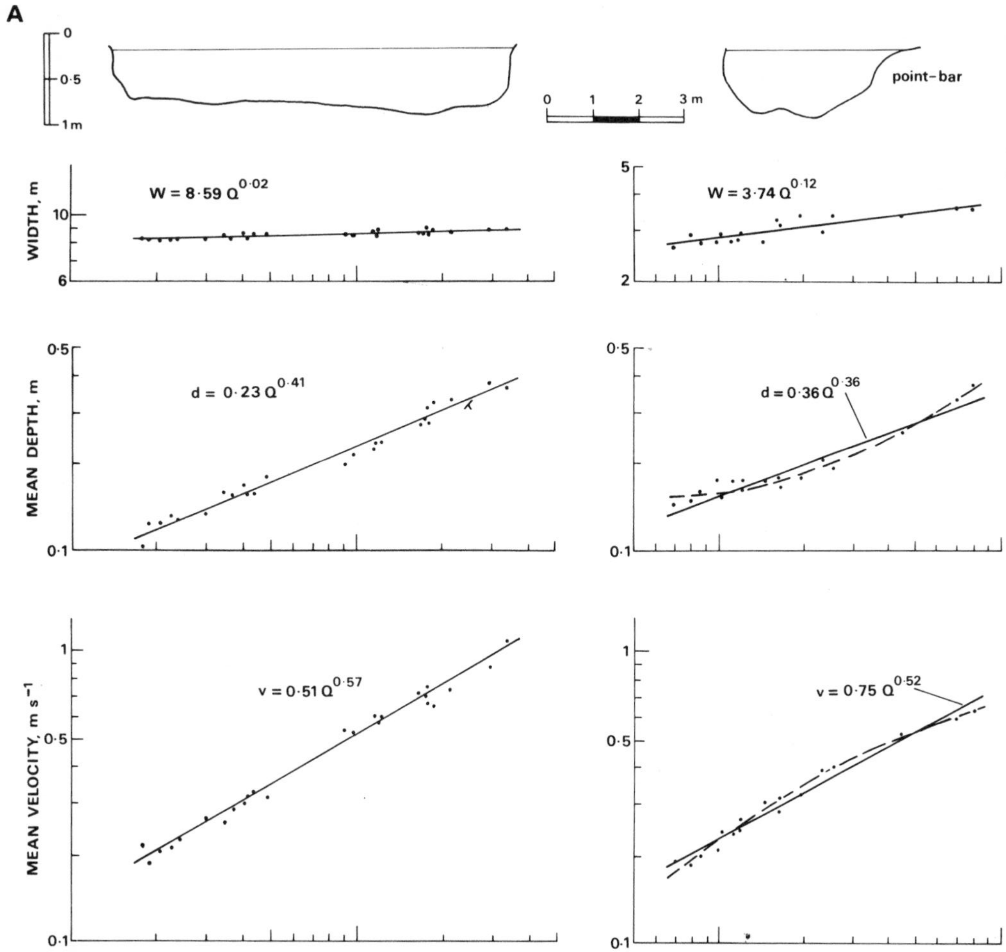

Fig 4.7 At-a-station hydraulic geometry:
A. Log-linear relationships of width, depth, velocity and resistance to discharge at two cross-sections, River Bollin-Dean. The cross-sections are shown at bankfull stage. The dashed lines in the second set of graphs indicate log-quadratic tendencies.

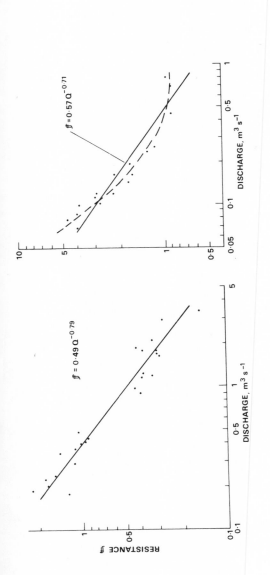

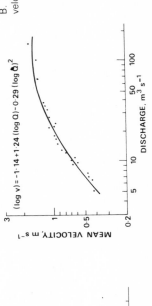

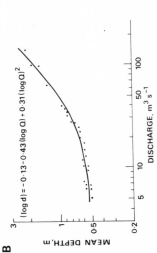

B. Log-quadratic relationships of depth and velocity to discharge (after Richards, 1977).

Table 4.6 An example of a minimum variance calculation

(1) Define the variables, constraints and variances involved:

	Variable	Relation	Variance	Constraint
Independent	Discharge	$Q \propto Q^1$	1	
	Width	$w \propto Q^b$	b^2	$b = 0.19f$
Dependent	Depth	$d \propto Q^f$	f^2	
	Velocity	$v \propto Q^m$	m^2	
	Slope	$s \propto Q^z$	z^2	$z = 0$ (slope constant)
	Shear	$\tau \propto Q^{(f+z)}$	$(f+z)^2 = f^2$ since $z = 0$	
	Darcy–Weisbach friction	$ff \propto Q^{(f+z-2m)}$	$(f+z-2m)^2 = (f-2m)^2$ since $z = 0$	

(2) Define the variance sum to be minimized:

$b^2 + f^2 + m^2 + z^2 + (f + z)^2 + (f + z - 2m)^2$

$= (0.19f)^2 + f^2 + m^2 + f^2 + (f - 2m)^2$ since $b = 0.19f$, $z = 0$

$= (0.19f)^2 + f^2 + (1 - 1.19f)^2 + f^2 + (3.38f - 2)^2$ since $b + f + m = 1 \Leftrightarrow m = 1 - 1.19f$

$= 14.88f^2 - 15.82f + 5$

(3) Set the derivative equal to zero and solve to find the minimum:

$\dfrac{d}{df} = 29.76f - 15.82 = 0$ $\therefore f = 0.53$

whence $m = 1 - 1.19f = 0.37$

$b = 0.19f = 0.10$

$(f - 2m) = -0.21$

The minimum variance adjustment for the given conditions is:

$w \propto Q^{0.10}$ $d \propto Q^{0.53}$ $v \propto Q^{0.37}$ $\tau \propto Q^{0.53}$ $ff \propto Q^{-0.21}$

(Scheidegger and Langbein, 1966) original choice of width, depth, velocity, shear and Darcy–Weisbach friction is the most reliable. Despite the criticisms, minimum variance theory provides a rationale for adjustment which predicts reasonably well the average exponent values of sections grouped according to boundary composition (Table 4.7). It is less accurate when applied to individual sections but then it was never intended for that purpose. The opportunity afforded by the theory to study the effects of different constraints on hydraulic geometry is a major advantage which has yet to be fully explored.

Numerous at-a-station analyses have now been carried out but no overall pattern has emerged regarding the variation in exponent values (Park, 1977), although Rhodes (1977) has identified the most common types of channel:
  (i) $m > f > b$ and $m > f + b$
  (ii) $f > m > \frac{2}{3}f$ and $f > b$
Such is the scale of variation that the relevance of an average or most probable flow geometry can be questioned. Rivers appear to adjust not in similar ways but in a large number of different ways (Rhodes, 1978). However, local factors may explain at least part of the considerable variety. Differences may be related to channel pattern (Knighton, 1975) or to bed topography (Richards, 1977) with adjacent riffle and pool sections being distinguishable by

$$f_{riffle} > f_{pool}$$
$$m_{riffle} < m_{pool}$$

Above all bank stability and the composition of the channel boundary seem to have a marked effect on at-a-station adjustment (Knighton, 1974; Williams, 1978a; Table 4.7).

At-a-station width exponents are usually much less than their downstream counterparts (Tables 4.3, 4.8). The composition of the channel banks significantly influences the rate of width adjustment so that, where banks are particularly cohesive and almost vertical, water-surface width remains approximately constant with changing discharge (Figure 4.7A; Knighton, 1974). In compensation, the velocity exponent (m) is generally much higher than in the downstream case.

The rates of change of depth and velocity depend on sediment load and flow resistance. Bed-load channels are characteristically wide and shallow with relatively small f and high m values, which are apparently required for an increase in competence with discharge (Wilcock, 1971). Certainly sediment load is sensitive to velocity changes (Colby, 1964). Leopold and Maddock (1953) obtained a direct correlation between the m/f ratio and the rate of change of suspended load (j in Table 4.8), suggesting that velocity must adjust more rapidly to accommodate higher rates of increase of suspended load.

Flow resistance cannot be measured directly but is commonly determined from one of the resistance equations (Table 3.2). In general resistance decreases with increasing discharge as the effects of grain roughness are drowned out (Figure 4.7A). Where other forms of roughness are also effective, the rate of decrease is lower, which tends to reduce the velocity exponent (Knighton, 1975). In sand-bed streams the behaviour of the variables is more complex because bed configuration changes in response to the flow (Figure 3.4C). There, in particular, log-quadratic relations

$$\log d = f_1 + f_2 (\log Q) + f_3 (\log Q)^2 \tag{4.27}$$
$$\log v = m_1 + m_2 (\log Q) + m_3 (\log Q)^2 \tag{4.28}$$

Table 4.7 A comparison of empirical and theoretical (minimum variance) rates of change for different channel types (after Williams, 1978a)

Type of channel		Theoretical exponent values					Average field values for n stations			
		Width b	Depth f	Velocity m	Shear f	Friction ff (f − 2m)	Width b	Depth f	Velocity m	n
Cohesive, near-vertical banks; sandy and gravelly beds		0	0.57	0.43	0.57	−0.29	0.01	0.52	0.47	22
Cohesive but non-vertical banks; sandy and gravelly beds	(i)	0.10	0.53	0.37	0.53	−0.21	0.08	0.50	0.42	74
	(ii)	0.09	0.53	0.38	0.53	−0.23				
Non-cohesive and readily eroded channel boundary		0.48	0.30	0.22	0.30	−0.14	0.54	0.26	0.21	16
One cohesive and one non-cohesive bank; sandy and gravelly beds		0.45	0.27	0.28	0.27	−0.29	0.40	0.31	0.30	51

Note: the theoretical exponent values are obtained by minimizing the variances of width, depth, velocity, shear and Darcy-Weisbach friction

(i) a constraint of b = 0.19f imposed
(ii) a constraint of b = 0.12–0.06f imposed

Table 4.8 At-a-station hydraulic geometry relations

Source	Location/Applicable conditions	Average exponent values						Number of stations
		b	f	m.	y	p	j	
(i) Empirical								
Leopold and Maddock (1953)	Mid-west USA	0.26	0.40	0.34			2	20
Wolman (1955)	Brandywine Creek, Pennsylvania	0.04	0.41	0.55			1.88	7
Leopold and Miller (1956)	Ephemeral streams, semi-arid USA	0.25	0.41	0.33	−0.20		1.3	10
Lewis (1969)	Rio Manati, Puerto Rico	0.17	0.33	0.49				10
Wilcock (1971)	R. Hodder, coarse bed, cohesive banks	0.09	0.36	0.53				9
Knighton (1975)	R. Bollin-Dean, coarse bed, cohesive banks	0.12	0.40	0.48	−0.24	−0.61	2.04	12
Harvey (1975)	R. Ter, cohesive banks	0.14	0.42	0.43				8
(ii) Theoretical								
Li et al. (1976)	Threshold theory	0.24	0.46	0.30				
Langbein (1965)/ Williams (1978a)	Minimum variance theory:							
	(i) Vertical banks (b = 0)	0	0.57	0.43	−0.05	−0.29		
	(ii) Cohesive but non-vertical banks	0.10	0.53	0.37	−0.01	−0.21		
	(iii) Non-cohesive boundary	0.48	0.30	0.22	−0.02	−0.14		

Symbols: $w = aQ^b$, $d = cQ^f$, $v = kQ^m$, $n = tQ^y$, $ff = lQ^p$, $Q_{ss} = rQ^j$ at a cross-section
Note: it is generally assumed that $s \propto Q^o$

are probably more appropriate than the traditional log-linear ones for describing depth and velocity changes (Richards, 1973). Subject to the requirement that $f_3 = -m_3$ (Knighton, 1979), depth curves tend to be concave-upward ($f_3 > 0$) and velocity curves concave-downward ($m_3 < 0$) (Figure 4.7B). The form of the latter can be explained by the declining rate of resistance decrease at higher discharges (Figure 3.4B; the drowning-out effect being more successful at lower flows), and by the increase in form roughness as dunes develop and enlarge at higher flows (Richards, 1977).

The complexity of at-a-station adjustment inhibits the drawing of simple conclusions. In broad outline, the width exponent (b) appears to be largely a function of channel geometry and therefore boundary composition, while the rates of change of depth and velocity are dependent partly on cross-sectional form and partly on transport and resistance-related factors which tend to be more variable. It is perhaps significant that the most consistent set of at-a-station relations, that of Wolman (1955), was obtained for straight-reach sections along a single stream flowing through relatively uniform bank material. Although hydraulic geometry has proved to be a valuable method for analysing flow behaviour at a cross-section, the original log-linear form may not be capable of handling the more complex situations which are coming to light, thereby casting some doubt on the validity of a mean hydraulic geometry defined in terms of the original formulation. Perhaps the time is ripe for greater flexibility not only in the relations themselves (Richards, 1973) but also in the basic approach.

Adjustability

The evidence available from studies of rivers subject to high flood discharges or altered hydrologic conditions indicates that cross-sectional form is one of the most adjustable components of channel geometry, at least in the width dimension. Burkham's (1972) study of historical changes along the Gila River in Arizona shows that, between 1905 and 1917, a series of large winter floods carrying low sediment loads significantly widened the channel from about 90 m to 610 m (Figure 5.3). The following period was characterized by smaller floods and higher sediment loads so that by the 1960s the channel had almost regained its former width.

Marked changes in channel form have been observed downstream of reservoirs whose construction tends to reduce flood peaks and sediment load. Decreases in bankfull cross-sectional area of over 50 per cent are not uncommon (Petts, 1979). In the Platte River system, bankfull width has continued to decrease during this century as new regulation schemes have been introduced (Williams, 1978c; Figure 5.8A). There, also, large but inconsistent changes in bed elevation and therefore channel depth have occurred, the pattern of bed aggradation and degradation reflecting the complex regulation of discharge and sediment load conditions. Although the scale and rate of adjustment are bound to be variable, it is clear that depth and in particular width can respond rapidly to changes in the dominant controls.

The implications for equilibrium adjustment are twofold. If a stream is seeking to attain some form of equilibrium, then the initial approach at least may be made largely through the adjustment of cross-sectional form over a time scale of 10^1–10^2 years. On the other hand, the sensitivity of cross-sectional form suggests that fluctuations about any mean state may be larger than in the case of other channel components, and that a few large events could produce substantial changes. Whether or not such transient behaviour represents the norm rather than the exception, it is interesting that the Gila River returned approximately to its pre-flood condition even though the process took 50 years (Figure 5.3). In more humid environments floods of comparable recurrence interval may have less effect (Costa, 1974; Gupta and Fox, 1974) so that a mean channel geometry is more readily maintained.

Bed configuration

Natural streams rarely have flat beds. Shear stresses above the critical for transport mould cohesionless beds into discernible forms whose geometry depends on various flow parameters which in turn are influenced by those forms, giving rise to complex feedback relations. In effect bed forms represent an important means of adjustment in the vertical dimension, related nevertheless to the transverse and horizontal adjustments which natural streams can also make.

Numerous classifications of bed forms have been proposed, the main elements of which are summarized in Table 4.9. Bars are larger-scale features having lengths of the order of the channel width or greater and are generally classified according to their shape and position. Composed of a wide range of grain sizes, these several types of bar are usually exposed at certain stages of flow. At a smaller scale are various concealed bed forms commonly associated with sand-bed streams, the most widely used sequence being ripples, dunes, plane bed and antidunes (Figure 3.4C). Because of its link with sediment transport and flow resistance, considerable effort has been invested in the study of this sequence, particularly in laboratory flumes. The formation of these various bed features indicates the presence of systematic tendencies in the ability of natural streams to sort and transport material over a wide range of flow and bed material conditions.

Ripples, dunes and antidunes

Simons and Richardson (1966) have defined conditions for the occurrence of ripples, dunes, etc., in terms of unit stream power ($\tau_o v = \gamma qs$) and particle diameter (Figure 4.8). The diagram shows that, for a given bed material size in the sand range, the sequence of ripples, dunes, plane bed and antidunes is correlated with increasing stream power or increasing velocity at constant depth and slope. Ripples form at relatively low shear stresses and rarely occur in sediments coarser than 0.6 mm, whereas dunes, the commonest type of bed form, develop at intermediate stresses and have a geometry which is closely related to the depth of flow. Antidunes are low-amplitude bed waves broadly in phase with water-surface waves. They are much less common than dunes, forming in broad, shallow channels of relatively steep slope when the sediment transport rate and flow velocity are high. The degree of regularity in these bed forms is variable and often a wide range of wavelengths and heights is present, even under the controlled conditions of a laboratory flume. Also, smaller forms may be superimposed on larger ones. However, there is usually enough regularity for a distinct pattern to be recognized.

Although the mechanisms responsible for their formation are not fully understood, the bed forms do possess certain common characteristics. All are the result of an orderly pattern of scour and deposition. In particular, ripples and dunes move downstream through erosion of their upstream face and deposition on their downstream face at velocities which are small compared with the flow (Figure 3.8C). In sliding down the steeper lee face grains orientate themselves so that bedding planes parallel to the face are formed.

Table 4.9 A classification of bed forms

Bed form	Dimensions	Shape	Behaviour and occurrence		
Bar	Lengths comparable to channel width	Variable	Five main types: (1) Point-bars: form particularly on the'inner bank of meanders (2) Alternate bars: distributed periodically along one and then the other bank of a channel (3) Channel junction bars: develop where tributaries enter a main channel (4) Transverse bars (include riffles): may be diagonal to the flow (5) Mid-channel bars: typical of braided reaches		
Ripples	Wavelength less than 0.6 m; height less than 0.04 m	Triangular profile; gentle upstream slope, sharp crest and steep downstream face	Generally restricted to sediment finer than 0.6 mm; discontinuous movement; at velocities much less than that of the flow	Lower regime of roughness; form roughness dominant	Particularly sand-bed streams
Dunes	Wavelength of 4 to 8 times flow depth; height up to $\frac{1}{3}$ flow depth; much larger than ripples	Similar to ripples	Upstream slope may be rippled; discontinuous movement; out of phase with water surface		
Plane bed			Bed surface devoid of bed forms; may not occur for some ranges of depth and bed material size		
Antidunes	Relatively low height dependent on flow depth and velocity	Sinusoidal profile; more symmetrical than dunes	Less comon than dunes, occurring in steep steams; in phase with surface water waves; bed form may move upsteam, downstream or remain stationary	Upper regime of roughness; grain roughness dominant	

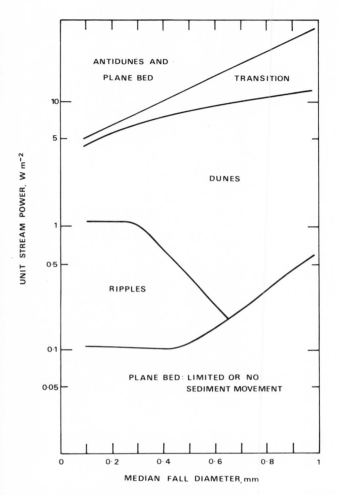

Fig 4.8 Existence fields for bed forms defined in terms of unit stream power and median fall diameter of bed material (after Simons and Richardson, 1966).

The bed forms are the effect of instability at the water–sediment interface. Deformation of an initially flat bed may lead to concentrations of grains which move intermittently when shear stresses are just above the threshold for movement. These small disturbances will under certain conditions influence the flow and local sediment transport rate in such a way that scour and deposition occur in the troughs and over the crests respectively, thereby increasing the amplitude of the initial bed undulations. Such increases disturb the local transport rate still further, promoting additional growth through positive feedback until a limit is reached and an equilibrium amplitude attained. Bagnold (1956) has shown theoretically that the formation of ripples and dunes is necessary if some degree of stability is to be achieved during sediment transport. Without the additional resistance provided by these bed forms, the channel could be destroyed as a structure for carrying the water and sediment supplied from upstream. Both the type of bed form and the geometry of each individual form depend on the prevailing flow, sediment transport and bed material properties. In particular, dune dimensions are strongly related to the depth of flow.

Bed forms exert a drag on the flow additional to that associated with the grains themselves. Flume data obtained by Simons and Richardson (1966) show how resistance, expressed by the Darcy–Weisbach friction factor ff ($= 8gRs/v^2$), varies with the type of bed form:

Lower flow regime
  (i) Ripples: $0.052 \leqslant ff \leqslant 0.13$
  (ii) Dunes: $0.042 \leqslant ff \leqslant 0.16$
Upper flow regime
  (iii) Plane bed: $0.02 \leqslant ff \leqslant 0.03$
  (iv) Antidunes: $0.02 \leqslant ff \leqslant 0.07$

Regarding plane-bed friction as indicative of the grain roughness component, the data show that form roughness can make a large contribution to total flow resistance, especially in the lower flow regime. A stream can thus alter the local resistance to flow and consequently the magnitude of any resistance-dependent variable by modifying its bed configuration.

On the one hand, bed form adjustment represents a response to changing discharge and load conditions during, for example, the passage of a flood wave, although there is always a time lag between a change of flow and a corresponding change of bed form because of the redistribution of sediment involved. On the other, bed form adjustment represents a means of regulating, principally through its effect on resistance, certain hydraulic variables, notably velocity and depth (hence its relevance to at-a-station hydraulic geometry relations (Richards, 1973)), which influence the local transport rate. Under certain conditions a given discharge can be transmitted at two or more different depths and velocities, depending on the type and size of bed form produced. Bed configuration in sand-bed streams is one of the most adjustable components of channel morphology which regulates in particular the short-term interaction of hydraulic variables and thereby promotes a kind of equilibrium in stream behaviour.

The riffle–pool sequence
The development of alternating deeps (pools) and shallows (riffles) is characteristic of both straight and meandering channels with heterogeneous bed material in the size range of 2–256 mm. Pools are especially associated with meander bends and often have a side or point-bar even in straight reaches, giving the cross-section an asymmetric profile. The gravel bars which form the intervening riffles are generally lobate in shape and frequently slope alternately first toward one bank and then toward the other so that the flow tends to follow a sinuous course even in a straight channel. The definition of individual pools and riffles in a sequence can be problematic and no one method is entirely satisfactory. One simple method deals directly with the bed topography itself and defines pools and riffles as, respectively, negative and positive residuals from a trend line fitted to bed height data (Richards, 1976b).

The most significant feature of riffle–pool geometry is the more or less regular spacing of successive pools or riffles at a distance of 5 to 7 times channel width (Figure 4.9A). The spacing distance is thus scale-related. This oft-quoted proportionality needs to be viewed against the background that both channel width and spacing distance are inherently variable even in short lengths of stream and that both present problems of consistent definition and measurement. It describes at best an average condition. The most extensive data set has values of pool-to-pool spacing ranging from 1.5 to 23.3 channel widths with an overall mean of 5.9 (Keller and Melhorn, 1978). Despite these problems, the opinion of rhythmic change in the bed topography of gravel-bed streams is now firmly entrenched. Similar tendencies have even been observed in supraglacial streams (Dozier, 1976; Knighton, 1981c). The riffle–pool sequence can be regarded as a pseudo-cyclic oscillation of stream bed height representing a combination of periodic and random elements (Richards, 1976b).

Riffle–pool development is apparently favoured by particular bed material conditions, although Keller and Melhorn (1978) regard it as a fundamental characteristic of many streams independent of boundary composition. Riffles and pools tend to be absent from or poorly developed in boulder-bed streams (Miller, 1958; Leopold *et al.*, 1964), where they may however be replaced by a pool–step sequence (Whittaker and Jaeggi, 1982), and show little tendency to form in channels that carry uniform sand or silt. Concentrations of coarser particles analogous to riffles and spaced at 5 to 7 times channel width have been observed in otherwise sandy ephemeral streams even though the concentrations had no topographic expression (Leopold *et al.*, 1966). Depending on the range of grain sizes present, riffles tend to have coarser bed material than do adjacent pools, indicating the action of local sorting mechanisms (Keller, 1971; Lisle, 1979). Thus bed topography and particle size characteristics are interrelated. Longitudinal distinctions in particle size may not always be present at this local scale, however, or be small relative to lateral differences (Milne, 1982). Upper slope as well as bed material limits have also been suggested (Keller, 1978) but are probably less critical. The degree of riffle–pool development varies with bed material size relative to the dominant flow conditions in a reach (Figure 4.6B) since the ability of a stream to modify its bed depends on the mobility of the available material and therefore the frequency with which competent flows occur.

A growing body of evidence suggests that riffles and pools have distinctive channel and flow geometries. Riffles tend to be wider and shallower at all stages of flow (Richards, 1976a). As regards response to at-a-station increases in discharge, riffle and pool sections appear to be distinguishable by (Richards, 1976a; Lisle, 1979):

$$f_{riffle} > f_{pool}$$
$$m_{riffle} < m_{pool}$$
$$z_{riffle} < 0, z_{pool} > 0$$

where f, m and z are respectively the rates of change of depth, velocity and water-surface slope. Since at low flows velocity and slope are greater and depth is less over a riffle than in a pool, the net effect of these differences in flow geometry is to produce a convergence or more even distribution of these flow variables along a reach at high flows. Competence, expressed by a bed velocity or boundary shear stress ($= \gamma Rs$), will also tend to become more evenly distributed or may even be reversed so that, contrary to the low-flow condition, it is higher in the pools at those discharges which transport most material in gravel-bed streams (Figure 4.9B; Keller, 1971; Lisle, 1979). In combining high-flow transport through pools and low-flow storage on riffles, such reversal provides a sorting mechanism for the concentration of coarser material in riffles, although it does not by itself explain their formation.

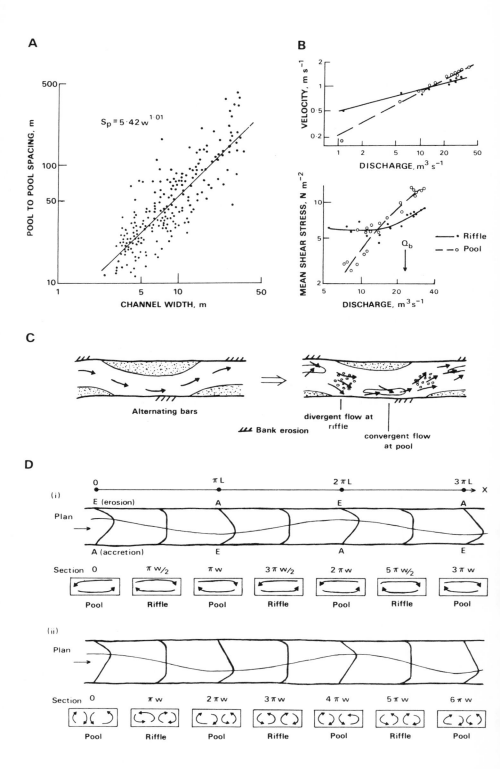

A

$S_p = 5.42\,w^{1.01}$

POOL TO POOL SPACING, m

CHANNEL WIDTH, m

B

VELOCITY, m s^{-1}

DISCHARGE, m^3 s^{-1}

MEAN SHEAR STRESS, N m^{-2}

Q_b

—— • Riffle
– – – Pool

DISCHARGE, m^3 s^{-1}

C

Alternating bars

⊥⊥⊥ Bank erosion

divergent flow at riffle

convergent flow at pool

D

(i)

0   πL   2πL   3πL   X

E (erosion)   A   E   A

Plan

A (accretion)   E   A   E

Section 0   πw/2   πw   3πw/2   2πw   5πw/2   3πw

Pool   Riffle   Pool   Riffle   Pool   Riffle   Pool

(ii)

Plan

Section 0   πw   2πw   3πw   4πw   5πw   6πw

Pool   Riffle   Pool   Riffle   Pool   Riffle   Pool

A complete explanation of riffle–pool formation needs to consider not only how they develop but also why they develop within the broader context of stream behaviour. Basically, given an initially flat bed, a riffle–pool sequence forms through a combination of scour and deposition, organized spatially to give a more or less regular spacing between consecutive elements. In the initial stages at least, a key question is sediment mobility since that influences the extent to which coarser fractions can be concentrated into incipient bars. Such concentrations probably occur at high discharges (bankfull and above), while lower flows (up to bankfull) may be sufficiently competent to amplify and maintain the initial undulations once they have reached a critical height. A distinction is thus drawn between those flows which form and those which maintain a riffle–pool sequence, the ranges of which will tend to vary with the quantity and grain size of sediment supplied.

The development of riffle–pool sequences has been explained in terms of various processes. In so far as riffles represent concentrations of units (coarser particles), Langbein and Leopold (1968) likened them to kinematic waves in traffic flow. As a result of grain–grain interactions, any random influx of particles will not remain random during downstream transport but will tend to accumulate in groups having wave-like forms and a more or less regular spacing. Bed material continues to move downstream during suitable flows but the position of these groups (riffles) remains fixed. Once the perturbations have been formed, they themselves generate the flow conditions necessary for their continued development. Kinematic wave theory explains how material moves through riffle–pool sequences and why they are relatively stable but it does not completely explain their origin or the characteristic spacing that tends to develop.

Yang (1971c) has explained riffle formation as a combined process of dispersion and sorting, arguing that greater dispersive stresses at potential riffle sites force larger particles to the surface and thereby raise the bed. The finer grains are washed out to leave concentrations of coarse particles at the riffles which are further accentuated by this combined process until a dynamic equilibrium is reached. The hypothesis contains several unverified assumptions which make the process rather unlikely.

Keller and Melhorn (1973) envisaged a multi-stage process involving convergence and divergence of flow. An initial deposition of alternating bars is followed by the development of pools against the opposite banks (Figure 4.9C). The asymmetric cross-profile of the incipient pools gives rise to convergent flow which induces scour and enhances pool development, while the flow diverges on leaving each pool, producing a more symmetric profile and deposition in the form of riffles. Although the approach is qualitative and several relevant points are not covered, this mode of development does seem plausible, especially when allied with Yalin's (1971, 1972) fundamental treatment of the behaviour of macroeddies in turbulent flow.

Yalin's argument is that a discontinuity at some point x = 0 disturbs the larger eddies in such a way that the velocity field will behave similarly at sections x = 2πL, 4πL, ... but with an opposite tendency at sections x = πL, 3πL, ... where

Fig 4.9 A. Relationship of pool-pool spacing to channel width (after Keller and Melhorn, 1978).
B. Velocity and shear stress reversal at riffle and pool sections (after Andrews, 1979 and Lisle, 1979).
C. Transformation of alternating bars to riffles and pools with divergent flow at riffles and convergent flow at pools (after Keller and Melhorn, 1973).
D. Models relating macroturbulent eddies to riffle-pool (and meander) development with (i) a single cell (after Yalin, 1971, 1972), and (ii) twin cells giving surface flow convergence at pools and surface flow divergence at riffles (after Hey, 1976); —, surface velocity profiles at sections.

L is the length of the disturbances (Figure 4.9D). As a result of these downstream fluctuations in the velocity field, a smaller sediment transport rate at x = 0 will be associated with a smaller rate at x = $2\pi L$, $4\pi L$, . . . but a larger rate at x = πL, $3\pi L$, . . ., thereby giving rise to alternating accretion and erosion. The alternating accretions and erosions will subsequently interact with the flow to maintain the initial perturbations in the velocity field. One problem with this treatment is to determine the scale variable to which the turbulent macrostructure is most likely related. Although the original derivation was applied to the formation of dunes and meanders with characteristic wavelengths of $2\pi d$ and $2\pi w$ respectively (i.e. L = d and L = w in each case), Richards (1976b) has argued that the fundamental velocity perturbation of $2\pi w$ ($\sim 6w$) is more appropriate to the development of riffles and pools than meanders. Hey (1976) reached a similar conclusion. Assuming that to be the case, the diagram for the horizontal plane (Figure 4.9D) bears a striking resemblance to the mode of development proposed by Keller and Melhorn (1973) if the accretions are interpreted as alternating bars and the erosions as scour at pools. In this way can the development of an alternating bed topography be related to oscillations in the velocity field of turbulent flow. A link with meandering is also provided, which emphasizes the interdependence of vertical and horizontal transformations in the channel.

No one explanation of riffle–pool formation is entirely satisfactory and many of the ideas remain rather speculative. Indeed more than one process may be involved. The problem is to identify an initiating mechanism which will ultimately produce a quasi-regular alternation of bed topography. Once initiated, the bed perturbations interact with the flow to generate conditions necessary for their maintenance. In particular, the hypothesis of velocity (Keller, 1971) or shear stress (Lisle, 1979) reversal in which flow competence in pools exceeds that over riffles above a certain range of flows (Figure 4.9B) offers a plausible mechanism for a pattern of scour and deposition capable of producing areal sorting of stream bed material and of maintaining the pre-existing bed topography.

As regards its broader implications, the riffle–pool sequence is seen as a means of self-adjustment in gravel-bed streams with significance firstly for the attainment and maintenance of quasi-equilibrium, and secondly for the development of meandering. Yang (1971c) has maintained that riffle–pool formation is the way in which a natural stream minimizes its time rate of potential energy loss in the vertical direction, while Cherkauer (1973) has provided limited evidence to show that flow over a riffle–pool bed satisfies the equilibrium or most probable condition of Langbein and Leopold (1964, 1966). Observation and theory testify to the relative stability of a riffle–pool bed (Leopold *et al.*, 1966; Langbein and Leopold, 1968; Keller and Melhorn, 1973, 1978), with riffle position remaining fixed during transport through a process of particle replacement in which the larger particles tend to move from riffle to riffle. Indeed the largest particles in the riffles may be essentially static except during extreme flows (Lisle, 1979). Dury (1970) found that little change had occurred in the riffle–pool morphology of a bedrock river over 100 years. Large floods can destroy a riffle-pool bed (Stewart and La Marche, 1967) but this need not necessarily be the case and the amplitude of the bed forms may indeed be increased (Gupta and Fox, 1974; Baker, 1977). In short, the riffle–pool sequence appears to be a valid equilibrium form.

Its link with meandering is based partly on the fact that the spacing of 5 to 7 times channel width is approximately half the straight-line meander wavelength and that riffles and pools in straight reaches have analogous points in meanders, namely points of inflection and pools at bend apices. Consequently several models of the transformation from a straight to a meandering pattern incorporate riffle–pool development as a significant element (Tinkler, 1970; Keller, 1972; Figures 4.6A and 4.13B).

Langbein and Leopold (1966) have argued that, whereas energy loss is concentrated at riffles in a straight reach, a more uniform rate of energy expenditure is produced in meanders by the development of bends at pool sections, a transformation which also minimizes the variance of flow properties. To that extent a meandering pattern represents a closer approximation to the most probable state. Field data comparing riffle and pool sections lend support to this conclusion (Cherkauer, 1973; Richards, 1976b). However, this explanation of meander development can only be a partial one since meanders occur in channels without a riffle–pool bed. Also, straight reaches with a riffle–pool sequence can be stable against the tendency for meanders to form (Keller and Melhorn, 1973). Richards (1976a) has contended that equilibrium can be achieved in a straight reach with alternating pools and riffles provided there is systematic variation in width with a wider channel developing at the riffles. Greater emphasis is thus placed on the sympathetic adjustment of cross-sectional rather than planimetric geometry with bed topography.

Many of the various claims regarding the riffle–pool sequence have yet to be fully tested. Hydraulic data from gravel rivers at high stage are particularly meagre. Nevertheless, this bed form does illustrate the strong relationship between flow and channel geometry, and the interdependence of the several modes of channel form adjustment. In particular, the riffle–pool sequence and meandering planform represent two sources of flow resistance capable of modifying the rate and distribution of energy loss at the reach scale, the difference between them being the plane in which the roughness principally operates.

Synthesis
Uniform beds are unstable and deform to give a wide range of forms adjustable over relatively short time periods, particularly in the case of ripples and dunes. Although sand-bed and gravel-bed forms have here been treated separately, they have important elements in common. They represent sources of flow resistance which influence the nature of energy loss. They have strong relationships with other form elements, notably channel pattern. Both dunes and riffles can be likened to kinematic waves developed at the local scale. Distinct patterns can usually be recognized although the degree of regularity can be highly variable, suggesting that a combination of deterministic and probabilistic modelling is required for the adequate description of the features.

The development of a particular form depends on local flow and sediment conditions. Given the tendency for bed material size to decrease and discharge to increase downstream, systematic changes in bed configuration may also be expected in that direction, with poorly developed riffles and pools in the headwater reaches giving way, first to better-defined riffle–pool sequences where the material is gravelly, then to a mixture of gravel-bed and sand-bed forms, and finally to ripples and dunes as the sand fraction becomes dominant. Such zonation is an idealization, although Smith (1970) has observed downstream changes in the dominant type of bar as bed material became finer grained and better sorted. Also, it emphasizes the influence of boundary composition on this element of channel form adjustment.

Channel pattern

Channel pattern represents a mode of channel form adjustment in the horizontal plane which is additional to but nevertheless linked with transverse and lengthwise modes. It influences resistance to flow and can be regarded as an alternative to slope adjustment when valley slope is treated as constant at the short and medium time scales. The effect of a meander, for example, is to increase resistance and reduce channel gradient relative to a straight reach between the same fixed points.

The conventional classification into straight, meandering and braided patterns is not entirely satisfactory. The terms are not mutually exclusive in that braiding can be superimposed on straight or meandering patterns and single channels can vary in their degree of sinuosity and regularity. The distinction between straight and meandering channels tends to be somewhat arbitrary. Also, the characteristics used to differentiate between the patterns are not consistent. Whereas braiding is distinguished by the multiplicity of channels, meandering is recognized by the tortuosity of the course.

A more logical classification starts with single-channel and multi-channel patterns. The first can be further classified according to:

(i) sinuosity, defined by

$$S = \frac{\text{channel length}}{\text{straight-line valley length}} \tag{4.29}$$

(ii) degree of regularity (Figure 4.11A) – Kellerhals *et al.* (1976) recognized three categories of meander regularity: irregular meanders with only a vague repeated pattern; regular meanders with a clearly repeated pattern and a maximum deviation angle (between the channel and downvalley axis) of < 90°; and tortuous meanders with a more or less repeated pattern and a maximum deviation angle of > 90°;

(iii) level of mobility – Popov (1964) distinguished between embedded (incised non-meandering), freely meandering and limited (confined) meandering patterns; a distinction can also be drawn between active and inactive channels, the latter being common in lowland Britain where they vary markedly in sinuosity (Ferguson, 1981).

Thus single-channel patterns include straight channels with medial bars, straight channels with alternating lateral bars and a meandering thalweg, incomplete meandering, and various forms of meandering.

Multi-channel patterns present a different problem in that their form is partly stage-dependent. Bars which are exposed at most flows may be inundated at higher discharges to give the appearance of a single channel, so that multi-channel patterns need to be described at some appropriate flow such as mean annual discharge. A subclassification based on the degree of island development may then become relevant, ranging from occasional (widely separated single islands) to fully braided (many channels divided by bars and islands).

The continuum concept

Despite the problems with the tripartite subdivision into straight, meandering and braided patterns, it remains the primary means of classification, partly because of its association with the continuum concept introduced by Leopold and Wolman (1957). Assuming that channel pattern is controlled by interactions among a set of continuous variables and that all channel patterns intergrade, Leopold and

Wolman argued that a continuum of channel patterns should exist each of which is associated with a particular combination of those variables. Although the continuum concept does not deal directly with the question of continuous deformation between channel types and rather assumes that streams are freely able to adjust their planimetric geometry, it fits the observation that channel pattern can be transitional over relatively short distances.

Slope–discharge relationships have been widely used to discriminate between the three types of channel pattern (Figure 4.10A; Table 4.10). Despite differences in the form of the relationships, which may reflect different environmental conditions, a picture emerges of braided channels occurring at steeper slopes than do meandering or straight channels. If, as laboratory experiments suggest (Ackers and Charlton, 1970b; Schumm and Khan, 1972), a further threshold exists between straight channels and meanders, then, since discharge and slope are the two variable quantities in stream power (= γQs), these results imply a sequence of channel pattern from straight to meandering to braided associated with increasing power. Chang (1979b) has introduced additional refinements to this sequence and shown analytically in terms of his concept of minimum stream power that within braided channels the number of braids actually tends to increase with stream power. Since stream power and sediment load are related (Bagnold, 1977), the sequence can also be associated with increasing sediment transport.

Table 4.10   Slope, discharge and bed material size in relation to channel pattern

Source	Relevant equations	Comments
Leopold and Wolman (1957)	$s = 0.012 \, Q^{-0.44}$	Natural streams. Braided channels plot above the line, meanders plot below the line, and straight channels occur throughout the range of slopes.
Lane (1957)	$s = 0.0007 \, Q^{-0.25}$ $s = 0.004 \, Q^{-0.25}$	Meanders Braided channels with sandy bed
Ackers and Charlton (1970b)	$s < 0.001 \, Q^{-0.12}$ $0.001 \, Q^{-0.12} < s < 0.0014 \, Q^{-0.12}$ $s > 0.0014 \, Q^{-0.12}$ $s = 0.00085 \, Q^{-0.21}$	Straight channels ⎫ Laboratory Straight channels with ⎬ experiments alternating bars ⎪ with 0.15 mm Meanders ⎭ sand Meanders plot above the line and straight reaches below; field data
Henderson (1963)	$s = 0.00012 \, D^{1.15} \, Q^{-0.46}$	Applied to the type of threshold channel — the type B channel gives way to the type A channel (allied to braiding) at slopes greater than this value, and to the type C channel (allied to meandering) at slopes lower than this value (Figure 4.4B)
Osterkamp (1978)	$s = 0.001 \, Q^{-0.24}$ $s = 0.0019 \, Q^{-0.31}$	Includes all types of channel pattern. Coefficient value tends to increase as (i) sinuosity decreases, and (ii) bed material size increases. Braided channels

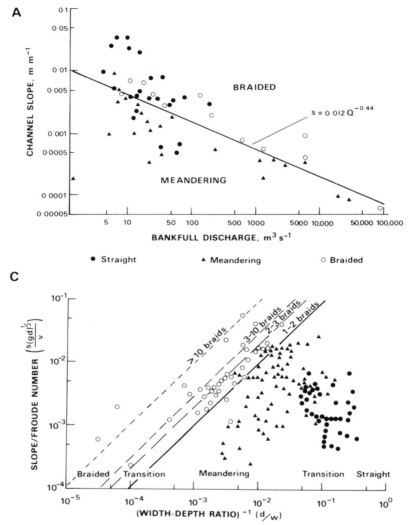

The experiments of Schumm and Khan (1972) support the slope–pattern link (Figure 4.10B) and include the effects of sediment load. Slope here represents an imposed variable akin to valley slope in the natural context. The laboratory channel remained straight until a threshold slope was reached when secondary currents became sufficiently effective in eroding and redistributing sediment to form alternating bars and a meandering thalweg. At the upper threshold (change from meandering to braided) the secondary flow was destroyed. Stream power became high enough to widen the channel significantly and induce braided-channel development. Between these two thresholds was a meandering-thalweg channel with sufficient bank resistance to preserve a sinuous pattern. Throughout the experiments sediment load had to be increased as the slope was increased in order to maintain channel stability. Consequently changes in channel pattern could be related not only to threshold slopes but also to threshold values of sediment load.

B

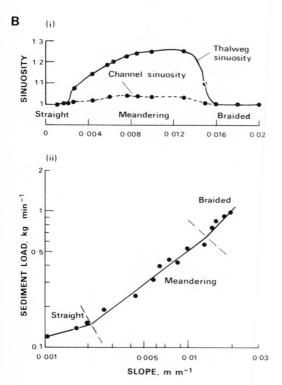

D

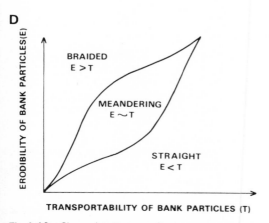

Fig 4.10 Channel pattern graphs:
A. Distinction between meandering and braided channels on the basis of a slope-discharge relationship (after Leopold and Wolman, 1957).
B. Channel pattern thresholds defined in terms of sinuosity-slope (i) and sediment load-slope (ii) relationships from flume experiments (after Schumm and Khan, 1972).
C. Straight, meandering and braided streams, and the degree of braiding, defined in terms of slope-Froude number and depth-width ratios (after Parker, 1976).
D. Straight, meandering and braided patterns defined in terms of the erodibility and transportability of bank particles (after Brotherton, 1979).

Supporting field data are largely unavailable but flume studies suggest that straight channels are unstable except at small sediment loads (Ackers and Charlton, 1970b; Schumm and Khan, 1972). The relationship between pattern, boundary composition and sediment load has been emphasized by Schumm (1963b) who found that, in the mid-west United States, meandering was associated with cohesive sediments and wash-load transport, braiding with coarser non-cohesive sediments and bed-load transport. The type of load as well as the total amount may therefore be important, although Schumm's data specifically exclude gravelly channels.

The ability of a stream to modify its channel pattern depends partly on the resistivity of bank material to erosion. Meandering depends on the availability of sufficient energy for bank erosion and sediment transfer, and experiments show a tendency for meandering channels to be wider than comparable straight ones (Ackers and Charlton, 1970b). However, excessive bank retreat may result in wide, shallow channels with multiple cells of secondary circulation which lead to braiding. Bank stability may thus be an important criterion for separating channel patterns (Figure 4.10D). Indeed Engelund and Skovgaard (1973) have analytically defined a threshold value of width below which a river meanders and above which it braids. Also, Antropovskiy (1972) has separated types of channel pattern in terms of empirical relationships between width (w) and shear stress (τ):

free meandering: $w < 0.013\tau^{-1.40}$
incomplete meandering: $0.013\tau^{-1.40} \leqslant w \leqslant 0.041\tau^{-1.40}$
braiding: $w > 0.041\tau^{-1.40}$

Parker (1976) has used a similar approach to Engelund and Skovgaard (1973) in treating meandering and braiding as an instability problem. Assuming an inherent tendency for rivers to form bars, a regime diagram is defined (Figure 4.10C) which shows that meandering is favoured where slope (s) and width–depth ratio (w/d) are sufficiently low and braiding where these variables are sufficiently high. Straight channels occur only at low width–depth ratios.

The available evidence suggests that the sequence of straight, meandering and braided patterns is related to:
(i)   increasing width–depth ratio, which is generally associated with decreasing bank stability and increasing bed-load transport;
(ii) increasing stream power, which implies increasing discharge at constant slope or increasing slope at constant discharge; and
(iii) increasing sediment load and in particular bed load.

To the extent that slope means valley slope in this context, it is regarded as an imposed constraint adjustable only over relatively long time periods. Straight reaches are possibly restricted to low-energy environments where the available stream power is not sufficient for bank erosion at formative discharges and cross-channel currents are relatively weak. At the other extreme lies the braided pattern with its characteristically wide, shallow channel in which any flow discontinuity tends to create localized circulations conducive to sub-channel development (Chitale, 1973). Between these extremes is the range of meandering channels in which there is sufficient energy for bank erosion but sufficient bank resistance to maintain a sinuous course. The action of secondary currents over the entire flow section, which is needed for sediment transfer, requires a relatively narrow, deep channel which is commonly associated with higher sinuosity. Thus has the three-fold sequence of channel pattern been represented as a continuum in terms of continuous variables, although the change from one pattern to another may be more abrupt than the continuum concept suggests as critical thresholds are crossed (Schumm and Khan, 1972).

The concept is limited in other respects. It is overly dependent on the results of laboratory experiments. While single-thread channels can be continuously deformed to give any degree of sinuosity, they cannot be continuously deformed in the horizontal plane to give multi-thread channels since the distinction between them is more a function of bed than plan geometry. The tripartite classification on which the concept is largely based oversimplifies the range of channel patterns found in natural streams. Various transitional patterns having particular char-acteristics exist, while distinctions can be drawn between active and inactive channels, confined and unconfined channels (Ferguson, 1981). Despite uniform conditions of stream power and sediment load along a length of stream, channel pattern may vary, possibly because valley slope is close to a threshold value (Schumm and Khan, 1972). Although the continuum concept has been modified since its inception, there is as yet no adequate model which can predict channel pattern from given information about significant controlling variables.

Meanders

The absence of long straight reaches and the presence of sinuous flow in straight reaches are regarded as evidence of an inherent tendency in natural streams to meander. However, the definition of a meander remains somewhat arbitrary, even though a sinuosity value in excess of 1.5 is often used. There is no guarantee that the feature will be particularly regular (Figure 4.11A), even though definition sketches often show symmetrical bends. Indeed meanders have been regarded as the outcome of random changes in direction (Langbein and Leopold, 1966) but in reality they are neither completely regular nor purely random. They are a com-promise between the two (Ferguson, 1979). If the meandering process is assumed to be deterministic and capable of producing regular forms, then the random element is provided by the environmental conditions in which that process operates.

Meander geometry has been analysed using two main approaches: the tradi-tional parametric approach which deals with individual bend statistics such as meander wavelength (λ) and radius of curvature (r_c) averaged over a series of bends (Figure 4.11B); and the series approach which spans sequences of bends and treats the stream trace as a spatial series of direction (θ) or direction change ($\Delta\theta$) in terms of distance (x) along the path (Figure 4.11C). The latter is more objective and offers greater flexibility both for analysing meander traces of varying regularity and for developing descriptive models. Ferguson (1975, 1979) considers that meandering in a broad sense can be characterized by three planimetric properties: a scale variable such as wavelength (λ or λ_*), sinuosity or wiggliness, and degree of irregularity. All three can be estimated from the analysis of direction or curvature (direction-change) series.

A simple descriptive model of meandering is provided by the equation for a sine-generated curve

$$\theta = \omega \sin kx \tag{4.30}$$

in which channel direction (θ) is expressed as a sinusoidal function of distance (x) with parameters ω (the maximum angle between a channel segment and the mean downvalley axis) and k ($= 2\pi/\lambda_*$) (Figure 4.11D(i)). Introduced by Langbein and Leopold (1966), this equation has been widely accepted as a satisfactory model of

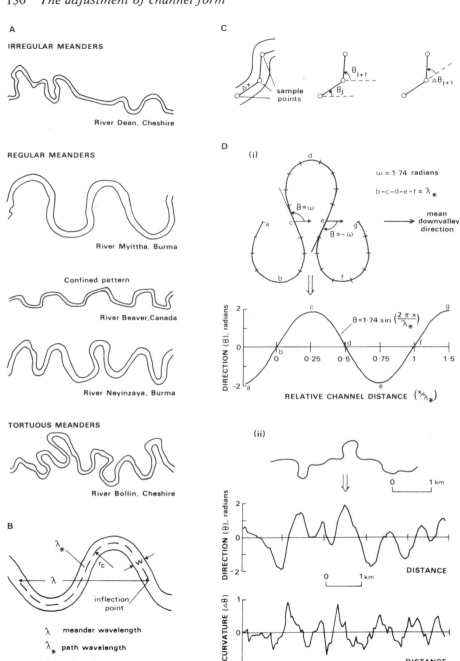

A

IRREGULAR MEANDERS

River Dean, Cheshire

REGULAR MEANDERS

River Myittha, Burma

Confined pattern

River Beaver, Canada

River Neyinzaya, Burma

TORTUOUS MEANDERS

River Bollin, Cheshire

B

λ_*

r_c

w

λ

inflection point

λ meander wavelength

λ_* path wavelength

r_c radius of curvature

C

θ_{j+1}

θ_j

$\Delta\theta_{j+1}$

$\Delta+$ sample points

D   (i)

$\omega = 1.74$ radians

$b\text{-}c\text{-}d\text{-}e\text{-}f = \lambda_*$

mean downvalley direction

$\theta = \omega$

$\theta = -\omega$

$\theta = 1.74 \sin\left(\dfrac{2\pi x}{\lambda_*}\right)$

DIRECTION (θ), radians

RELATIVE CHANNEL DISTANCE $\left(\dfrac{x}{\lambda_*}\right)$

0   0.25   0.5   0.75   1   1.5

(ii)

0   1 km

DIRECTION (θ), radians

0   1 km

DISTANCE

CURVATURE ($\Delta\theta$)

DISTANCE

Table 4.11 Meander wavelength–discharge relationships

Source	Relationship	Comments
Dury (1964)	$\lambda = 54 \, Q_{ma}^{0.5}$	Q_{ma} = mean annual flood
Carlston (1965)	$\lambda = 166 \, Q_{m}^{0.46}$	Q_{m} = mean annual discharge
	$\lambda = 126 \, Q_{mm}^{0.46}$	Q_{mm} = mean monthly maximum discharge
Ackers and Charlton (1970b)	$\lambda = 62 \, Q_{b}^{0.47}$	Q_{b} = constant 'bankfull' discharge in laboratory streams
Ferguson (1975)	$\lambda_s = 57 \, Q_{d}^{0.58}$ $\lambda_a = 36 \, Q_{d}^{0.63}$	Q_{d} = 'dominant' discharge of 1% duration; λ_s, λ_a are wavelengths estimated respectively from direction-change spectra and autocorrelograms rather than direct measurement
Dury (1976)	$\lambda = 33 \, Q_{1.58}^{0.55}$	$Q_{1.58}$ = most probable annual flood

meander bends, at least when they are regular. It is less applicable to non-regular bends or to lengthy meander patterns since a string of identical bends (constant ω and k) is unlikely (Figure 4.11D(ii)).

It has long been recognized that consistent relationships exist between meander parameters and channel width (w), where the latter operates as a scale variable of the channel system (Figure 1.2C). In particular, results from a variety of fluvial environments suggest that wavelength and radius of curvature are respectively about 10 to 14 and 2 to 3 times channel width, although there is less agreement as to the generality of the second. Hey (1976) found no constancy in bend tightness (r_c/w) in two British rivers; rather, it increased with the arc angle measured between inflection points. However, r_c/w appears to have a lower limit of approximately 2 which, once reached by a meander, influences subsequent erosion and deposition in such a way as to ease the curvature (Hickin and Nanson, 1975).

Since width is approximately proportional to the square root of discharge, it is not unreasonable to expect that meander wavelength will also vary as $Q^{0.5}$. Although this approximate relationship is now well established (Table 4.11), controversy has existed as to whether discharge has a direct influence on wavelength or only an indirect one through width (Leopold and Wolman, 1960) and, of more importance, as to which discharge is physically the most significant in shaping meanders. This issue, which is related to the dominant discharge concept, is reflected in the wide range of discharge indices used in the relationships (Table 4.11). The argument has centred on whether bankfull discharge or a more frequent range of flows is more important (Carlston, 1965), being based more on the strength of statistical relationships than physical reasoning. Meander geometry is probably related not to a single dominant discharge but to a range of discharges

Fig 4.11 A. Degrees of meander regularity in natural rivers.
B. Definition sketch of standard meander bend parameters.
C. Definition of path direction (θ) and change of direction or curvature ($\Delta\theta$) for series analysis.
D. Stream traces and their corresponding plots of direction and curvature against distance: (i) A hypothetical regular meander with a maximum deviation angle of 1.74 radians (110°) and the corresponding sine-generated curve (after Langbein and Leopold, 1966); (ii) Irregular meander pattern of the River Trent and the corresponding plots (after Ferguson, 1979).

whose competence varies with the materials in which the channel is cut. However the issue is resolved, meander wavelength is clearly scaled according to the dimensions of the channel (w) and flow (Q) systems.

To reflect the influence of boundary composition, Schumm (1967) has obtained multiple regression equations for a sample of non-gravelly channels

$$\lambda = 1935 \ Q_m^{0.34} M^{-0.74} \tag{4.31}$$

$$\lambda = 394 \ Q_{ma}^{0.48} M^{-0.74} \tag{4.32}$$

which show that, for a given discharge, meander wavelength decreases as the boundary and particularly the channel banks become more cohesive (increasing M). Combining these equations with Schumm's (1963b) sinuosity relation

$$S = 0.94 \ M^{0.25} \tag{4.33}$$

and equations (4.17)–(4.20), the implication is that λ is influenced by material properties through both w and S, varying directly with the first and inversely with the second, a view anticipated by Ferguson (1973). Channels with more cohesive materials will tend to be relatively narrow, deep and sinuous and have smaller wavelengths, at least for a range of materials up to medium sand. Larras (1968) has shown that for fine sand and coarser material wavelength increases as bed material size decreases, suggesting a reversal in the form of the relationship caused by grain size.

To the extent that M reflects the type of sediment load (p. 65), larger values of λ are associated with a higher proportion of bed-load transport. Information on the effect of the amount of sediment load is both meagre and conflicting. Whereas Shahjahan (1970) noted an inverse relation between wavelength and sediment charge (Q_s/Q), Ackers and Charlton (1970a) reported little improvement in their wavelength–discharge relation when a sediment concentration variable was included. The influence of boundary composition as well as sediment load can be properly evaluated only when better data sets become available.

These various relationships emphasize a regularity in meander geometry which is not everywhere apparent. Lowland rivers with gently sinuous courses and upland ones with confined meanders often have an irregular planform whose wavelength is difficult to define (Ferguson, 1981). One answer to this problem is to use a series approach and obtain direction or direction-change spectra. A perfectly regular meander train should have a spectrum with a single sharp peak. Whereas Speight (1967) found that Australasian rivers seldom have a single dominant wavelength, most of the spectra obtained by Ferguson (1975) for 19 British rivers have a single peak which is strongly correlated with dominant discharge (Table 4.11), leading him to conclude that environmental irregularities distort an underlying regular process to give an observed geometry which combines random and deterministic components in varying proportions.

One important element of that process is the **flow pattern** through meander bends. The main features of the flow are:

   (i) superelevation of the water surface against the concave (outer) bank;

  (ii) a transverse current directed toward the outer bank at the surface and toward the inner bank at the bed to give a cell of secondary circulation; and

 (iii) a maximum velocity current which tends toward the inner bank in the upstream limb of the bend, crosses the channel at the apex and descends below the surface as it goes round the curve.

These characteristics can be explained by the need to maintain equilibrium between centrifugal and pressure forces as water follows a curved path. A combination of

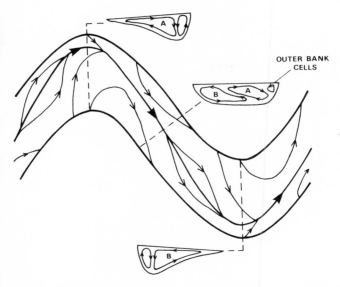

Fig 4.12 Surface flow in a meander bend with convergent flow at the bend apex and divergent flow at the inflection point (after Hey and Thorne, 1975). The cross-sections show the pattern of secondary circulation in which a new cell (B) grows beneath an old one (A) as the next bend is approached (after Thorne and Hey, 1979; Bathurst et al., 1979).

the transverse current with the main downstream velocity component gives a spiral or helicoidal motion to the flow.

Secondary currents, which can be defined in more than one way, are usually much weaker than primary ones but are nevertheless significant in that they influence the distribution of velocity and boundary shear stress. Their magnitude varies with discharge, the tightness of the bend and cross-sectional form. Provided the flow is deep enough relative to its width, it appears that more than one cell of secondary circulation may develop (Callander, 1978). Recent field observations (Thorne and Hey, 1979; Bathurst *et al.*, 1979) suggest the following pattern (Figure 4.12):

   (i) at the apex of a bend two cells of opposite rotation may exist, a major one which carries surface water toward the outer bank and a minor one which develops close to that bank provided the bank is steep; downwelling at the junction of these cells is associated with bed scour;

  (ii) between bends the circulation in the upstream bend must decay and be replaced by one of opposite rotation in the downstream bend, a process accomplished by the growth of a new cell beneath the old one at the inflection point with divergence at the surface and convergence at the bed;

 (iii) the new cell grows at the expense of the old one as the downstream bend is approached.

Since similar secondary flow patterns have been observed in straight channels with meandering thalwegs (Einstein and Shen, 1964), they appear not to be a direct consequence of meandering. The generation of a new cell close to the bed is related to the curving of streamlines as the bed topography changes from highly asymmetrical at the bend apex to almost symmetrical at the inflection point.

The complex system of primary and secondary currents in meanders influences the pattern of erosion and deposition. In broad outline bend apices are characterized by surface flow convergence and scouring, points of inflection by surface flow divergence and deposition, a pattern which parallels that proposed for pools and riffles (Figure 4.9C; Keller and Melhorn, 1973). Erosion in the bend tends to be concentrated against the outer bank immediately downstream of the apex where velocities are high and secondary flow is downward. In a parallel position against the opposite bank point-bar building predominates with material being carried by both longitudinal and transverse currents. This pattern gives a largely downvalley component to meander migration and underlines the intimate relation between deformation of the channel bed and meandering. Hooke (1975) has maintained that the importance of secondary circulation is often overstated but the flow pattern in natural rivers is difficult to replicate in laboratory flumes where most of the work has been carried out.

As yet the links between the flow and meander geometry are rather tenuous. Most progress has been made with the radius of curvature–width relation. Bagnold (1960) has shown that at $r_c/w \sim 2$ water filaments begin to separate from the inner bank. Resistance to flow through the bend is at a minimum immediately prior to breakaway but increases rapidly at $r_c/w < 2$ because the separation zone breaks down and generates large eddies. Evidence suggests that there is a corresponding reduction in the rate of erosion at the concave bank (Hickin and Nanson, 1975), possibly because the force applied to the bank also decreases rapidly as r_c/w falls below about 2 (Begin, 1981). Through its relation to flow resistance and the shear stress exerted on the outer bank, channel curvature (r_c/w) controls the rate of erosion (Figure 4.14B). Erosion increases as r_c/w decreases from higher values (>6), reaching a maximum in the approximate range $2 < r_c/w < 3$. Bends thus become tighter (r_c/w decreases at constant width). Below this range erosion decreases and subsequent adjustments tend to reduce the curvature (Hickin, 1974). These separate studies emphasize the regularity rather than the randomness of meander geometry and show how it can be explained in terms of deterministic flow behaviour.

The **initiation of meanders** requires localized bank retreat which, if a series of bends is to develop, must alternate from one side of a channel to the other in a more or less regular fashion. Associated changes in bed topography are regarded by many as the fundamental cause of meandering, preceding erosion of the channel banks (Callander, 1978). As yet there is no completely satisfactory explanation of how or why meanders develop. The ubiquity and underlying regularity of natural river bends suggest that they are not simply the result of random disturbances. Most explanations fall into two broad categories which focus respectively on the properties of the flow itself and the mechanics of sediment transport. The question is whether meandering is an inherent property of the flow and the role of sediment transport is largely collateral or whether sediment transport is an essential factor in the meandering process.

Helicoidal flow has long been recognized as an important influence on the pattern of erosion and deposition through meander bends. It is a natural consequence of flow in a curved channel. In addition, it has been argued that this type of secondary flow develops spontaneously in straight channels where turbulence is non-isotropic, the case in natural streams, as a result of vortices generated at the boundary walls (Einstein and Shen, 1964; Shen and Komura, 1968). Whether or not secondary currents are strong enough to effect major changes in the geometry

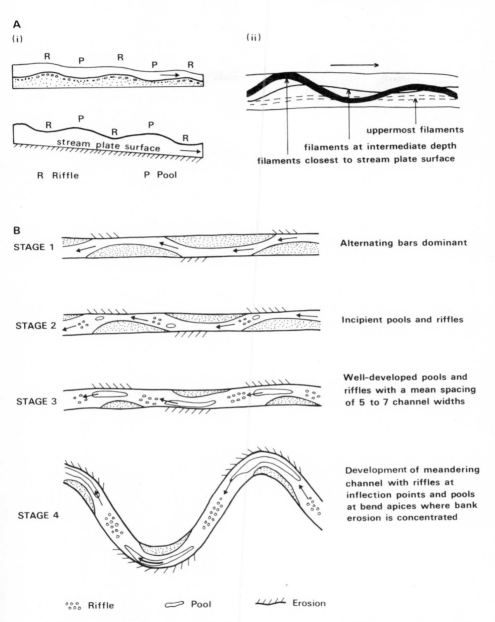

A
(i)

R   P   R   P   R

R   P   P   R   R
stream plate surface

R   Riffle   P   Pool

(ii)

uppermost filaments
filaments at intermediate depth
filaments closest to stream plate surface

B

STAGE 1   Alternating bars dominant

STAGE 2   Incipient pools and riffles

STAGE 3   Well-developed pools and riffles with a mean spacing of 5 to 7 channel widths

STAGE 4   Development of meandering channel with riffles at inflection points and pools at bend apices where bank erosion is concentrated

°°° Riffle   ⊂⊃ Pool   ∠∠∠∠ Erosion

Fig 4.13 A. Stream plate experiment (after Gorycki, 1973): (i) Water surface undulations (lower diagram) akin to pools and riffles in natural streams (upper diagram); (ii) Vertical variation in the extent of filament sinuosity with maximum sinuosity in those filaments closest to the plate surface where hydraulic drag is at a maximum.
B. Transformation of a straight channel with a riffle-pool bed to a meandering channel (after Keller, 1972).

of natural channels, they can develop meanders in laboratory flumes. Einstein and Shen (1964) recognized two types of meandering: a diagonal dune pattern which travelled rapidly downstream without developing scour holes, and a series of alternating scour holes through which the flow meandered. Both have natural equivalents (Keller, 1972).

Stream-plate experiments in the absence of sediment support the helicoidal mechanism as a cause of meandering (Tanner, 1960; Gorycki, 1973). Gorycki's results are particularly interesting. In an initially straight stream, a side view reveals upper surface undulations akin to pools and riffles in natural streams (Figure 4.13A(i)). Also, a vertical structuring is apparent in which the flow becomes more sinuous toward the plate surface where the frictional resistance is at a maximum (Figure 4.13A(ii)). As the velocity and discharge are increased, progressively more of the flow depth is involved in sinuous flow until the stream itself becomes distorted and develops meanders with a characteristic geometry. Meanders thus evolved from the effect of hydraulic drag on the flow and required the attainment of a critical velocity or discharge. Although these small laboratory streams can hardly match natural conditions, they did develop many comparable features.

Yalin's (1971, 1972) hypothesis discussed previously in the context of riffles and pools again emphasizes the importance of flow properties in meander development. He demonstrated that any discontinuity (for example, a ridge in the channel bed) disturbs the structure of the largest eddies to give a velocity field which induces alternating accretions and erosions of approximately constant wavelength, resulting in the relationship

$$\lambda \sim 2\pi w \tag{4.34}$$

In natural channels with a large width–depth ratio, these eddies are unlikely to occupy the entire width and may disintegrate into smaller cells (Figure 4.9D(ii)). Assuming that to be the case, recalculation gives a repeating distance of $4\pi w$ (Hey, 1976) which is much closer to the wavelength of natural meanders. The value of $2\pi w$ then becomes more appropriate to the riffle–pool sequence (Richards, 1976b). Whatever the merits of these modifications to Yalin's original derivation, the main point is that, given a tendency for a regular pattern of alternating regions of high velocity to develop, the resulting secondary flow is sufficient to explain meander initiation in any erodible material. This tendency is regarded as an inherent property of turbulent flow and not dependent on the presence of a deformable boundary. A deformable boundary merely allows us to observe the underlying wave-like structure in the flow. The reason for meanders is thus a horizontal version of the reason for regular alternations in bed topography.

These various explanations concentrate on flow properties and emphasize the importance of secondary currents. Field and in particular laboratory observations have frequently been cited as evidence that sediment transport is a fundamental requirement of meander development. In a series of flume experiments Friedkin (1945) observed that localized bank erosion caused overloading of the stream and the consequent deposition of sediment in the form of a point-bar a short distance downstream of, and on the same side of the channel as, the initial incision. Point-bar deposition disturbed the flow and induced erosion of the opposite bank where the same process was repeated. Thus meanders were initiated as a result of the orderly transfer of sediment from eroding banks to depositional bars which formed a downstream sequence along alternate sides of the channel. Although a channel with a meandering thalweg was produced, the channel itself had a low sinuosity at high flows because the alternate bars were submerged. Indeed most laboratory studies of river meanders have failed to duplicate the field condition of a truly sinuous bankfull channel.

The experiments of Schumm and Khan (1972) partly overcome this limitation. Once a threshold slope or shear stress was attained and secondary currents became effective in redistributing sediment, the typical meandering-thalweg channel developed. With the addition of suspended sediment and a commensurate reduction in bed-load transport, the submerged bars were stabilized and the thalweg was scoured throughout its length to leave a channel in which the banks as well as the thalweg had a meandering pattern. These results imply that the development of meandering depends on changes in the type of sediment load being carried by a stream.

Lewin (1976) has described the rapid initiation of meanders in an artifically straightened gravel-bed stream without any change in sediment load conditions. Emphasizing the intimate relationship between sedimentation and meandering, he ascribed the immediate cause of bank erosion at regularly spaced intervals and thus the creation of meanders to secondary flow patterns related to modifications in the bed of the initial channel. Once a sinuous channel had formed, however, flow patterns and bank erosion became less dependent on initial forms so that lateral accretion became more a result than a precursor of bank erosion. Thus cause–effect relationships would be reversed during the multi-phase development of meanders.

To the extent that deformation of the channel bed precedes erosion of the channel banks, Lewin's observations support the results obtained from mathematical modelling (Engelund and Skovgaard, 1973; Parker, 1976), the basic aim of which is to identify a cause from which meandering follows as an effect. The main thesis is that the mobile bed of a channel with straight banks is unstable. This instability takes the form of alternating bars which tend to grow in amplitude, leading eventually to the formation of meanders provided $w/d \ll \dfrac{v}{s(gd)^{\frac{1}{2}}}$ (braiding develops if $\dfrac{w}{d} \gg \dfrac{v}{s(gd)^{\frac{1}{2}}}$, Parker, 1976, Figure 4.10C). Sediment transport is regarded as an essential rather than simply a collateral factor in this process. Parker has further argued that secondary flow is a result rather than a cause of meandering tendencies and is therefore not essential. Although the need for sediment transport is largely a consequence of the mathematics and mathematical models are at best approximations to physical reality, the formation of alternating bars is a significant element in models of meander development based on field observations (Keller, 1972; Figure 4.13B).

The standard evidence against sediment-related hypotheses is the presence of meanders in environments where there is no material to form bars (supraglacial streams) and where there are no confining banks (Gulf Stream currents, streamplate experiments). Parker (1976) has attempted to explain each of these three cases by invoking special conditions. Although not explicitly stated, the implication is that meanders are not necessarily the outcome of a single cause. Indeed similarity of form is no guarantee of similarity of process. However, even in alluvial streams where sediment transport does occur, the orderly transfer of material must be related to an underlying pattern in the behaviour of flow.

Other explanations have been less concerned with specific processes and rather more with why streams meander in the broader context of channel form adjustment. Yang (1971b) has hypothesized that a stable unbraided channel must adopt a sinuous meandering course in order to satisfy the so-called 'law' of least time rate of potential energy expenditure. Since this law is equivalent to minimization of the velocity–slope product, meandering is principally regarded as a means of slope reduction for given external constraints. Chang (1979b) has argued in a similar vein, where the relevant quantity to be minimized is γQs rather than vs. Although the derivations contain inconsistencies, they do underline the relationship between meandering and slope adjustment. Along a stretch of river with essentially uniform water and sediment discharges but a variable valley slope, a river can maintain a relatively constant gradient by lengthening its course where the valley slope is locally steep. Consequently, if no other adjustments are made, higher values of sinuosity should reflect steeper valley slopes. Along the Red River in the southern United States, a smooth river profile is maintained despite valley slope irregularities by such changes in sinuosity (Lee and Henson, 1977).

Langbein and Leopold (1966) postulated that meandering is the most probable channel form in that it satisfies as closely as possible the condition of minimum variance. As in Yang's (1971b) hypothesis, meanders are regarded as features in dynamic equilibrium. Variance minimization was recognized in two ways: through adjustment of the plan geometry, and through adjustment of hydraulic variables. Dealing with the first, Langbein and Leopold proposed that the typical shape of a meander pattern is the most probable random walk between two fixed points. If changes in direction ($\Delta\theta$) per unit distance are normally distributed, then the most probable path is the one with minimum variance of curvature and its equation is closely approximated by the sine-generated curve (equation 4.30). However, this model is unrealistic (Ferguson, 1979). In particular, the proposition that changes in direction from one channel segment to the next are independent random variables (ϵ_j) in the form

$$\Delta\theta_j = \theta_j - \theta_{j-1} = \epsilon_j \qquad (j = 1, 2, \ldots) \tag{4.35}$$
$$\text{or} \quad \theta_j = \theta_{j-1} + \epsilon_j \qquad (j = 1, 2, \ldots) \tag{4.36}$$

gives rise to untenable channel patterns. A model which recognizes that events in neighbouring segments are dependent on one another provides a more realistic picture of behaviour in meandering reaches. Ferguson's (1976) disturbed periodic model

$$\theta_j = b_1\theta_{j-1} + b_2\theta_{j-2} + \epsilon_j \qquad (j = 1, 2, \ldots) \tag{4.37}$$

reproduces many of the main features of meander geometry in fulfilling this requirement.

With respect to the adjustment of hydraulic variables, Langbein and Leopold (1966) argued that, whereas energy loss is concentrated at riffles in a straight reach, it is more uniformly distributed in meanders because of the additional resistance provided by curvature at pools. Thus the condition of minimum variance is satisfied. Support for this hypothesis has come from comparisons of flow conditions in neighbouring curved and straight reaches in both a supraglacial stream (Dozier, 1976) and a gravel-bed stream (Richards, 1976b). Although incomplete, this approach provides some explanation for the meandering habit and, through its emphasis on the distribution of energy loss in streams, offers opportunities for further development.

There is no general agreement as to how or why streams meander. The problem is to account for the development of the first bend which, once formed, will influence flow conditions and induce further meandering downstream. Explanations which require the formation of alternating bars as an initial condition cannot be universally applicable because of meandering in streams which carry no sediment load. Nevertheless, deformation of the channel bed appears to be an important prerequisite which modifies the pattern of flow prior to meandering. That deformation may take the form of a more or less regular variation in the degree of cross-sectional asymmetry (Figure 4.6A; Knighton, 1982). In line with Yalin (1971, 1972) and Gorycki (1973), meandering is here regarded as the external manifestation of a wave-like structure inherent to water flow. Sediment factors act largely as modifying influences on the underlying flow mechanism. Too much reliance has been placed on the results of laboratory experiments which cannot faithfully reproduce natural conditions and there is a need for more systematic studies in the field (see Thorne and Hey, 1979; Bathurst *et al.*, 1979).

Finally, the **stability** of the meandering planform needs to be considered. By analogy with vibrating spring systems, Quick (1974) defined three possible states:

(i) a tendency for meanders to be damped out, implying that some form of straight or slightly curved channel is maintained (the straight channel with a riffle–pool bed and an oscillatory width proposed by Richards (1976a) would fall in this category);
(ii) stable meanders; and
(iii) increasingly unstable meanders which will eventually develop cut-offs.

As shown previously, meandering in alluvial rivers seems to require sufficient energy for bank erosion and sediment transfer but sufficient bank resistance to prevent overwidening. Beyond critical levels of slope, stream power and bank resistance, meanders give way to braided channels as the dominant planimetric form.

The underlying regularity of meander geometry suggests that, for a given range of conditions, meanders are stable forms in dynamic equilibrium. However, they do have a tendency to migrate. Point-bar deposition on the convex bank complements erosion of the concave bank which, being concentrated in the downstream limb beyond the bend apex, gives a predominantly downvalley component to migration. On average, deposition keeps pace with erosion to maintain an approximately constant width but local imbalances are possible to give complex patterns of change. At a larger scale, areas that have experienced tilting may have a regional trend to meander migration additional to the main downvalley component (Nanson, 1980).

Migration occurs at widely different rates which vary directly with discharge and indirectly with bank resistance (Daniel, 1971). It can involve various types of movement (Figure 4.14A): translation when the bend shifts its position upstream or downstream without altering its basic shape; rotation when the bend axis changes its orientation; and extension when the path length increases. Although Hooke (1977) has shown that, of 444 eroding bends in Devon rivers, 55 per cent either translated downstream, extended laterally, or both, in a generally consistent way, in different combinations these types of movement could produce a wide range of meander shapes and varying degrees of pattern irregularity. Given the tendency for migration, the question is whether a stable geometry can exist, related in some way to the distribution of effective stresses.

Channel curvature (r_c/w) seems to have an important effect on the rate of channel migration. From a detailed study of scroll bars developed over 250 years along the Beatton River in British Columbia, Hickin and Nanson (1975) demon-

A

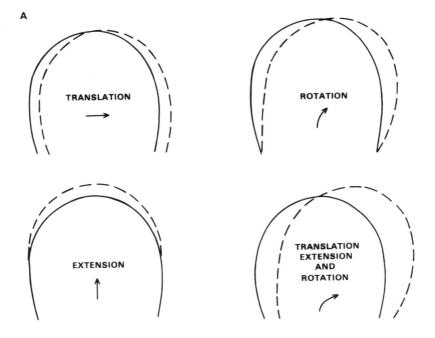

B

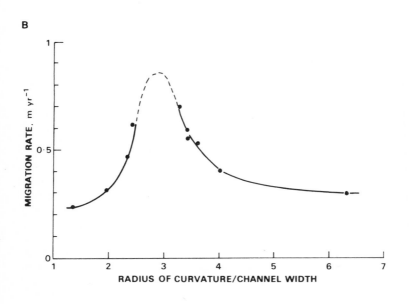

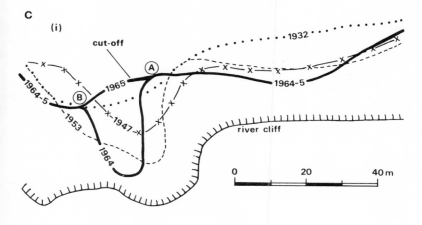

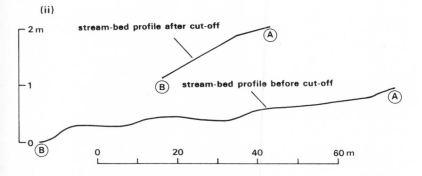

Fig 4.14 A. Types of movement of meander bends.
B. Relationship between the average rate of channel migration and the ratio of radius of curvature to channel width (after Hickin and Nanson, 1975).
C. Development of a cut-off, River Irk, Lancashire (after Johnson and Paynter, 1967): (i) Course changes prior to the cut-off; (ii) Increase in channel gradient resulting from cut-off development.

strated that the rate of migration was at a maximum for $2.4 < r_c/w < 3.3$, decreasing rapidly on either side of this range (Figure 4.14B). The decrease at the lower end of the range may be attributable to the large increase in resistance (Bagnold, 1960) or decrease in radial force exerted on the outer bank (Begin, 1981) as r_c/w falls below 2, a slightly smaller value than Hickin and Nanson's lower limit. Based on studies in a meandering flume, Hooke (1975) has argued that a uniform down-valley migration and therefore a stable meander geometry require a curvature in the range of 2 to 3. Too shallow a curve (r_c is too large) gives rise to a shear stress distribution which induces a faster rate of migration in the upstream than in the downstream limb, thereby leading to an increase in curvature. Conversely, if r_c is too small, the downstream limb migrates more rapidly and the bend becomes less arcuate. When combined, these separate studies suggest that a natural stream can control both the rate of migration and the pattern of erosion and deposition in meander bends by adjusting its channel curvature. They provide evidence of a self-regulating mechanism by which a stable geometry can be attained despite down-valley migration.

Curvature is but one mode of adjustment available to a natural stream. Indeed the preceding discussion assumed that width remained constant while r_c alone was changed. Wide, shallow channels tend to have a lower sinuosity (flatter bends) than do narrow, deep ones (equations 4.17 and 4.33) and Chitale (1973) has used this tendency to show how the cross-sectional shape (width–depth ratio) of a channel can influence the distribution of erosion in meander bends and hence their stability. In particular he argued that the location of erosion in narrow, deep channels helps to increase sinuosity until eventually a cut-off develops across the narrowed neck. In wide, shallow channels erosion is concentrated beyond rather than at the bend apex so that meanders travel downstream rather than increase in curvature. If the conditions for stable meandering are to be better defined, both planform and other elements of adjustment need to be linked more effectively with flow behaviour. The development of theoretical models (Engelund, 1974) is one means toward this end.

Not all meandering rivers migrate. The meander pattern of the lower Ohio River has changed little over the past 1000 years (Alexander and Nunnally, 1972). How-ever, where flow and bank material conditions are conducive to a continued increase in the amplitude and tightness of bends, a threshold sinuosity may be reached which the river can no longer maintain and a cut-off develops (Figure 4.14C). Cut-offs are therefore a symptom of instability (state (iii) of Quick, 1974). They can be regarded as a response to excessive sinuosity which so lowers the channel gradient that the stream cannot transport the load supplied, although they do develop in supraglacial streams which carry no sediment load (Knighton, 1981c). The net effect of cut-off development is to increase channel gradient and therefore local transporting ability, so that selective cut-offs may return a river to a more stable sinuosity which enables a balance to be maintained between curvature and transport. Meandering is one means whereby a river can adjust its rate of energy loss and transporting ability. In both respects a meandering channel may be more efficient than a straight one (Onishi *et al.*, 1976).

Braided channels

Braided reaches consist of two or more channels divided by bars or islands, with one channel usually being dominant. They are characterized by relatively high width–depth ratios, steep slopes and large bed loads. The containing channel generally has a more or less straight alignment, although individual channels may be quite sinuous. Distinctive topographic levels can often be identified across the channelled area, ranging from the most active channels to elevated, abandoned areas. Former channels may be reoccupied and enlarged during high discharges when rapid shifts in channel position are not uncommon.

In comparison with meanders, the geometrical properties of braided channels have received little attention. Consequently few relationships exist between braided channel geometry and variables of any causative significance. Part of the problem stems from the fact that the degree of braiding is not constant in the short term but tends to decrease at high stages as channel bars are drowned out (Figure 4.15A). For that reason Howard *et al.* (1970) chose to use only those variables that can be determined from topographic maps, which may account for the poor correlations between their indices of braiding and hydraulic regime. However, they did show that braided streams tend to be less sinuous than single-thread channels and that the number of channels in a braided reach increases with slope. The latter result agrees with theoretical analyses of channel pattern (Figure 4.10C; Parker, 1976; Chang, 1979b). In particular Parker's analysis emphasizes how adjustments to braided channel geometry can alter resistance properties and indicates that, if a number of multi-channel forms are possible, those with the least excess energy are the most likely to occur.

The distinctive feature of the braided pattern is the complex of bars and islands which occupy the channelled area. Central bars elongate in the flow direction and rhomboidal in outline are typical of braided rivers which carry a coarse gravel load. Their formation in a laboratory flume has been described by Leopold and Wolman (1957). The lag deposition of coarser material which the stream is locally incompetent to transport provides a locus for further deposition so that the incipient bar grows surfaceward and downstream by successive addition (Figure 4.15B). When the bar is large enough, the main flow becomes concentrated in the flanking channels which erode their banks and scour their beds until eventually the central bar emerges as an island. In rivers, the growth of vegetation helps to stabilize the island by preventing erosion and promoting the deposition of finer material. This process may be repeated in one or both of the flanking channels to give further subdivision along the reach. A similar mode of formation has been observed in natural streams (Krigstrom, 1962).

Lateral bars of diverse morphology can also develop (Figure 4.15C), particularly where individual channels are relatively sinuous. They begin as arcuate masses of sediment attached to one bank in the same way as a point-bar but, unlike the point-bar, do not grade upward into the adjoining flood-plain (Bluck, 1976). They extend across the stream to meet the opposite bank at an acute angle and have a steep downstream face behind which a bar platform is constructed. The diagonal form of these bars directs the flow obliquely across the channel and the bed is scoured downstream of the face where the flow is concentrated (Krigstrom, 1962). Dissection of the bar platform and downstream face at high discharges enhances the braided appearance.

Bars generally consist of sand and gravel in varying proportions. With the tendency for grain size to decrease downstream, the dominant type of bar may also vary longitudinally (Smith, 1970). Although not always the case, the materials forming more stable bars tend to become finer upwards, reflecting the progressively lower energy regimes of inundating flows as bars grow vertically (Figure 3.11). Although within-channel deposition is a dominant process in the formation of braiding, it occurs in association with both vertical and lateral erosion as the flow becomes concentrated in flanking channels and is diverted sideways against confining banks. Indeed the creation of new channels by erosional rather than depositional processes can also give rise to a braided pattern. Although based on laboratory experiments, it was suggested by Hong and Davies (1979) that this mode of development is dominant in rivers having a lower slope and carrying finer, more homogeneous material. Certainly former channels can be reoccupied at high stages where the channelled area is relatively wide, thereby reinforcing the braiding process.

Although not as frequent as single-thread channels, braided channels occur in a wide range of environments, from proglacial to semi-arid, and at a large range of scales, from the small streams on sandy beaches to the largest continental rivers.

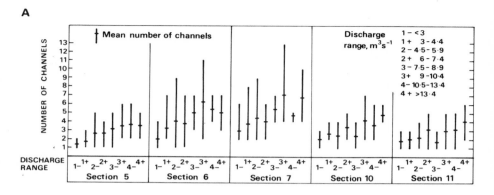

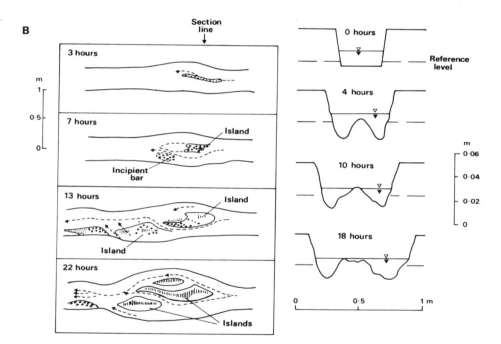

Fig 4.15   A. Changes in the number of channels with discharge at cross-sections in a braided stream (after Fahnestock, 1963).
B. Stages in the plan and cross-sectional development of a braided channel in a laboratory flume (after Leopold and Wolman, 1957).
C. Types of bar in Scottish rivers: (i) Lateral bar; (ii) Medial bar (after Bluck, 1976).

Various conditions have been suggested as conducive for the development of this planimetric form:

(i) **An abundant bed load** – Although it is generally assumed that braiding is not symptomatic of overloading, the availability of large amounts of sediment is regarded as necessary. In addition, the load should contain size fractions which the

C

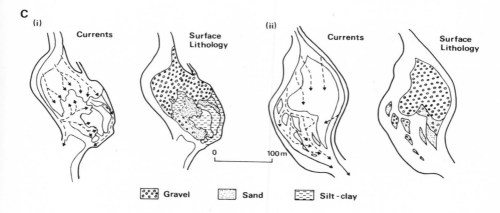

(i)

Currents

Surface Lithology

(ii)

Currents

Surface Lithology

0   100 m

Gravel   Sand   Silt - clay

stream is locally incompetent to transport as they provide the initial deposits. Concentrated deposition in the form of bars diverts the flow against the channel banks and thus contributes to the bank erosion needed for the development of the wide, shallow channel commonly associated with bed-load transport. Changes in the channel pattern of the Rangitata River in New Zealand illustrate the importance of sediment availability (Schumm, 1980). The river descends from the mountains to the Canterbury Plain through a narrow bedrock gorge, above which there is a plentiful supply of sediment and a braided pattern. In common with the other rivers which cross the Canterbury Plain, it seems that the Rangitata should also be braided below the gorge but the reduced sediment supply there has caused it to adopt a meandering planform. However, further downstream where the river has cut into poorly consolidated materials, it rapidly converts from a meandering to a braided form which then persists to the sea.

(ii) Erodible banks – Banks composed of readily erodible material are an important source of sediment as well as being necessary for the channel widening characteristic of braided reaches. The opportunity for localized deposition is greater in a wider channel in which any non-uniformity in the flow tends to affect part rather than all of the cross-section. Without erodible banks, any incipient bar deposits would tend to be destroyed rather than added to. Examples exist to show that rivers with resistant banks meander rather than braid even though bed-load transport may be dominant (Miall, 1977). Mackin (1956) attributed a sequence of meandering – braided – meandering along the Wood River in Idaho to changes in bank resistance as the river passes through a corresponding sequence of forest – prairie – forest environments. The Turandui River in New Zealand has changed over a period of years from a braided to a meandering pattern as a result of the planting of willow shrubs at appropriate places (Nevins, 1969). Although this factor is not by itself sufficient since braided and non-braided patterns can coexist along reaches where bank erodibility does not vary markedly (Fahnestock, 1963), it may be critical where conditions are close to the meandering – braided threshold suggested by regime diagrams (Figure 4.10).

(iii) A highly variable discharge – Rapid fluctuations in discharge are often associated with high rates of sediment supply, particularly in proglacial areas. They also contribute to bank erosion and irregular bed-load movement, both of which are conducive to bar formation. At a longer time scale, braiding seems to have developed as a direct result of historic flooding (Schumm and Lichty, 1963; Burkham, 1972). However, the fact that braided reaches can be interspersed with meandering ones and that braiding can be produced in the laboratory under steady flow conditions (Leopold and Wolman, 1957; Hong and Davies, 1979) suggests that rapid discharge variation is not of primary importance in braided channel development.

(iv) Steep slopes – The evidence from empirical and theoretical studies indicates that braiding develops when the slope is above a threshold value (Leopold and Wolman, 1957; Schumm and Khan, 1972; Parker, 1976). Also, the degree of braiding seems to increase as the slope steepens, at least in theory (Parker, 1976; Chang, 1979b). However, the critical factor is possibly a high stream power (γQs) rather than simply a steep slope, since braiding can persist at low slopes in large rivers (the Ganges at Patna has a braided pattern but a slope of only 0.000066 m m^{-1}, Leopold and Wolman, 1957) and channel subdivision is characteristic of deltaic areas where gradients are often low. A river must be sufficiently powerful to erode its banks and achieve the high bed mobility which is a crucial requirement for braiding. None of these conditions appears to be sufficient on its own to produce braiding, although an abundant bed load, erodible banks and a relatively high stream power are probably necessary. Where these factors occur in association, as in proglacial areas, braiding tends to be most prevalent.

Braided streams are characterized by frequent shifts in channel position. Between 1736 and 1964 the Kosi River in India has migrated westward over a distance of 112 km, reworking its own deposits and maintaining a braided pattern in the process (Gole and Chitale, 1966). Shifts of up to 90–120 m day^{-1} have been reported along the lower Yellow River in China where the amount of lateral shifting is controlled by the spacing of valley-side constrictions (Chien, 1961). Major floods may indeed be responsible for the onset of braiding as well as triggering large shifts in channel position. At a more modest scale, the formation and destruction of individual bars and channels can be observed over a few hours or days as discharge fluctuates (Fahnestock, 1963). Where juxtaposed channels differ in flow competence, rapid changes are not unexpected. The subsidiary one may be plugged with coarser material at its upstream end so that the flow becomes concentrated in the main channel which scours its bed and erodes its banks preparatory to a new phase of braiding. Given the transitory nature of braided channels, it seems reasonable to regard them as unstable.

Ackers and Charlton (1970b) have argued that the braided pattern is unstable since it develops where a river cannot transport the total load supplied. Aggradation occurs until an equilibrium slope is achieved when presumably braiding must cease and give way to a straight or meandering pattern. However, increases in slope tend to exacerbate braiding rather than damp it and many regard the braided pattern as a valid equilibrium form, even though individual channels might be transient. Leopold and Wolman (1957) found braided reaches showing little change over several decades, although the reaches are single channels with vegetated islands rather than active braids. They maintained that braiding is merely the type of adjustment made by rivers with erodible banks and a debris load too large to be carried by a single channel. It represents a particular combination of the adjustable variables which, once established, can be maintained thereafter with only slight modification.

There is now some theoretical justification for this opinion (Parker, 1976; Chang, 1979b), although Chang does differentiate between braiding due to overloading and channel-bed aggradation and braiding due to steep slopes, only the latter of which is deemed capable of maintaining a quasi-equilibrium between discharge, sediment inflow and transport capacity. Progress has been made toward defining the channel and hydraulic geometry variables which characterize braiding as a stable state. Also, both analyses suggest that the degree of braiding can be adjusted in order to satisfy specific energy relationships. Bagnold (1977) has shown that bed-load transport is directly related to stream power and that it is more efficient in channels which are shallow relative to the size of bed material (equation 3.18). To the extent that braiding is favoured where stream power and width-depth ratio are sufficiently high, it would seem to fulfil the requirements needed for transportation of a large bed load. In common with meandering, braiding involves changes in form elements other than strictly planimetric ones and represents a mode of adjustment that can modify the way in which a stream consumes its energy. Such modification has implications for transporting ability.

Channel gradient and the longitudinal profile

River profiles are an important element of drainage-basin geomorphology in that, together with the channel network, they fix the boundary conditions for slope processes. The longitudinal profile is a graph of height (H) against distance downstream (L) expressed formally by

$$H = f(L) \tag{4.38}$$

Given a tendency to treat the profile as an ideal shape, the initial problem is to determine the possible form that this functional relation might take.

Hack (1957) has argued that slope (s) and distance (L) are related by a power function,

$$s = k\,L^n \tag{4.39}$$

where the exponent n is an index of profile concavity. Since $s = -dH/dL$ (the minus sign denotes decreasing gradient downstream), equation (4.39) can be integrated to give the two profile equations:

$$H = H_1 - k \ln L \qquad \text{where } n = -1 \tag{4.40}$$

$$H = H_0 - \frac{k}{n+1} L^{n+1} \qquad \text{where } n \neq -1 \tag{4.41}$$

where H_0 and H_1 are the heights at $L = 0$ and $L = 1$ respectively. For gravel-bed and boulder-bed streams in Virginia and Maryland, Hack believed that the two equations applied to different conditions, the first where grain size remains constant along a stream and the second where grain size changes systematically downstream. However, the association of a logarithmic profile (equation 4.40) with constant grain size is unlikely to apply generally. In particular equation (4.40) describes reasonably well the profile of the River Bollin (Figure 4.16C) along which bed material size decreases markedly.

Assuming that slope is proportional to height,

$$\frac{-dH}{dL} = k_1 H \tag{4.42}$$

a simple model of profile form can be derived in which height decreases exponentially downstream:

$$H = H_0 e^{-k_1 L} \tag{4.43}$$

Since the particle size model (equation 3.25) has a similar form, a close link between channel gradient and bed material size is already implied (note that

$$s = s_0 e^{-\delta L} \tag{4.44}$$

can be reduced to equation 4.43 for appropriate changes to parameters). A similar approach can be used to describe profile development if distance is replaced by time (t) to give:

$$H = H_0 e^{-k_2 t} \tag{4.45}$$

which suggests that erosion at any point slows down exponentially over time. Given the underlying complexity of reality, it would be surprising if such simple formulations provided accurate solutions.

More complex treatments have been based on equations of the diffusion type (Devdariani, 1967; Begin *et al.*, 1981):

$$\frac{\partial H}{\partial t} = K \frac{\partial^2 H}{\partial L^2} \tag{4.46}$$

where height is a function of both distance and time. Such equations seem to provide the correct basis for modelling river profiles whose development is subject to external constraints and random influences (Scheidegger, 1970). However, a solution of sufficient generality has yet to be obtained and the exponential model (equation 4.43) serves as a first approximation to the typical river profile. Indeed Leopold and Langbein (1962) attempted to justify its applicability by demonstrating with a random-walk model that the most probable profile should have an exponential form if there are no constraints on channel length (Figure 4.16F(i)).

Longitudinal profiles tend to be concave upward (Figure 4.16) but they are rarely smooth. They may contain evidence of past events. Based on the assumption that convexities in compound profiles (those with concave segments separated by convex steps) indicate the position of rejuvenation heads, attempts have been made to estimate former sea levels by downvalley extrapolation of curves fitted to profiles and terrace remnants (e.g. Jones, 1924; Figure 4.16E). However, convexities can be produced other than by headward recession following a fall in base-level. The profile of Nigel Creek in the Canadian Rockies provides an extreme example (Figure 4.16D). The large step toward the basin mouth reflects the discordant junction of two pre-existing glaciers, while the smaller convexities upstream are related

Fig 4.16 Longitudinal stream profiles:
A. River Amazon, illustrating how Langbein's (1964b) index of concavity is calculated where H is total fall and A is the height difference between the profile at mid-distance and a straight line joining the end points of the profile.
B. River Rhine.
C. River Bollin (dashed line) and a logarithmic profile (solid line) calculated on the basis of equation (4.40).
D. Nigel Creek, Canadian Rockies.
E. River Towy and its main tributaries, with profiles (dashed lines) fitted to indicate previous base-levels (after Jones, 1924).
F. Random walk profiles generated without (i) and with (ii) length constraints (after Leopold and Langbein, 1962).

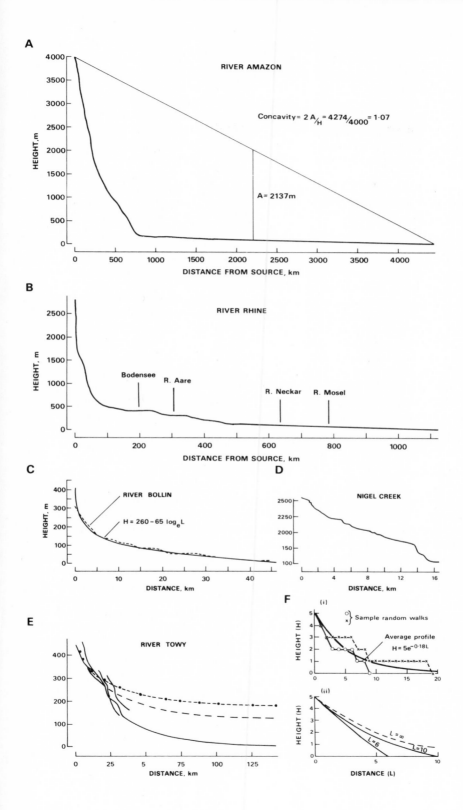

to resistant bedrock outcrops. Interestingly, well-defined knickpoints have developed in small channels tributary to Nigel Creek in response to recent down-cutting by the main stream as it passes through braided reaches (Knighton, 1976). In addition to major convexities, smaller-scale fluctuations related in particular to local bed topography and channel pattern underlie the main downstream tendency for gradient to decrease. Thus both the degree of concavity and average gradients can vary within and between rivers as a result of geological and hydrological effects.

Controls on channel gradient
Rubey's (1952) equation for 'large adjusted streams',

$$s^3 = k \; \frac{Q_s^2 M}{Q^2 X} \tag{4.47}$$

summarizes the main factors controlling channel gradient. For a constant cross-sectional shape X (= d/w), slope varies directly with sediment load (Q_s) and the size of material in the load (M), and inversely with discharge (Q). Since sediment load data are sparse, subsequent empirical work has tended to focus on the effects of M and Q, with M being characterized by bed material size (D) and drainage area (A_d) often being used as a surrogate for Q.

The size and sorting of bed material at any point are determined by the initial conditions of supply and the subsequent action of sorting and abrasion processes during downstream transport (Figure 3.6). Both initial size and resistance to wear are influenced by bedrock lithology. Working in an area of diverse lithology, Hack (1957) found no simple relation between channel slope and median bed material size. Only when sites of equivalent drainage area (approximately equal discharge) were compared was a significant relationship obtained:

$$s = 0.006 \left(\frac{D_{50}}{A_d} \right)^{0.6} \tag{4.48}$$

The implication is that slope depends not on grain size or discharge alone but on their combined effect. The influence of lithology was reflected in the progressively steeper slopes and coarser debris of similar-sized streams flowing on limestone, shalè and sandstone bedrock.

Subsequent work has tended to confirm that positive relationships between slope and average bed material size remain rather weak, even along single streams (Wilcock, 1967), unless some index of discharge is also included (Cherkauer, 1972; Penning-Rowsell and Townshend, 1978). However, Wilcock (1967) did find that slope correlated well with residual bed material size, defined as that fraction which is too coarse to be moved by present-day bankfull flows. This raises the question of the physical significance of different grain size parameters. Debris size influences bed mobility and hydraulic roughness, both of which affect the adjustment of channel gradient. For British gravel rivers in which slope is relatively free to adjust, Charlton et al. (1978) suggested that slope is better related to D_{65} (the threshold grain diameter at bankfull stage) than to D_{90} (the diameter used to represent the size of roughness elements). Certainly the exponent associated with D_{65} is positive and much higher in absolute terms in multiple regression equations (Table 4.12).

Following a similar line, Howard (1980) has argued that a small range of grain sizes coarser than the mean is critical in determining required channel gradients.

Table 4.12 Multivariate relationships with channel slope as the dependent variable

Source	Relationship	Comments
Wolman and Brush (1961)	$s = 0.0011\ C_s^{0.25}\ Q^{-0.47}$	Laboratory experiments in coarse sand
Cherkauer (1972)	$s = k_1\ R_f^{0.80}\ \overline{D}^{0.20}\ (w/d)^{0.14}\ A_d^{-0.40}$	Concave segments on sedimentary rocks
	$s = k_2\ R_f^{0.38}\ \overline{D}^{0.26}\ A_d^{-0.19}$	Straight segments on sedimentary rocks
	$s = k_3\ R_f^{1.02}\ \overline{D}^{0.28}\ (w/d)^{0.22}\ A_d^{-0.51}$	Concave segments on granitic rocks
	$s = k_4\ R_f^{0.42}\ \overline{D}^{0.06}\ A_d^{-0.21}$	Straight segments on granitic rocks

Ephemeral streams in Arizona; concave segments are upstream, straight ones downstream

| Charlton et al. (1978) | $s = 0.40\ Q^{-0.42}\ D_{65}^{1.38}\ D_{90}^{-0.24}$ | $d/D_{90} > 3$: relatively smooth channels |
| | $s = 0.12\ Q^{-0.25}\ D_{65}^{1.22}\ D_{90}^{-0.55}$ | $d/D_{90} < 3$: relatively rough channels |

British gravel rivers: negligible sediment load, slope assumed to be freely adjustable

Symbols: s, channel slope;
C_s, sediment concentration (total load);
Q, discharge;
R_f, basin relief;
$\overline{D}$, mean grain size;
w/d, width–depth ratio;
A_d, drainage area;
D_{65}, grain size at which 65% of the particles are smaller;
D_{90}, grain size at which 90% of the particles are smaller

Using 15 different transport equations he has calculated the gradient required to transport the load supplied. When required gradient is plotted against grain size, the various equations give the same basic pattern: a maximum in the range of 0.1–2 mm, a minimum near 5–10 mm, and a continuous increase in required gradient for grain sizes larger than 10 mm (Figure 4.17A). In effect the minimum at 5–10 mm separates gravel-bed from sand-bed streams. In the former the required gradient is determined by the supply of coarse grains. If, for some critical grain size, the required gradient is greater than the fine-grained maximum (A in Figure 4.17A), the bed will be dominated by that coarse fraction. On the other hand, if the required gradient for that critical size is less than the fine-grained maximum (B in Figure 4.17A), the bed will be dominated by grains in the size range of 0.1–2 mm because of differential transport. By keeping other factors constant, Howard has gone on to show how required gradient varies directly with sediment concentration (or sediment load with Q fixed) and indirectly with unit discharge $q = Q/w$ (Figure 4.17B, C, D). Also increasing the range of grain sizes in transport alters the gradient curves (Figure 4.17E). In particular it broadens the curve of the fine-grained maximum while simultaneously reducing the depth of the valley at intermediate sizes and therefore the distinction between coarse and fine beds.

Slope is in general negatively correlated with discharge but both exponent (z) and coefficient (g) values in $s = gQ^z$ tend to vary over a wide range. For four major rivers in the United States z ranges from -0.50 to -0.93 with a mean of -0.65 (Carlston, 1968), while Osterkamp (1978) obtained an average value of -0.25 for 76 Kansas channels. Of particular interest in the latter case is the dependence of g on bed material properties. Although differences are small, coefficient values tend to increase not only with particle size but also with the sorting index. An increase in the index, signifying poorer sorting, may reflect armouring of the bed by larger particles in these sand-bed channels, to which a stream responds by steepening its gradient in order to maintain bed mobility as suggested by Figure 4.17E. In this way could the better correlation of slope with coarser bed material fractions be explained.

Osterkamp's results underline the multivariate character of relationships demonstrated initially by equation (4.47) and subsequently (Table 4.12). Cherkauer's (1972) relationships for small gravel-bed streams, separated according to lithology and position along the profile (concave upstream segments, straight downstream segments), confirm the association of steep slopes with coarse debris, small drainage areas (or discharge) and wide, shallow channels, although the correlation with width–depth ratio is either weak (concave segments) or not significant (straight segments). Indeed channel slope may have little or no relation

Fig 4.17   Curves of required gradient against grain size calculated from sediment transport equations (after Howard, 1980):
A. The curves for four equations using nominal parameter values: $Q = 1000$ m^3 s^{-1}, Sediment concentration (C) = 0.01, w = 100 m, n = 0.02, $D_{50} = 0.3$ mm, Variance of grain size distribution (θ) = 0.87. The dashed line emanating from the fine-grained maximum of the Einstein-Brown curve separates regions A and B described in the text.
B – E. The effects of changing input parameters on the shape of the Einstein-Brown curve:
B. Variations in sediment concentration (C = Q_s/Q);
C. Variations in specific discharge (q = Q/w);
D. Variations in specific discharge and concentration with specific sediment discharge (q_s = C.Q/w) fixed;
E. Variations in the variance of grain size distribution (or degree of sorting).

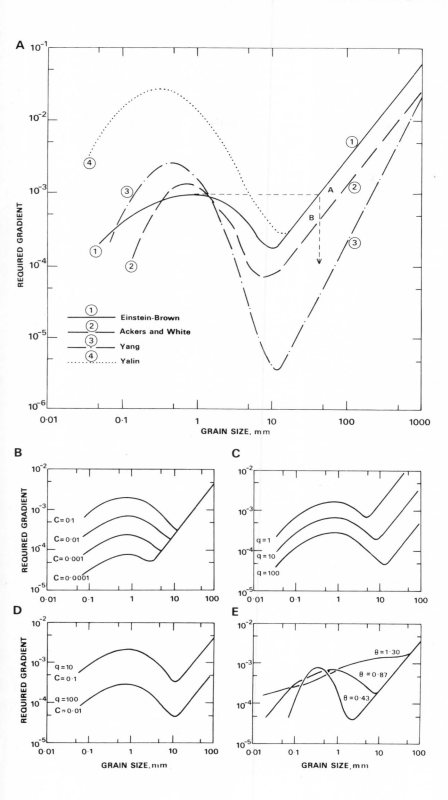

to channel shape unless the analysis is carried out at a detailed scale where discharge is essentially constant (Penning-Rowsell and Townshend, 1978). The transport of a larger bed-material load could be accommodated by an increase in width–depth ratio or an increase in slope or both but, if slope adjustment is constrained, then changes in channel shape become more likely. To emphasize its basically dependent character, the shape factor X in equation (4.47) should appear on the left hand side as in Rubey's original formulation.

Of the major variables, discharge and bed material size, the former appears to have the dominant influence if degree of correlation is accepted as the criterion (Miller, 1958; Cherkauer, 1972). However, their relative importance may vary with the scale of analysis. Penning-Rowsell and Townshend (1978) found that their index of discharge was more significant at the reach scale but of less importance relative to bed material size at the local scale when, however, many of the correlations were rather weak. If real, their results emphasize the need to choose an appropriate spatial scale when relating form elements to control variables. Most of the studies considered above deal with variation in channel gradient over regions of diverse geology and hydrology, but truly consistent relationships may be expected only along single streams where the conditions of sediment supply and discharge addition remain relatively similar.

Causes of profile concavity
Initially at least, the location and height of the end points of a longitudinal profile and therefore its average gradient are determined by tectonic and other historical events. From an analysis of 115 British rivers Wheeler (1979) found a positive correlation between profile concavity and total fall, while the random-walk model of Leopold and Langbein (1962) suggests that a constraint on stream length reduces concavity (Figure 4.16F(ii)). However, profile form is only partly dependent on incident relief and available length. Since slope at any point is related to bed material size and discharge, it is logical to explain variations in profile concavity (or the downstream rate of change of channel gradient) in terms of the downstream behaviour of those variables.

Downstream changes in sediment properties reflect a complex history of sediment transport through the fluvial system. To the extent that a negative exponential function adequately describes downstream changes in both grain size and channel gradient (equations 3.25 and 4.44), their respective rates of change (α and δ) ought to be related. Empirical data (Hack, 1957; Ikeda, 1970; Cherkauer, 1972) confirm that profiles are more concave where bed material size decreases more rapidly and, in addition, suggest that profiles have little concavity if particle size remains constant or increases downstream. In so far as bedrock type influences initial size and its downstream rate of reduction, different lithologies could give rise to profiles of different concavity. Although based on data from several streams, the slope–length relations obtained by Brush (1961) provide some support for this argument:

$$s = 0.050 \, L^{-0.81} \quad \text{(shale)} \quad (4.49)$$

$$s = 0.027 \, L^{-0.71} \quad \text{(limestone)} \quad (4.50)$$

$$s = 0.063 \, L^{-0.67} \quad \text{(sandstone)} \quad (4.51)$$

Thus the distribution of bedrock types along a stream may influence profile form overall and the concavity of individual segments in compound profiles. More resistant outcrops can act as local base-levels.

Further evidence of profile–particle size relations comes from the study of profiles having a marked discontinuity. In an analysis of nine Japanese rivers Yatsu (1955) identified a distinct break of slope in the longitudinal profiles which corresponded to a rapid transition from gravel-bed to sand-bed conditions. Both slope and grain size decreased more rapidly above the discontinuity than below. The deficiency of intermediate grain sizes (2–10 mm) at the break can be explained as an effect of differential sorting (Howard, 1980; Figure 4.17), although the rapid breakdown of gravel into sand may also have been a contributory factor. Profile and grain size discontinuities do not always correspond (Ikeda, 1970) but a reanalysis of Yatsu's data has shown that real differences in the behaviour of channel slope do exist between upstream and downstream segments in at least two of the rivers (Bennett, 1976). In particular, changes in bed height become less variable and less subject to random influences in the sand-bed channel of the downstream segments.

Based on a mathematical model of sediment sorting, Rana *et al.* (1973) have also shown that the curves describing downstream change in slope and bed material size have two distinct limbs. For various discharges and bed-material loads considered in the model, the ratio α/δ in the upper limb remained nearly constant with an average value of 1.70, signifying a more rapid decrease in grain size than slope. In the lower limb, on the other hand, α/δ did vary but was approximately constant at the same bed-material discharge, values being mostly less than unity.

Profile form appears to reflect quite closely downstream changes in particle size. In particular, a significant threshold related to the mechanics of sediment transport seems to exist between gravel-bed and sand-bed channels, upstream and downstream segments. Translating his results into a downstream context, Howard (1980) found that the variation of slope with length and grain size was similar within each type but differed considerably between the two types of channel in parallel with Yatsu's results, with slope decreasing more rapidly in gravel-bed streams. Although it is easy to appreciate the need for steeper slopes in the transport of coarser debris, especially in the gravel range, the underlying relationships are unlikely to be simple given the influence of other factors and the complex way in which bed material size and sorting interact with transport and resistance.

In common with bed material size, the downstream rate of change of discharge is not necessarily constant from one river to another. Although rivers with relatively uniform discharge can have concave profiles provided they are long enough, increasing discharge is a major cause of concavity (Langbein, 1964b). Not only do profiles tend to be more concave where discharge increases more rapidly (Wheeler, 1979), but breaks of slope separating segments of different concavity have been associated with a change in the rate of discharge increase (Cherkauer, 1972).

In broad terms increasing discharge implies an ability to transport the same bed-material load over progressively lower slopes. However, a river can accommodate that increase in various ways and different combinations of the adjustable variables may be associated with different profile forms. Following Leopold *et al.* (1964), simple deductions about the effects of different combinations can be made in terms of downstream hydraulic geometry by holding certain factors constant and then successively relaxing them. Although downstream relations are not as straightforward as originally supposed, width tends to vary consistently as the square root of discharge. For simplicity decreasing z in $s = gQ^z$ is equated with increasing concavity, although the actual profile associated with a given slope–discharge relation depends on the rate at which discharge increases with stream length.

STATE 1.   Without any reference to sediment load and assuming constant resistance, increasing profile concavity requires that depth accommodates progressively more of the downstream change in discharge and velocity correspondingly less (Table 4.13). Being one of the most sensitive variables, velocity is perhaps least likely to show consistency of downstream adjustment. However, near constancy or a slight increase of velocity may be common over long distances (Carlston, 1969), which is here associated with a profile of moderate concavity.

Apparently the requirement of constant resistance can be satisfied by realistic adjustments of the dependent variables and still be reflected in a concave profile. Since such a requirement could be associated with constant grain size or increasing grain size if the change in depth is sufficient to render relative roughness (d/D) constant, it is confirmed that decreasing bed material size is neither a sufficient nor a necessary condition for profiles to be concave.

STATE 2.   There is evidence to suggest that on average resistance decreases slightly downstream. However, relations are never based on the direct measurement of resistance and the separate effects of different resistance components remain obscure. Grain roughness should decrease downstream because of decreasing grain size and increasing depth, its rate of change being largely determined by the behaviour of those two variables. As regards form roughness the situation is less clear. In moving from a gravel-bed to a sand-bed channel, the resistance due to bed forms may assume a greater relative significance through the development of dunes in particular. Also the resistance offered by channel bends may increase downstream if the channel becomes more sinuous as a larger proportion of the load is carried in suspension (Schumm, 1963b). Consequently resistance may change less rapidly than expected if grain roughness was the sole component. Although hydraulic efficiency generally improves downstream, the behaviour of total resistance could vary considerably within and between rivers depending on how each component changes longitudinally.

A more rapid rate of resistance decrease leads to a larger m/f ratio for a given profile form (constant z) or greater profile concavity for constant velocity (m = 0) (Table 4.13). Large decreases in resistance are perhaps most likely in small basins or the headwaters of large streams, where also the flattening of channel gradient is usually most marked. A constant or slightly increasing velocity can be maintained along more concave profiles than was the case for constant resistance (STATE 1).

STATE 3.   The inclusion of sediment load as a variable markedly increases the complexity of the analysis. Rarely are the requisite data available as a downstream series and even then only for suspended sediment. Also transport equations derived originally for cross-sectional conditions translate with unknown efficiency to the downstream case. Yet both the competence and capacity for transport may be expected to vary longitudinally.

The adjustment of slope to sediment load is closely bound up with the concept of a stream at grade or in equilibrium. Mackin (1948) believed that graded alluvial streams with a stable flow regime have slopes which are just sufficient to transport the load supplied. Aggradation may increase a slope that is too small, while degradation decreases one that is too large. Evidence for this comes largely from laboratory experiments conducted under steady flow conditions, where gradients are adjusted to equalize the input and output of sediment load over short distances. However, the situation in natural streams with variable discharge and fluctuating sediment supply is infinitely more complex. Setting aside the possibility that any imbalance in sediment transport can be accommodated by other adjustments, an

Table 4.13 Downstream changes in channel slope deduced for various states

	Assumptions	Implications	Results
STATE 1	$w \propto Q^{\frac{1}{2}}$	$f + m = \frac{1}{2}$ (from continuity equation)	$z = 0 \Leftrightarrow f = \frac{3}{10}, m = \frac{2}{10}$
	resistance constant $(y = 0)$	$z = 2m - \frac{4}{3}f$ (from Manning equation)	$z = -\frac{1}{2} \Leftrightarrow f = \frac{9}{20}, m = \frac{1}{20}$
			$z = -\frac{2}{3} \Leftrightarrow f = \frac{1}{2}, m = 0$
STATE 2	$w \propto Q^{\frac{1}{2}}$	$f + m = \frac{1}{2}$	
	(i) $y = -0.15$	$z = 2m - \frac{4}{3}f - \frac{3}{10}$	$z = 0 \Leftrightarrow f = 0.21, m = 0.29$
			$z = -\frac{1}{2} \Leftrightarrow f = 0.36, m = 0.14$
			$z = -\frac{3}{4} \Leftrightarrow f = 0.435, m = 0.065$
	(ii) $y = -0.30$	$z = 2m - \frac{4}{3}f - \frac{6}{10}$	$z = 0 \Leftrightarrow f = 0.12, m = 0.38$
			$z = -\frac{1}{2} \Leftrightarrow f = 0.27, m = 0.23$
			$z = -\frac{3}{4} \Leftrightarrow f = 0.345, m = 0.155$
STATE 3	$w \propto Q^{\frac{1}{2}}$	$f + m = \frac{1}{2}$	
	bed-load discharge constant	$z = \frac{1}{2}\alpha' - \frac{1}{6} - f$ (from equation 4.52)	
	(i) $y = 0$, $\alpha' = 0$	$z = 2m - \frac{4}{3}f$	$z = -0.67 \Leftrightarrow f = 0.5, m = 0$
	$\alpha' = \alpha_1 < 0$		$z = -0.76 \Leftrightarrow f = 0.53, m = -0.03$
	(ii) $y = -0.15$, $\alpha' = \alpha_1 < 0$	$z = 2m - \frac{4}{3}f - \frac{3}{10}$	$z = -0.63 \Leftrightarrow f = 0.4, m = 0.1$
	$\alpha' = \alpha_2 = 2\alpha_1$		$z = -0.73 \Leftrightarrow f = 0.43, m = 0.07$
	(iii) $y = -0.30$, $\alpha' = \alpha_1$	$z = 2m - \frac{4}{3}f - \frac{6}{10}$	$z = -0.52 \Leftrightarrow f = 0.27, m = 0.23$
	$\alpha' = \alpha_2 = 2\alpha_1$		$z = -0.60 \Leftrightarrow f = 0.30, m = 0.20$

Symbols: f, m, y and z are respectively the downstream rates of change of depth, velocity, Manning's resistance coefficient and slope with discharge; α' is a nominal exponent intended to express the downstream rate of change of debris size but give a particular value at STATE 3(ii) to enable comparisons to be made.

assumption of continuity in bed-material transport enables some deductions to be made regarding channel slope.

For this purpose a simplified version of the Einstein–Brown bed-load function is used:

$$Q_{sb} = K \frac{w\,(d.s)^3}{D^{\frac{3}{2}}} \qquad (4.52)$$

To maintain a constant bed-load discharge (Q_{sb}) where w and d increase and D decreases downstream, slope must decrease. The profile of a graded river must therefore be concave. The degree of concavity will depend in particular on the rates at which w, d and D change in the downstream direction, although the variation in other related factors will also be important. Since downstream hydraulic geometry requires that all variables are related to discharge, further analysis is limited. By assigning nominal values to the rate of change of bed material size, it can be shown that a more rapid decrease in grain size is associated not only with more concave profiles but also with a larger rate of change of depth relative to velocity for a given value of y (Table 4.13). However, the rate of change of resistance is also likely to be affected by such changes.

The simplified nature of this analysis cannot be overemphasized. However, it should have illustrated that increasing discharge and decreasing bed material size provide only a general explanation of profile concavity. Underlying those changes are adjustments to many variables whose interaction in different combinations can lead to a wide variety of profile forms. Given that there are more dependent factors than independent ones, deterministic approaches may be able to go only so far in resolving the issue. Also the definition of a graded stream needs to recognize that adjustments to form elements other than slope can be made in order to provide the conditions necessary for the transport of the load supplied, as Bagnold (1977) has shown with respect to cross-sectional form.

Adjustability of channel gradient
To reflect the opinion dominant particularly before 1950 that gradient is the principal means of adjustment whereby a river attains a state of grade or equilibrium, channel gradient has thus far been treated as a response element. However, that adjustment may be constrained. Because of the interdependence of successive channel segments, major changes in gradient require the redistribution of immense quantities of material. Valley slope and non-alluvial controls such as bedrock outcrops place limits on the possible range of gradient adjustment. For selected rivers in Australia and the mid-west United States, Schumm (1968a) has shown that valley slope and channel gradient are almost identical in channels with a low silt–clay content, although the valley slope/channel gradient ratio does become progressively larger as the silt–clay content increases. Channel gradient can be adjusted by, for example, a river adopting a more sinuous course (the direct relation of sinuosity and silt–clay content (equation 4.33) explains why in Schumm's channels valley slope is steeper than channel gradient where silt–clay content is higher), but only within the limits imposed by valley slope, an inherited characteristic reflecting a history of past discharges and sediment loads.

Rates of adjustment are likely to vary with the type of channel and scale of the system. Bedrock channels are the slowest and fine-bed channels the most rapid to respond, with gravel-bed channels occupying an intermediate position. The fact that slope correlates well with residual bed material size but not average bed material size along the gravelly River Hodder in Lancashire (Wilcock, 1967) suggests that the river is graded to conditions which are a legacy of the past (Pleistocene) and that therefore slope is largely an imposed characteristic. Response time will also tend to increase with the scale of the system as well as boundary resistance. Small sand-bed channels in Virginia ($A_d < 0.005$ km^2) undergo seasonal cycles of aggradation and entrenchment with winter/summer gradient ratios of up to 1.5 (Howard, 1982). At the other end of the scale Howard has estimated a response time for the Mississippi ($A_d \sim 3,200,00$ km^2) of 50,000–80,000 years.

An example of change in a small basin ($A_d = 179$ km^2) is provided by Haible's (1980) study of Walker Creek in the Coast Range of California. In response to fluctuating climatic and watershed conditions over the past 5000 years, the valley has experienced one episode of infilling followed by two episodes of incision, the most recent beginning about 100 years ago (Figure 4.18A). Despite the removal of large quantities of material during these episodes, profile concavity has remained essentially constant. Gradient adjustments of 2 to 4 per cent have been made but are insignificant when compared with cross-sectional changes. It appears that, even when conditions allow, a river does not necessarily change its channel gradient.

River profiles can be affected by conditions other than those directly associated with watershed controls (notably flow regime and sediment supply). Since the effects of tectonic activity can be very variable, consideration is given only to changes in base-level at the downstream end of a stream. Based on a mathematical model and laboratory experimentation, Begin *et al.* (1981) have shown what the main effects of a base-level lowering are likely to be (Figure 4.18B). Local steepening at the distal end increases transporting ability and over time the abrupt break of slope migrates headward, flattening as it does so. The rate of degradation not only reaches a peak relatively quickly and then declines slowly at any station but also decreases with distance from the outlet. If stream-bed lowering leads to bank heights which are unstable, excessive bank erosion may occur and supply the channel with sediments that are temporarily stored, preventing further degradation until they are flushed out. The results show that the ultimate effect of base-level lowering by a certain amount is degradation along the entire length of a channel by the same amount, leading to a new profile with essentially the same form as the original. This simple picture can be complicated by, for example, the exposure of resistant bedrock strata or armouring of the stream bed (Figure 4.18B(ii)). Also, since headcut retreat is likely to be a protracted process over long river distances, a profile may contain evidence of several base-level lowerings, an argument frequently used by denudation chronologists in constructing long-term histories of landscape development.

A rise in base-level whether eustatic or local may be similar in effect to the construction of a barrier across a river. From repeated surveys above man-made barriers, it seems that the aggradation which occurs as a result of reduced competence proceeds quickly at first but does not continue far upstream thereafter (Leopold and Bull, 1979; Figure 4.18C). Beyond the head of the depositional wedge the profile remains largely unaffected by the rise in base-level. Since the gradient of the wedge is usually less than that of the original channel, a stream must make adjustments as it flows over the wedge if the same load is to be carried at the same discharge. Increasing channel width and decreasing hydraulic roughness may be the main adjustments involved.

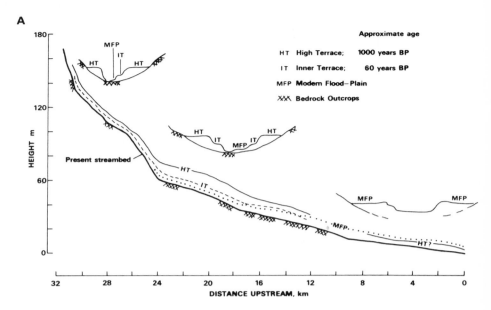

Fig 4.18   A. Stream-bed and terrace profiles, Walker Creek, California (after Haible, 1980).
B. Profile development after base-level lowering in laboratory models, without (i) and with (ii) channel bed armouring. Numbers denote time, in minutes, from start of the run (after Begin et al., 1981).
C. Profile changes following the construction of small dams in New Mexico channels (after Leopold and Bull, 1979).

Based upon this and other work, Leopold and Bull have concluded that changes in slope account for only a small part of the adjustment required to achieve a balance between the input and output of sediment load, most of the adjustment being accomplished by changes to other aspects of flow and channel geometry which respond more rapidly. This naturally assumes that those aspects are not themselves limited in their range of adjustment, which is not always the case. However, except in small responsive basins (e.g. Rendell and Alexander, 1979), channel slope can be regarded either as an imposed parameter or, if valley slope is imposed, as a parameter adjustable only over a limited range (Church, 1980). Consequently Mackin's (1948) definition of a graded stream (p. 92) might be rephrased as '. . . one in which, over a period of years, slope, velocity, depth, width, roughness, pattern and channel morphology . . . mutually adjust to provide the power and the efficiency necessary to transport the load supplied from the drainage basin without aggradation or degradation of the channels' (Leopold and Bull, 1979, p. 195).

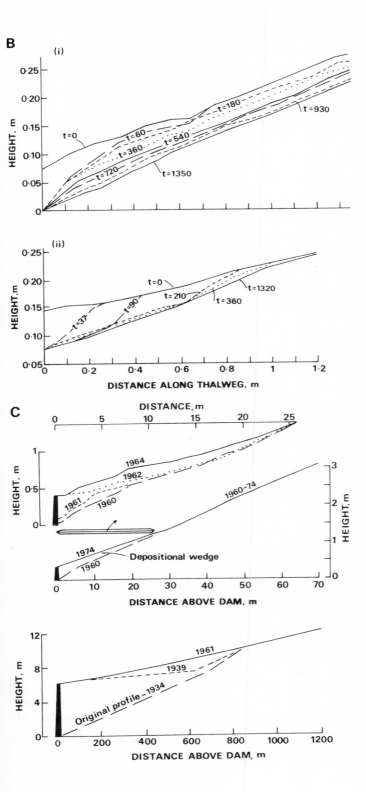

5
Channel changes through time

The fluvial system can be treated as either a physical system or an historical system (Schumm, 1977). At one time or another both viewpoints have held sway in geomorphological approaches to the study of river channels. The first focuses on how the system functions, usually over short timespans, while the second deals more directly with evolutionary tendencies or changes to the system over various time scales.

In reality, the fluvial system is a physical system with a history (Schumm, 1977). Present form is the product of past and present processes and conditions, where 'present' in this context could be defined as that time period over which input and output conditions have remained reasonably constant on average. Any assessment of the relative contributions made by past and present events is complicated by the fact that the existing state has been influenced to varying extents and in different ways by previous states. Many rivers were directly affected by events during and immediately after the last glaciation and may well have retained features from that time. The channel patterns and deposits of Amazon Basin rivers draining Andean source areas reflect the influence of Pleistocene glacial episodes when the uplands supplied large quantities of coarse bed load which only the major rivers are now able to rework (Baker, 1978). The fluvial system thus has a memory.

In broad terms the length of that memory depends on the ability of the system (or any component of the system) to absorb or respond to change, which is in turn dependent on the sequence of past events and on the inherent resistance of the system. As suggested in the previous chapter, different components of channel morphology adjust at different rates and presumably reflect the influence of past conditions to different extents. Where the response time is short, the historical legacy becomes proportionately less. Stevens *et al.* (1975) maintained that the influence of past flood events on river channel form varies with their absolute magnitude, more extreme floods having a longer-lasting effect, and with their magnitude relative to the 'normal' regime of the river expressed by the ratio of individual flood peaks to the mean annual flood. Where the ratio is large, the river channel should exhibit non-equilibrium tendencies at least over the timespans of up to 10^2 years which they considered. Recognition of an historical dimension switches attention from those treatments which assume quasi-steady and quasi-uniform conditions to those which emphasize the unsteady nature of river channel adjustment.

Ability to interpret the past is partly dependent on the level of understanding of the present. Brunsden and Thornes (1979) have maintained that geomorphologists are now in a better position to extrapolate the short-term record to timespans of 10^2–10^4 years and longer because of the knowledge of process action gained over the last few decades and the wider range of techniques now available. Such extrapolation is not without problems. Only rarely can initial and boundary conditions

Table 5.1 Changing status of river variables with time (modified from Schumm and Lichty, 1965)

Variables	Long timescale > 10^5 years	Medium timescale 10^3–10^4 years	Short timescale 10^1–10^2 years	Instantaneous time < 10^{-1} years
Geology	E	E	E	E
Climate	E	E	E	E
Regional relief	D	E	E	E
Slope morphology	D	D	E	E
Soil properties	D	D	E	E
Vegetation properties	D	D	E	E
Mean water and sediment discharge	I	D	E	E
Channel morphology	I	D	D	E
Instantaneous flow characteristics	I	I	I	D

E: environmental or independent variable
D: dependent variable
I: indeterminate or irrelevant variable

be accurately specified. Continuous or even irregular studies of process activity are usually limited to one or two decades at most, so that average rates may be unrepresentative of longer-term trends. Even when available, average rates of erosion and deposition reveal little about the complexity of landform change. Events are unlikely to be synchronous over large areas because the threshold conditions which partly determine the magnitude and direction of change are influenced by factors which are themselves spatially variable. Even in a single area there is no guarantee that two drainage basins and their constituent channels will respond in the same way to the same external stimulus.

Further problems are created by the changing status of environmental variables over time (Table 5.1). Geology and climate retain an independent status at all timespans but, whereas climate can be regarded as fixed in the short term, it ceases to be invariant over longer time periods. Sympathetic changes are produced in those environmental factors which together with geology and climate control the main variables (notably discharge and sediment load) influencing channel form. Not only does the number of dependent factors increase with time but so does the level of indeterminacy in the system. Specific details become more obscure and there is a greater danger of circular argument in which cause and effect or the effects of a common cause are confused.

A wide range of time scales is probably appropriate for the study of river channel changes since some features retain or are influenced by inherited characteristics to a greater extent than others. In choosing an appropriate scale, a primary need is independent assessment of: (i) the amplitude of environmental change at different time scales and how in particular it is related to discharge and sediment load conditions; and (ii) the adjustability of different form elements. By linking the two, it may be possible to determine firstly the potential of a particular element to achieve a state of approximate equilibrium with prevailing conditions, and secondly the likely response of a given element to a given level of change. In addition, distinctions need to be made between types of change. Intermediate between those changes associated with long-term evolutionary tendencies and short-term fluctuations about an average state are those induced by disturbances to external conditions and those initiated internally as critical thresholds are crossed. All may be present to a greater or lesser extent. The validity of reconstructions at whatever time scale depends on how well the historical record can be read, which is itself a variable as a wider range of techniques becomes available.

Evidence of change

The primary evidence for change in the fluvial system comes from morphologic remnants such as abandoned channels and from sediment sequences which reveal a complex and usually incomplete record of changing conditions. Geomorphologists in the past have relied heavily on longitudinal profile form and associated terrace remnants in reconstructing river histories but purely morphologic evidence needs to be supported by other information if ambiguous interpretations are to be avoided. Table 5.2 lists some of the methods available, wherein a distinction can be drawn between those methods which provide more direct evidence of change and those which relate to the dating of past events.

Table 5.2   Methods used in studying river channel changes

Direct observations	— Instrument records (rarely continuous)
	Photographic records
	Ground survey
Historical records	— Maps and photographs of different dates
	Historical documents
Sedimentary evidence	— Surface forms
	Internal structures
Dating techniques	— (1) Relative methods
	Relative height
	Organic remains
	Artifacts
	(2) Absolute methods
	Radioactive isotopes
	Dendrochronology

Direct observations can be used to monitor change at specific locations over periods of hours (Fahnestock, 1963), days (Smith, 1971), months (Knighton, 1972) or years (Leopold, 1973), and are particularly valuable when tied to measurements of streamflow and sediment properties. The scale of river channel adjustment to events of varying frequency, including extreme floods (Stewart and La Marche, 1967; Costa, 1974), can be directly determined, enabling a better assessment of such events in an historical context. Repeated field surveys play an important role in that they bring a general picture evident from other sources into sharper focus by concentrating on more detailed changes over shorter time periods.

   However, direct observations are seldom maintained for more than a decade or two. They may fail to include a wide enough range of erosional and depositional events to be representative of longer-term change. Almost no directly useful morphologic variable is regularly measured, although several important parameters (notably precipitation and discharge) are continuously monitored at an expanding network of sites. The main value of short-term records lies in establishing relationships between applied stresses and stream channel response, and in evaluating the significance of individual (extreme) events.

Historical records, including documents, survey notes, maps and photographs, can provide valuable information about channel and related changes particularly but not exclusively over the last 10^2 years. Thus Grove (1972) has used land rent records for the Josterdalsbre area in Norway to show how the incidence of mass movements and floods has varied since the sixteenth century (Figure 5.1A).

Maps and photographs of different dates have been increasingly used to identify changes in the planimetric properties of river channels. In many parts of Britain at least five separate surveys have been undertaken over the last 130 years and this type of historical map information enabled Hooke (1977) to chart the distribution of course changes along Devon streams as well as estimate rates of bank retreat (Figure 5.1B). Up to 40 per cent of the length of a single channel was found to be laterally mobile, with movements of up to 100 m in a 50-year period.

Direct comparisons of channels at different times are readily made using photographs, although most early photographs were not taken for that purpose. Various photographs taken of the Platte River in Nebraska show the spectacular reductions in channel width which have resulted from river regulation schemes since 1900 (Williams, 1978c). Using evidence from aerial and ground photographs taken between 1946 and 1977, Anderson and Calver (1977, 1980) identified how a natural channel has adjusted to a major flood (in 1952) and during the post-flood period of lower discharges. The recent advent of satellite photography raises the possibility of repeated, large-scale observations of river channels but as yet applications are few.

The potential use of historical sources has not been fully exploited. However, care needs to be exercised in using this type of information, particularly the earlier material which may be of doubtful accuracy. Since information is usually available only for specific dates, it has to be assumed that change was uniform between each pair of surveys. Without data for intervening periods when the channel may have been significantly altered, changes can seldom be related to the events which produced them. By themselves historical methods indicate only the general direction and rate of channel change, and then only for planimetric properties usually.

Since rivers must erode and deposit sediment in changing their elevation, course or channel form, *sedimentary evidence* is a primary source of information. It includes the forms developed in or on sedimentary surfaces as well as the internal structure and character of the deposits themselves. Thus Hickin (1974) has traced the pattern of meander development along the Beatton River in British Columbia over 250 years by mapping point-bar ridges formed during bend migration and defining erosional pathlines as orthogonals through the ridge systems (Figure 5.1C). Since the ridges could be dated dendrochronologically, it was possible to show how channel curvature (r_c/w) has influenced the rate of migration (Hickin and Nanson, 1975; Figure 4.14B). Remnants of former channels evident on the ground or from aerial photographs are frequently used in reconstructing river histories and, especially where they take the form of abandoned meanders, estimates of previous discharges can be made based upon contemporary wavelength–discharge relationships (Dury, 1976).

From studies of the sedimentation patterns developed by modern rivers, the stratigraphic and textural characteristics of older deposits can be used to interpret the conditions under which they were laid down. Schumm (1968b) has constructed idealized cross-sections which show how vertical differences in the texture of

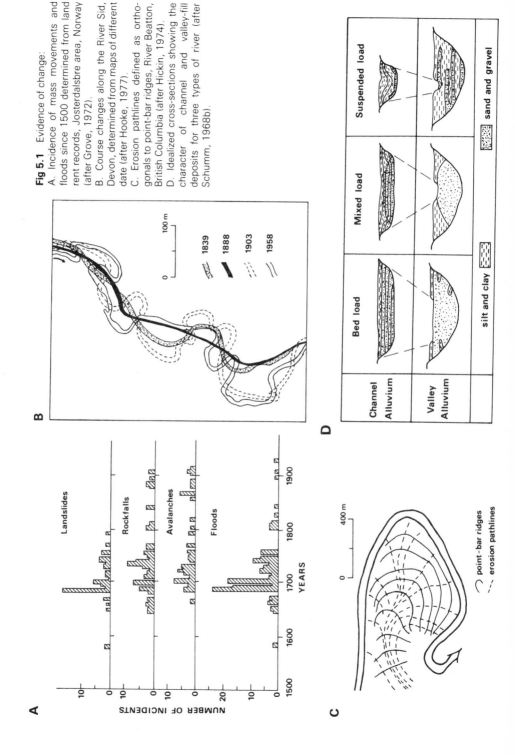

Fig 5.1 Evidence of change:

A. Incidence of mass movements and floods since 1500 determined from land rent records, Josterdalsbre area, Norway (after Grove, 1972).

B. Course changes along the River Sid, Devon, determined from maps of different date (after Hooke, 1977).

C. Erosion pathlines defined as orthogonals to point-bar ridges, River Beatton, British Columbia (after Hickin, 1974).

D. Idealized cross-sections showing the character of channel and valley-fill deposits for three types of river (after Schumm, 1968b).

channel and valley-fill deposits may indicate the dominant type of load carried by former streams (Figure 5.1D). Sedimentologists have developed a methodology for reconstructing the morphologic and flow characteristics of palaeochannels, which relies heavily on empirical equations obtained from measurements on modern rivers and in particular on those obtained by Schumm (1960, 1968a). To begin the process data are required on palaeochannel width, depth and silt–clay content in the channel boundary, none of which can be estimated with a high degree of certainty. Post-depositional modifications may have produced an incomplete or inconsistent record, especially where periodic erosion has occurred. Although flood-plain accumulations can remain stable for relatively long periods, the possibility of reworking of part or all of the depositional record may lead to misinterpretation. Illustrating how grain size data can be used in conjunction with tractive force theory to make palaeoflow calculations, Church (1978) has pointed out that reconstructions from such information can at best be an order-of-magnitude exercise.

Unless deposits are locally homogeneous, the sampling problem becomes very difficult. Frequently the analysis of sediments is constrained by the limited number of exposures. Rose *et al*. (1980) have identified the broad changes which occurred in the River Gipping in Suffolk over the last 13,000 years based upon an analysis of the sediments and forms exposed in a single gravel pit. Such detailed local studies need to be integrated if intra- and inter-regional correlations are to be established and greater reliability achieved. However, the larger the spatial scale, the more likely is the lack of synchroneity in events. Directions of change may vary not only from one area to another but also within the same basin where, for example, tributary streams are degrading while the main stream is aggrading. Alluvial sequences usually reflect complex fluvial histories whose interpretation at longer time scales requires a chronological framework.

A wide range of *dating techniques* is now available, only a sample of which is given in Table 5.2. Many depend on finding suitable remains which have been fortuitously preserved without contamination. Relative methods attempt to place events in their correct temporal sequence without giving any absolute dates, while absolute methods partly rectify this shortcoming in enabling a date to be attached to particular events.

Relative height has been one of the methods most often used to determine the relative position in time of morphological features, notably river terrace sequences. In that case height is usually taken relative to the present channel bed with the underlying assumption that the highest terrace is the oldest. Only isolated fragments remain in most cases and, without continuity of terrace surfaces along a valley, correlation on the basis of height alone is liable to large errors.

In addition to the relative chronology provided by sediments themselves, organic and artifactual remains contained therein can indicate relative position in time. Floral and faunal evidence has been primarily used to establish past environmental conditions but, if a particular assemblage can be identified as time-specific, its presence may be taken as indicating sediments of that age. Man-made objects have been extensively used to date fluvial sediments. By reference to the pottery chronology of the Rio Grande valley as a whole, Miller and Wendorf (1958) were able not only to date periods of deposition and erosion in a tributary valley but also to show that rates of sedimentation in the area have remained relatively uniform over the past 2000 years. Since artifacts are commonly dated by reference to their stratigraphic position, there is an increasing need for independent dating so that diagnostic types can be identified and the dangers of circular argument avoided. This type of information is likely to have an irregular distribution, as illustrated by the fortuitous recovery of car licence plates which enabled Costa (1975) to estimate the rate of overbank deposition in a Piedmont stream since 1924, but is potentially applicable over a wide range of time scales.

Absolute methods tend to be more specialized and more costly to use. Major advances in absolute dating have come from the development of various radiometric techniques based on the known rates of decay of radionuclides (notably radiocarbon). Most are applicable to timespans of 10^3–10^8 years and are particularly relevant to Pleistocene and early Holocene studies but some are suitable for shorter periods (Wise, 1980). Provided suitable materials can be found, they are often used in combination with stratigraphic methods to date particular levels in deposits and thereby provide reference horizons (e.g. Rose *et al.*, 1980). Haynes (1968) revised the alluvial history of the southwestern USA largely on the basis of radiocarbon dating and identified five depositional cycles over the past 10,000 years with some overlap between different valleys.

Dendrochronology, the study of tree rings to indicate time intervals or past variations in climate, is a very accurate method for dating events over the last 2000 years in particular. The progressive downcutting (totalling 3 m) over 800 years by a small ephemeral stream in southwestern Utah was traced from the position and growth characteristics of two trees flanking the incised channel (La Marche, 1966). The dating of flood-plain trees has been used as a basis for determining the form and rate of channel migration (Everitt, 1968; Hickin, 1974) and the effects of river regulation on downstream channel form (Petts, 1977). By relating tree age to flood-plain elevation along the Little Missouri River in North Dakota, Everitt was able to plot 25-year isochrones delimiting the dates of flood-plain reworking. Much of the flood-plain has been traversed by the stream over the past 200 years, requiring an average volume of sediment to be eroded annually from the channel banks of approximately 31,600 m³ per km of valley. The reliability of tree-ring data, especially in a climatic context, depends on an understanding of the factors which determine the thickness and growth rate of rings in individual tree species.

The range of techniques considered above is by no means exhaustive. Although discussed separately, it must be emphasized that techniques need to be used in combination if the possibility of misinterpretation is to be minimized. Dating methods are not of themselves direct evidence of change but, as the time scale increases and the resolution with which an event sequence can be reconstructed tends to diminish, the greater is the need for a chronological framework, especially when correlating events in different areas. Even then successive phases of development may be obscure if the information available allows only dated reconstructions at widely separated times. Sequences are invariably complex, involving events of varying frequency, magnitude and duration. Studies of fluvial history cannot be divorced from the broader context of past environmental conditions and therefore from explanations in terms of the factors producing environmental change.

Causes of change

Various types of change can be envisaged, the first of which is associated with the long-continued evolution of the fluvial system. Davis (1899) in his cycle of erosion assumed that landforms develop sequentially through time as relief is gradually reduced. However, since landforms are the net effect of many controlling factors, some of which change with time while others do not, reduction of relief does not of necessity lead to significant and progressive change in landscape geometry. In addition, this type of time-directed change needs to be assessed against the background of the major changes in environmental conditions which have occurred over the past millennia either naturally or as a result of man's activities.

In so far as the fluvial system can be represented as a set of outputs (specifically, channel form elements) related to a set of inputs or controls, changes in channel form can result from a change in either input conditions or input–output relationships. As regards the former, Brunsden and Thornes (1979) have distinguished between two types of external disturbance, pulsed and ramp, which may have different response characteristics. The first is associated with episodic events of low frequency and high magnitude, such as extreme floods, whose effects may be spatially and temporally limited. An approximate return to initial conditions may follow the imposed disturbance but extreme events can produce a lasting effect particularly if some significant threshold is crossed. Schick (1974) has attributed the formation of desert stream terraces to extreme floods which incise channels in the alluvium previously built up by more moderate flows, a mode of terrace formation which does not rely on classical concepts of rejuvenation or climatic change.

In the ramp type of disturbance controlling variables are sustained at a new level as a result of more permanent shifts in input conditions. Such changes are likely to apply over wider areas, although the response may not be spatially uniform. Much of the unsteadiness in the fluvial system is caused by fluctuations in climate which, through its influence on vegetation, the rainfall–infiltration–runoff relationship and process activity, affects the flow regime of rivers and the production, supply and transportation of sediment. Based on various forms of evidence, an impressive picture has been constructed of climatic fluctuations over the last million years (Figure 5.2). For time periods exceeding 10^4 years the scale of climatic fluctuations increases markedly but even over the past 10^3 years distinct variations have occurred, leading to unsteadiness of input behaviour and geomorphic activity (Figure 5.1A). Although the timing, level and direction of climatic change have varied from one area to another, all parts of the earth's surface have been affected to some extent by events during the Quaternary.

Most is known about palaeotemperatures. Geomorphologically more relevant information on past precipitation and runoff conditions is much more elusive, although Lamb (1977) has estimated average amounts for part of the post-glacial period (Table 5.3). These results are untested and should be treated as broad averages over many centuries within which considerable fluctuations must have occurred. In any case average amounts provide only a partial picture since the seasonal distribution and magnitude–frequency characteristics of rainfall are at least as significant geomorphologically. From an analysis of rainfall records for the south-west USA, Leopold (1951) has shown that, without any appreciable change in mean annual totals, the incidence of rainfalls of different intensity changed during the 1880s, a factor which may have contributed to the accelerated surface erosion observed at that time. Despite recent progress, detailed information on past precipitation conditions is generally lacking and geomorphologists have

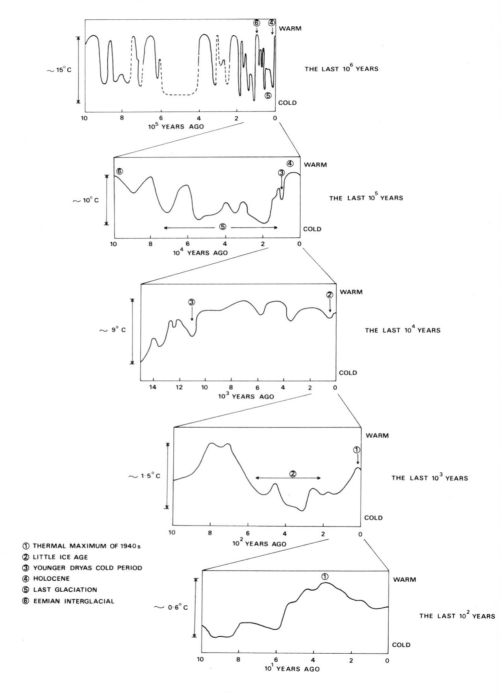

Fig 5.2   Main trends in temperature over different time spans in north-west Europe (after Zagwijn, 1975 and Lamb, 1977).

Table 5.3   Estimates of average rainfall (R), evaporation (E) and surplus water (D) in different epochs in England and Wales, expressed as percentages of 1916–1950 averages (after Lamb, 1977)

Approximate dates		Epoch	Estimate of average annual temperature, °C	R	E	D
				(% of 1916–1950 averages)		
7000	BC	Pre-Boreal	9.3	92– 95	94– 98	89– 94
4500	BC	Atlantic	10.7	110–115	108–114	112–116
2500	BC	Sub-Boreal	9.7	100–105	102–104	100–106
900– 450	BC	Sub-Atlantic (onset)	9.3	103–105	97	110–115
1150–1300	AD	Little Optimum	10.2	103	104	102
1550–1700	AD	Little Ice Age	8.8	93	94	92
1900–1950	AD	20th century warm decades	9.4	(932 mm)	(497 mm)	(435 mm)

largely argued in broad terms such as humid and dry phases.

Dury (1976) has suggested how previous discharges can be determined from morphologic evidence. By substituting measurements of former channel dimensions into the relationships

$$Q = (w/2.99)^{1.81} \tag{5.1}$$

or $$Q = (\lambda/32.86)^{1.81} \tag{5.2}$$

or $$Q = 0.83\ A^{1.09}.S \tag{5.3}$$

where w, λ and A are respectively the bed-width, meander wavelength and cross-sectional area of the former channel and S is the sinuosity of the present stream, estimates of past bankfull discharges (Q) can be obtained. Former discharges in some British rivers have been estimated at 33–115 times present discharge by this method. However, this scale of discharge change is doubtful. The soundness of any estimate depends heavily on the reliability of the original equations and on the accuracy with which the former channel can be defined. Based largely on anomalies between modern meanders and 'valley meanders' of a supposed ancestral origin, this methodology tends to ignore the fact that wavelength and width are related to sediment characteristics as well as discharge. Since braiding can be associated with large-scale sinuosity, some 'valley meanders' may represent the traces of former braided rivers in which the discharges were not much larger than those of today (Ferguson, 1981). There remains also the problem of dating previous discharge levels. This type of approach uses morphologic data to estimate past conditions rather than the reverse but, whenever possible, independent assessments of palaeoclimate and palaeohydrology need to be made.

The lengthiest records are for the River Nile in Egypt and extend back to AD 622. They indicate high flood levels in 630, 850–930, 1100–1150, 1400–1450 and the mid-1800s, and show that the river has been progressively aggrading its bed and flood-plain at an average rate of 0.1 m per century (Lamb, 1977). From miscellaneous reports of floods and droughts, it seems that many parts of Europe experienced a marked period of flooding from AD 1150–1500 with peaks about 1310 and 1450. More recently (1900–1964), the flow records for 30 rivers in the northern hemisphere reveal large variations in discharge (Goudie, 1972). Many show low levels in the 1930s and 1940s followed by a slight upward trend. At least for the period of historical records a more reliable picture of previous discharges is being built up but over more recent times in particular it becomes increasingly difficult to differentiate between the effects of climatic oscillation and man's activities. In mid-Wales, for example, recent increases in flooding have been triggered by an increased incidence of intense storm events but concomitant land-use changes have accentuated the tendency (Howe *et al.*, 1967).

The accumulated evidence points to the dynamic quality of climate. Major and minor shifts of climate and related vegetation changes have significantly altered input conditions and levels of fluvial activity over a range of time scales. In addition, important changes have occurred in the relative heights of land and sea, caused principally by eustatic fluctuations in sea-level and tectonic activity. Sea-level has risen by more than 50 m since the last glaciation, thereby altering the potential energy in the landscape and the position of the base-level to which streams may adjust. The Holocene marine transgression was largely accomplished by 6000 BP since which time minor oscillations have occurred of about 1-4 m, with possible maxima around 4000 BP and in the Early Middle Ages (Lamb, 1977). The effect of a change in sea-level will be felt first near the mouth of a river but may be transmitted far enough upstream to alter base-level conditions throughout the network, although Leopold and Bull (1979) have maintained that base-level only has a limited influence on upstream reaches and that the vertical position of a river is more the effect of aggradation and degradation in adjoining reaches than a base-level far removed in space. Tectonic activity can produce significant modifications to river channels of a more localized nature and in some parts of the world it represents a continuous source of instability. Adams (1965) attributed the progressive contraction in agriculture over 1000 years along the Dujala River in Iraq to the cumulative effects of uplift which steepened channel gradient, caused incision to a depth of 15 m and thereby led to the abandonment of irrigation canals.

Undoubtedly disturbances to external factors such as climate, vegetation, land use and base-level are a major cause of instability in the fluvial system. However, change can also be initiated internally during the continued operation of normal input levels, a type of unsteady behaviour commonly associated with the excedance of critical levels termed *intrinsic thresholds* by Schumm (1973). Without a change in external factors, a landform may through time reach a condition of incipient instability when a critical threshold may be crossed and significant change initiated. The development of meander cut-offs is a simple example of such instability. Although meanders are regarded as a stable form, they may attain a sinuosity and amplitude which cannot be maintained under existing conditions of flow and sediment transport. By increasing channel gradient, selective cut-offs may return a river to a more stable sinuosity in which there is a better balance between transporting ability and gradient. To the extent that functions such as Leopold and Wolman's (1957) slope–discharge equation (Figure 4.10A) discriminate between different types of channel pattern, they define thresholds and rivers which plot near the line could have a history characterized by transitions from braided to meandering and vice versa (Schumm, 1980). Although internal changes tend to be localized, their effects can be propagated away from the initial disturbance. They may not always be distinguishable from response to external change but their recognition adds a further dimension to understanding the course of fluvial history.

Adjustment to changing external or internal conditions (including the effects of man) contrast sharply with the type of progressive change conceptualized in the cycle of erosion. In the same way that such changes can vary in their frequency, magnitude, duration and spatial extent, so can the nature of adjustment. In terms of change through time, three possibilities can be envisaged: response to an impulse may be simply damped out and the previous state restored; it may be sustained at a new level of activity; or it may be reinforced by positive feedback in which one change leads autocatalytically to another (Brunsden and Thornes, 1979). Additionally, response may be spatially uniform or spatially variable. Thus, for example, the level of climatic change may be relatively uniform over large areas but all parts of an area need not be equally affected. Erosion in one part of a stream system can be associated with deposition in another to give alluvial chronologies which are temporally and spatially out of phase. On the other hand, highly localized changes to input conditions may have effects which are propagated throughout an entire system. These characteristics of adjustment make it difficult to interpret the historical record, to effect regional correlations, and to attach specific causes to specific events.

Philosophies of change

To some extent these various modes of change can be incorporated in conceptual frameworks which provide a means of assessing change through time in a unified way. Two philosophies have dominated developments in geology and geomorphology: catastrophism and uniformitarianism. As the name suggests, the first assumes that much of the erosional and depositional work carried out at the earth's surface is attributable to catastrophic events of large magnitude. This philosophy held sway up to the 1800s with Noah's flood being a favoured candidate as the major catastrophic event in earth history.

Largely through the work of Hutton, Playfair and Lyell, the tenets of the original catastrophe theory were undermined and replaced by the doctrine of uniformitarianism with its precepts:

(i) The basic laws of nature are time-invariant,
(ii) Similar processes and rates prevailed in the past as at present,
(iii) Change takes place gradually and progressively rather than suddenly.

Although the evidence now available refutes the second proposition, the main theme of gradual change has remained. That philosophy permeates Davis's model of landform development and the basic elements of climatic geomorphology. The more recent assertion of Wolman and Miller (1960) that events of moderate frequency and magnitude perform the bulk of fluvial work is in substantial agreement with the uniformitarian doctrine. The main theme can also be seen in the concept of dynamic equilibrium in which small-scale adjustments are continuously being made in order to maintain an approximate state of balance between processes and forms. For given environmental conditions, there is a tendency over time to produce a set of characteristic forms.

The idea of long-continued, low-amplitude change has been challenged on the grounds that geomorphic controls may not remain constant for a long enough period to allow the development of characteristic forms, and that a few extreme events may produce substantial change of lasting effect. In particular, recent studies have emphasized the role played by both ancient and modern floods in shaping the fluvial landscape. At one extreme of the spectrum, sudden failures of Pleistocene lakes have been invoked to explain valley morphology in the western United States, with discharges estimated as high as 21.3×10^6 m^3 s^{-1} (Baker, 1973). Modern floods, although of lesser magnitude, are better documented.

Stewart and LaMarche (1967) evaluated the effects of a flood with a recurrence interval greater than 100 years on a small upland catchment in California. The entire morphological character of the valley was modified as boulders up to 2 m in diameter were transported, with erosion dominant in narrow, steep reaches and deposition in broader, gently sloping ones. Natural levees were a prominent depositional feature, attaining widths of 15 m sufficient to constrain future channel migration during lesser flows. The authors concluded that valley morphology and channel pattern are largely determined by catastrophic events in this high-gradient stream.

One of the best examples is Burkham's (1972) study of channel changes in part of the Gila River, Arizona, over the period 1846–1970. Three distinct phases were identified: 1846–1904, 1905–1917 and 1918–1970. Prior to 1905 the river was sinuous, relatively stable and narrow, with an average width of 90 m. Between 1905 and 1917 (possibly the wettest period since 1650) a series of large winter floods carrying low sediment loads destroyed the flood-plain and widened the channel to about 600 m (Figure 5.3), when also channel sinuosity was decreased and gradient increased. Most of the widening was accomplished in 1905 and 1906 when the flow rate reached a peak of $4250\ m^3\ s^{-1}$. From 1918 onwards the flood-plain has been reconstructed by smaller floods carrying large loads, so that by 1964 the stream channel had developed a meandering pattern and narrowed to an average width of 60 m. This study is significant in that it indicates firstly the scale and rate of river channel adjustment, and secondly the importance of a sequence of flood events in modifying channel morphology.

The main changes induced by major floods appear to be channel straightening and widening, although factors such as antecedent conditions and valley width can modify the effects. Where the channel is confined, particularly in small headwater reaches, deepening may be the dominant change and adjustments to planimetric properties become somewhat limited (Anderson and Calver, 1977). Partly as a result of the recent interest in flood effects, it has been argued that the magnitude–frequency concept outlined by Wolman and Miller (1960) needs modification in order to cope with response to catastrophic events. However, major floods do not always produce large or lasting change. Localized channel widening occurred in response to floods having recurrence intervals exceeding 200 years in the Piedmont area of the United States (Costa, 1974; Gupta and Fox, 1974) but the effects were largely temporary and in one case (Costa, 1974) channel widths had almost recovered their pre-flood values within one year. Clearly there is a question as to the variable impact of extreme events and the persistence of their effects in the fluvial landscape.

The significance of extreme events can be related to climatic factors. Regions of continuous or seasonal aridity seem to have a high potential for catastrophic response. Flood-frequency distributions tend to be highly skewed and in consequence a larger percentage of the total work is carried out by less frequent flows (Wolman and Miller, 1960; Baker, 1977). Also, since vegetation is sparser, resistance to erosion is less and recovery times are likely to be longer than in more humid areas. Width increased greatly along the Cimarron River in Kansas after a major flood had followed a series of dry years when riparian vegetation was much reduced (Schumm and Lichty, 1963). It remained large until a series of wet years enabled the vegetation to become re-established.

Climate and vegetation are not the only controls. Channels cut in more resistant material such as limestone bedrock (Patton and Baker, 1977) may change little

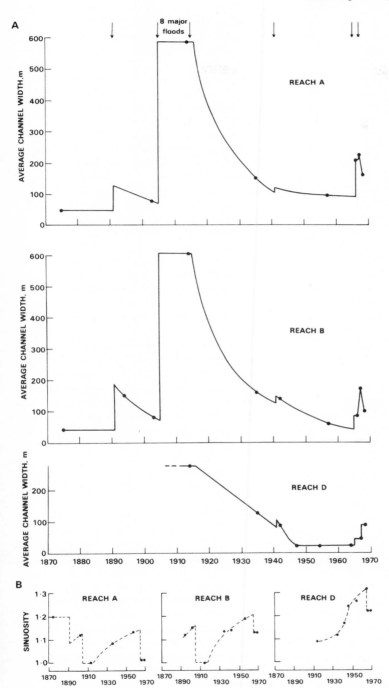

Fig 5.3 Historical changes in channel width (A) and sinuosity (B), 1875–1970, Gila River, Arizona (after Burkham, 1972). The vertical arrows indicate major floods.

except during rare catastrophic events whose effects are preserved thereafter for long periods of time. Basin size is important since, in common with more arid areas, smaller basins tend to have more variable flow regimes in which relatively large events have a dominant influence. To some extent a decrease in basin area in a humid region is comparable to a change from humid to arid conditions in that episodic rather than continuous processes assume greater importance (Wolman and Gerson, 1978). Climatic and physiographic factors produce a wide spatial variation in the response characteristics of river channels to major floods.

The effectiveness of an extreme event depends not only on its absolute magnitude but also on its magnitude relative to average values (e.g. Stevens *et al.*, 1975) and on the ability of subsequent flows to reconstruct the modified channel. Rivers in humid areas seem to be able to recover rapidly provided there is a plentiful supply of sediment. However, where major floods have so altered channel morphology and the distribution of sediment that subsequent flows cannot effect significant change (e.g. Stewart and La Marche, 1967), there may be either no return or a long-delayed return to previous conditions. The present form of Exmoor channels subject to a major flood (recurrence interval > 150 years) in 1952 is substantially the same as that of the early post-flood period (Anderson and Calver, 1977, 1980). The overall extent to which channel morphology reflects the influence of extremes cannot readily be assessed but certain rivers do seem to have long memories for past flood events.

Whether or not a major event has a large or lasting effect depends partly on whether or not a significant threshold is exceeded. Thresholds separate different system regimes each of which may have its own characteristic geometry, so that recovery may be difficult once a threshold has been crossed. Schumm (1973) has recognized two main types, extrinsic and intrinsic. The first is associated with change in an external factor such as climate, while the second reflects an inherent property of geomorphic systems to evolve to a critical state when adjustment or failure occurs. The concept of intrinsic thresholds recognizes that sudden changes in the fluvial system can be an inherent part of normal development and do not always require a change in external controls. One advantage of the threshold approach is that it focuses attention on those variables and mechanisms which are likely to cause a change in the mode of operation of a system.

To a certain extent the threshold concept reconciles the conflicting philosophies of catastrophism and uniformitarianism in that it is associated with a model of change in which periods of rapid adjustment are separated by periods of more gradual change or relative stability when characteristic forms may develop (Figure 4.2A). This episodic model underlines the role that extreme events can play in shifting the system to a new state and helps to explain discontinuities in the erosional and depositional record. It is well exemplified by the development of terrace sequences along Douglas Creek which drains an area of 1070 km² in Colorado (Womack and Schumm, 1977). Modern incision of the valley fill began about 1882, possibly as a result of overgrazing, and led to downcutting by tributary streams. Large quantities of sediment were delivered from the steep tributaries, causing localized deposition and over-steepening of the valley floor at the new level. Repeated entrenchments in these deposits produced flights of terraces at various locations along the main stream (Figure 5.4A). At one section six terraces have developed but both the number and continuity of terrace surfaces vary in the valley, indicating spatial and presumably temporal differences in the erosional and depositional history. Nevertheless the overall trend is episodic with incision to a

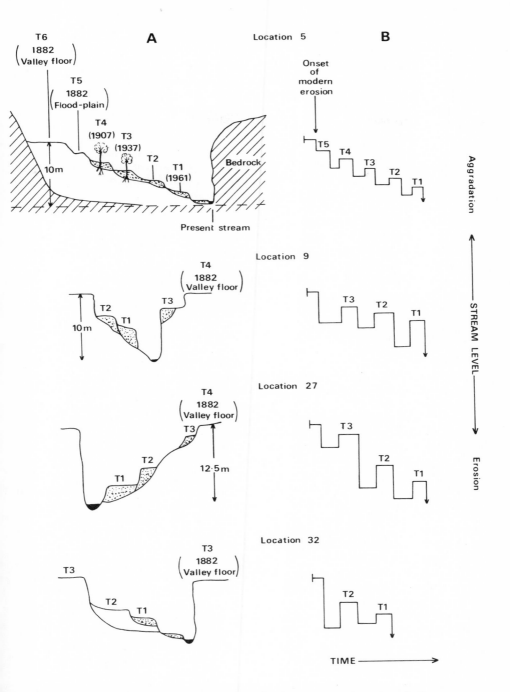

Fig 5.4 A. Diagrammatic cross-sections of Douglas Creek terraces; not drawn to scale. Terraces are numbered from lowest to highest, so that the 1882 valley floor may be assigned a different number depending on the number of terraces present at each location.
B. Schematic diagrams representing the episodic deposition and erosion at each location. Vertical segments indicate incision or deposition, horizontal segments periods of relative stability. At location 5 the surfaces were dated using tree-ring and historical data (after Womack and Schumm, 1977).

new level being followed by deposition, valley floor steepening and renewed down-cutting (Figure 5.4B). It appears that the changes are related to internal rather than external factors, although the initial period of erosion may be an effect of over-grazing in the 1880s. Since the episodic model as exemplified by Douglas Creek seems to require high rates of sediment supply, its applicability to longer time and larger spatial scales may be difficult to substantiate. However, it does emphasize that change need not be progressive and Schumm (1980) has suggested how the threshold and episodic erosion concepts may have practical implications for pre-dicting future erosion and deposition that will occur either as a result of man's activities or as a normal part of landscape evolution.

Reaction and relaxation times
A pervasive tendency of natural physical systems is for response to lag behind changes in process intensity. Conceptually at least, geomorphological time can be divided into (Brunsden, 1980):
  (i) the time taken for the system to react to a change in conditions (reaction time),
  (ii) the time taken for the system to attain a characteristic (equilibrium) state (relaxation time), and
  (iii) the time over which that state is expected to persist (characteristic form time).
Considering the complexity of the fluvial system in which a hierarchy of form elements is related to a set of controls having space-dependent and time-dependent qualities, response curves could show a wide range of forms with variable reaction and relaxation times.

Figure 5.5A shows the basic elements of response to a step-like change in a single control variable, assuming that the change is sustained at a new level. The step function, which implies a rapid transition in input conditions from one regime to another, is one of the simplest models that can be devised but it does seem to have merit for describing changes in climatic parameters in particular. Evidence from Greenland cores indicates that temperature changes from full temperate to full glacial can occur in as little as 10^2 years, even though the resulting ice-sheets may take 10^4 years to reach their maximum extent (Dansgaard *et al.*, 1971). Major dis-continuities in the botanical and cultural record of the Holocene identified from an analysis of radiocarbon dates from the northern hemisphere support an abrupt rather than smooth transition of climate, with vegetation lagging climate by about 10^2 years (Wendland and Bryson, 1974). If the assumption of step-like change is not unreasonable, then its extension over time leads to a square-wave function for describing change.

Evaluating the likely response in fluvial systems involves two major phases: changes in the external environment need to be related firstly to changes in the flow and sediment conditions in the stream, which must then be related to the morphological response of the channel. Both phases involve temporal lag. Con-sequently, even if climate changes in a step-like fashion, channel morphology need not behave similarly, although channels may respond rapidly to pulsed inputs. The scale of the problem can be appreciated from Knox's (1972) work which illustrates part of the first phase. Adopting a square-wave function for climatic fluctuations (Figure 5.5B), he has suggested that maximum sediment yields would be associated with a change from arid to humid conditions when increased precipitation falls on a surface as yet unprotected by an effective vegetation cover. Then also larger

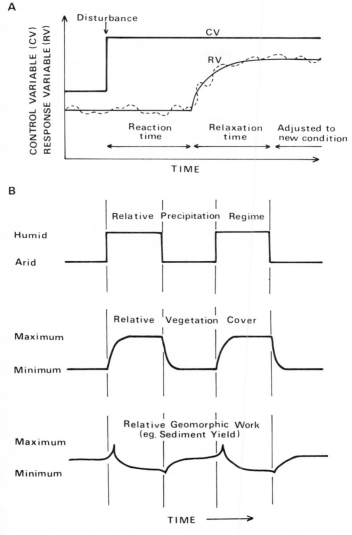

A

Disturbance

CONTROL VARIABLE (CV)
RESPONSE VARIABLE (RV)

CV

RV

Reaction
time

Relaxation
time

Adjusted to
new condition

TIME

B

Relative Precipitation Regime

Humid

Arid

Relative Vegetation Cover

Maximum

Minimum

Relative Geomorphic Work
(eg. Sediment Yield)

Maximum

Minimum

TIME

Fig 5.5 A. Diagrammatic representation of response to a step-like change in a control variable, where the solid line of the response curve indicates the mean condition about which fluctuations occur (dashed line).
B. Suggested vegetational and geomorphic responses to abrupt changes in climatic regime (after Knox, 1972).

floods may be expected. After this initial period, sediment yields would decline as the higher precipitation induces an increased vegetation density and better protection. Even this simple model of environmental change produces quite a complex variation in sediment yield when relaxation effects are introduced. Extension of the model to include other control variables and stream channel response would add considerably to the complexity so that at this stage only general tendencies can be indicated.

Following the format set out by Chorley and Kennedy (1971), reaction and relaxation times can be considered in terms of four main factors:

(i) The resistance to change offered by the various morphological components of the system and by the system as a whole. A hierarchy of increasing resistance and therefore response time can sensibly be constructed according to the dominant type of boundary material: from sand-bed, to gravel-bed, to bedrock streams. The last are particularly slow to change and catastrophic events may be required to effect significant response. Since change in the fluvial system requires work to be done in the form of material transfer, similar hierarchies can be envisaged for both the scale of the system (larger networks and channels adjusting more slowly) and the type of morphological component in the order: bed configuration in sand-bed streams, channel width, channel depth, bed configuration in gravel-bed streams/planimetric geometry, channel bed slope and the overall shape of the longitudinal profile (Figure 4.1). Although no direct calculations have been made of the amount of work required to move from one state to another as regards these components so that their position in the hierarchy may be debatable, their variable resistance and sensitivity to change cannot be denied. River channel width appears to be one of the most adjustable components and available data, albeit for extreme floods, suggest relatively short relaxation times (Table 5.4).

Table 5.4   Adjustment of river channel width to extreme events

River	Frequency of event, years	Maximum widening, %	Relaxation time, years	Source
Patuxent River, Maryland	200	64	15	Gupta and Fox, 1974
Baisman Run	200	160 (average of 10–20)	1–10	Costa, 1974
Appalachian rivers	100	300–400	10	Hack and Goodlett, 1960
Gila River	200	600	45–50	Burkham, 1972

(ii) The complexity of the system, which includes the number of components involved and the character of their interconnections. In the fluvial system where many possible adjustments exist, response to changing discharge and load in the system as a whole may be relatively rapid, particularly if change is concentrated in more sensitive components. Schumm (1968a), for example, has suggested that the Murrumbidgee River in Australia responded to changes in hydrologic regime by selectively altering its channel width and sinuosity without significant aggradation or entrenchment. Relaxation times are dependent on the ability of a system to transmit impulses. Where drainage densities are high, effects may be propagated downstream and, to a lesser extent, upstream quite quickly. Howard (1982) has compared the response times in a long, unbranched channel and a channel network, and found that, whereas they increase with the square of channel length in the former, the rate of increase is much lower in the latter.

(iii) The magnitude and direction of change in input conditions. Smaller-scale changes may have noticeable effects only in more sensitive areas or be absorbed by the system in such a way that the overall effect is reduced. Response times and the type of response depend partly on whether the changes reinforce existing tendencies or produce counteractive effects. In evaluating the impact of climatic change, the initial climate is of critical importance. Baker and Penteado-Orellana

(1977) have argued that the Colorado River in Texas adjusted rapidly with the onset of more arid conditions but more gradually during arid-to-humid transitions, although Knox's diagrammatic model (Figure 5.5B) associates more sudden changes with the latter as far as sediment yield is concerned. Directions of change are considered in more detail below.

(iv) The energy environment of the input. To the extent that rates of change are determined by permissible rates of material transfer, relaxation times are strongly influenced by the prevailing levels of energy available to perform work. A distinction can be drawn between headwater and downstream areas, where the former have more variable flow regimes, higher potential energy and stronger links between hillslopes and channels. They therefore tend to be more responsive. Howard (1982) has suggested that response time is more dependent on the magnitude of input variables than the magnitude of change and, in particular, that it decreases as water and sediment discharges increase. Consequently there is an asymmetry of adjustment in that an increase in discharge or load causes a more rapid change than does a decrease of the same amount.

Even though the discussion above is rather general, the difficulty of defining representative reaction and relaxation times should be clear. Sensitivity to change varies not only between one climatic and physiographic environment and another but also between the various components which characterize river channel form. Notwithstanding this complexity, it has been widely assumed that geomorphic systems respond rapidly at first after disruption but at a steadily declining rate thereafter as a new equilibrium state is approached. In other words, relaxation paths have a basically exponential form. Graf (1977) has used such an argument for studying gully development in the Colorado Piedmont. Based partly on an analogy between adjustment in geomorphic systems and the decay of radioactive isotopes, he has proposed a model for relaxation paths with the form,

$$A_t = A_o e^{-bt} \qquad (5.4)$$

where, in his study, t ($<$ 150 years) equals the time since disruption, A_o equals the potential equilibrium length of a gully, and A_t is the length yet to be eroded before that equilibrium is reached. Dendrochronologic and photographic evidence enabled gully length to be determined at various dates and in the main system it seems that episodic erosion has occurred with the initial development of a protogully (about 1826) being followed by later dissection (about 1906) when a second gully began to form within the first (Figure 5.6A). Headward extension was rapid at first in both cases so that by 18.7 and 15.4 years respectively the older and younger gullies had reached half their new equilibrium length. Thereafter the rate of headward growth steadily declined as the drainage area at the headward end and therefore the amount of energy available for erosion progressively fell. Although data from the test gullies fit equation (5.4) quite well, the universality of the underlying principle remains to be proven.

Relaxation paths and times have a key role to play in assessments of river channel adjustment to externally or internally generated change over a wide range of time scales. They indicate not only the potential for recovery after disturbance but also the conditions under which system equilibrium might be attained and the extent to which the effects of past events might persist in the fluvial landscape. In terms of a transient form ratio,

$$TF = \frac{\text{mean relaxation time}}{\text{mean recurrence time of events}} \qquad (5.5)$$

A

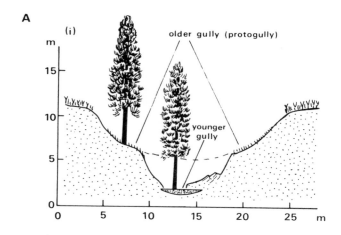

(i)

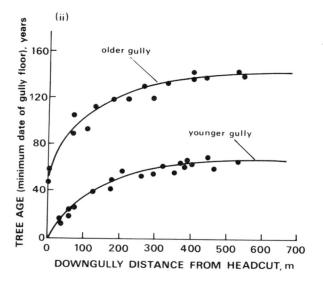

(ii)

Fig 5.6   A. Gully development in Colorado: (i) A typical cross-section illustrating the two phases of gully development; (ii) Dendrochronologic data obtained from trees growing on the gully floors show an exponential decline in the rate of gully extension, where younger trees grow on more recently exposed surfaces further headward (after Graf, 1977).
B. Diagrammatic representation of stability and instability defined by the ratio (TF) of the mean relaxation to the mean recurrence times (after Brunsden and Thornes, 1979).

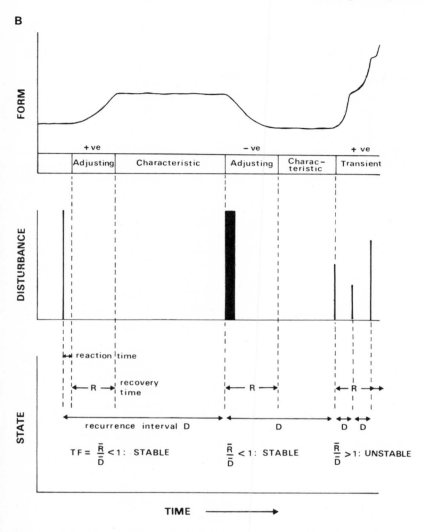

Brunsden and Thornes (1979) define two possible states (Figure 5.6B):

(i) TF > 1: because the mean recurrence time of events capable of producing change is shorter than the time taken for the system (or component of the system) to recover or equilibriate, there is likely to be a poor correspondence between process agents and resulting landforms; that is, forms will be predominantly transient;

(ii) TF < 1: the system has the potential to adjust to new conditions before the next major disturbance occurs so that characteristic forms will tend to prevail after the initial recovery period, leading to more reliable process-response relationships.

Neither of the times given in equation (5.5) can be specified with any assurance for the components of river channel morphology or the fluvial system as a whole, although various estimates can be made (Table 5.4; Howard, 1982). In general river channels respond relatively rapidly except possibly in the profile dimension, but even so scale and environmental differences produce a large range of sensitivities. Where relaxation times are short, geohistorical influences become progressively less important.

Directions of change
Predicting directions of change can be visualized as a procedure which involves two main phases: firstly, environmental change (basically climate) is related to runoff and sediment yield conditions; and secondly, changes to discharge and sediment load are related to the morphological response of river channels. The procedure is illustrated using empirical relationships based largely on United States data.

The first phase is based on curves assembled by Schumm (1968a), in which mean annual runoff and sediment yield are respectively related to mean annual precipitation with suitable corrections for temperature. From these curves the possible effects of climatic change have been determined (Table 5.5), where + denotes an increase, – a decrease and 0 no change. Clearly the initial climate is an important factor. In a temperate climate such as Britain's a shift to cooler and wetter conditions would lead to an increase in runoff and a decrease in sediment yield but, if the climate was originally semi-arid, a similar change would produce increases in both variables, although a denser vegetation cover may eventually become effective in reducing erosion (Figure 5.5B). Because the sediment yield curve is at its steepest for precipitation amounts characteristic of semi-arid environments (Figure 3.7A), those areas are likely to be particularly sensitive to repeated fluctuations in climate and even small changes might induce a marked response.

Climatic change usually alters both runoff and sediment yield but by variable and different amounts. However, predicting the magnitude of change is liable to error given the approximate nature of the curves. In addition, mean annual precipitation and mean annual runoff have limited value as indices of climate and flow regime respectively. Thus, a shift from relatively wet to dry may produce lower runoff totals but a greater incidence of flooding sufficient to cause significant channel widening (Knox, 1972). Despite the higher average runoff associated with a change in the opposite direction, the magnitude of flood flows may decline and vegetation may become more effective in stabilizing channel margins. The relationships between changing climate on the one hand and hydrologic regime and sediment yield on the other are not straightforward so that, although the main directions can be deduced, specific details remain obscure.

The second phase of the procedure is highly dependent on relationships assembled by Schumm (1969) for largely sand-bed channels of assumed stability in semi-arid and sub-humid regions of the United States and southeastern Australia (Table 5.6). M is assumed to indicate not only the type of sediment load (p. 85) but also the quantity of bed load (Q_{sb}) provided only moderate changes in discharge are involved (Schumm, 1977). If M varies inversely with the quantity of bed load, then $1/Q_{sb}$ can be substituted for M in the equations. This set of relationships is one of the few to include a sediment load factor, albeit indirectly, but others (Table 5.6) can be used as a partial check on the consistency of predicted directions of change.

Table 5.5 Possible effects of climatic change on mean annual runoff and sediment yield

Original climate	New climate			
	Cooler $(T_m - 5°C)$, Wetter $(P_m + 250mm)$	Warmer $(T_m + 2.5°C)$, Wetter $(P_m + 250mm)$	Cooler $(T_m - 5°C)$, Drier $(P_m - 125mm)$	Warmer $(T_m + 2.5°C)$, Drier $(P_m - 125mm)$
Temperate:				
$T_m = 10°C$	$R_u{}^+$	$R_u{}^+$	$R_u{}^0$	$R_u{}^-$
$P_m = 750mm$	$S_y{}^-$	$S_y{}^-$ or $S_y{}^0$	$S_y{}^0$	$S_y{}^+$
Sub-humid:				
$T_m = 12.5°C$	$R_u{}^+$	$R_u{}^+$	$R_u{}^0$	$R_u{}^-$
$P_m = 500mm$	$S_y{}^-$	$S_y{}^-$	$S_y{}^0$	$S_y{}^0$
Semi-arid:				
$T_m = 15°C$	$R_u{}^+$	$R_u{}^+$	$R_u{}^-$	$R_u{}^-$
$P_m = 350mm$	$S_y{}^+$	$S_y{}^+$	$S_y{}^0$	$S_y{}^-$

Symbols: T_m, mean annual temperature;
   P_m, mean annual precipitation;
   R_u, mean annual runoff;
   S_y, mean annual sediment yield.

Table 5.6 Empirical equations relating channel variables to flow and sediment characteristics

Channel variable	Schumm's (1969) equations	Other equations	Source
Width	$w = 44Q_m{}^{0.38} M^{-0.39}$	$w = 5.6Q_b{}^{0.51} S^{-0.30}$	Rundquist (1975)
	$w = 5.5Q_{ma}{}^{0.58} M^{-0.37}$	$w = 2.4Q_b{}^{0.41} s^{-0.10*}$	Charlton *et al.* (1978)
Depth	$d = 0.51Q_m{}^{0.29} M^{0.34}$	$d = 0.08Q_b{}^{0.26} S^{0.50} s^{-0.22}$	Rundquist (1975)
	$d = 0.12Q_{ma}{}^{0.42} M^{0.35}$		
Width-depth ratio	$w/d = 255 M^{-1.08}$		
	$w/d = 80Q_m{}^{0.10} M^{-0.74}$		
	$w/d = 41Q_{ma}{}^{0.18} M^{-0.74}$		
Meander wavelength	$\lambda = 1935Q_m{}^{0.34} M^{-0.74}$	$\lambda = 1.2Q_b{}^{0.30} s^{-0.58}$	Derived from equations given by Larras (1968)
	$\lambda = 394Q_{ma}{}^{0.48} M^{-0.74}$		
Sinuosity	$S = 0.94M^{0.25}$		
Channel gradient	$s = 0.0036Q_m{}^{-0.32} M^{-0.38}$		

Symbols: Q_m, mean annual discharge;
   Q_{ma}, mean annual flood;
   Q_b, bankfull discharge;
   M, silt-clay in channel perimeter;
   w, width;
   d, mean depth;
   λ, meander wavelength;
   S, channel sinuosity;
   s, channel gradient
*(assumed to apply to gravelly rivers with an imposed slope and appreciable sediment load)

Using a + or − sign again to denote an increase or decrease, the effects of a change in discharge (Q) or bed load (Q_{sb}) on channel form variables can by hypothesized:

$$Q^+ \rightarrow w^+, d^+, (w/d)^+, \lambda^+, s^- \tag{5.6}$$

$$Q^- \rightarrow w^-, d^-, (w/d)^-, \lambda^-, s^+ \tag{5.7}$$

$$Q_{sb}^+ \rightarrow w^+, d^-, (w/d)^+, \lambda^+, S^-, s^+ \tag{5.8}$$

$$Q_{sb}^- \rightarrow w^-, d^+, (w/d)^-, \lambda^-, S^+, s^- \tag{5.9}$$

The changes appear to be in the right direction except that Larras's (1968) equation suggests that the signs attached to wavelength and slope should be of an opposite sense which they are not in (5.8) and (5.9). However, there is some compensation elsewhere in that a higher sinuosity which implies a lower gradient is associated here with a smaller wavelength.

Changes in discharge or sediment load rarely occur alone because of their joint dependence on watershed variables. Four combinations are possible:

$$Q^+, Q_{sb}^+ \rightarrow w^+, d^\pm, (w/d)^+, \lambda^+, S^-, s^\pm \tag{5.10}$$

$$Q^-, Q_{sb}^- \rightarrow w^-, d^\pm, (w/d)^-, \lambda^-, S^+, s^\pm \tag{5.11}$$

$$Q^+, Q_{sb}^- \rightarrow w^\pm, d^+, (w/d)^\pm, \lambda^\pm, S^+, s^- \tag{5.12}$$

$$Q^-, Q_{sb}^+ \rightarrow w^\pm, d^-, (w/d)^\pm, \lambda^\pm, S^-, s^+ \tag{5.13}$$

The net effect of an increase in discharge and bed-material load is to produce wider, less sinuous channels with a higher meander wavelength (equation 5.10). Changes to depth and gradient are less clearly defined but, since width–depth ratio increases, depth may remain constant or decrease. The projected changes are reversed when both discharge and bed load decrease, as might occur following reservoir development.

The predictions made earlier (Table 5.5) suggest that changes in discharge and sediment load of an opposite sense could be relatively common. Equation (5.12) shows that increasing discharge and decreasing bed load tend to result in narrower, deeper channels of larger sinuosity and lower gradient. In the case of the Colorado River in central Texas (Figure 5.7), such changes have been equated with a return to more humid conditions when streamflow becomes more evenly distributed and catchment erosion is reduced (Baker and Penteado-Orellana, 1977). With the onset of a more arid climate when aggradation follows a period of limited incision, equation (5.13) is more applicable. Although runoff declines as a whole, high magnitude flows become increasingly dominant, transporting coarser and larger sediment loads and forming broad channels of low sinuosity (Figure 5.7).

The relationships (5.10–5.13) suggest no more than possible directions of change. The equations on which they are based (Table 5.6) cover a limited range of conditions and their universality is by no means proven. The use of M as an index of both the type of sediment load and the quantity of bed load is questionable and reflects an expediency conditioned by the lack of suitable data. No consideration is given directly to the differential rates of adjustment of the various form elements or to possible changes in channel pattern other than through sinuosity and wavelength. The development of braiding, for example, is often linked with a plentiful supply of coarse sediment and, in the case of the Colorado River, was associated with more arid phases (Baker and Penteado-Orellana, 1977). Finally, it should be stressed that the initial and ultimate response of river channels depend not only on

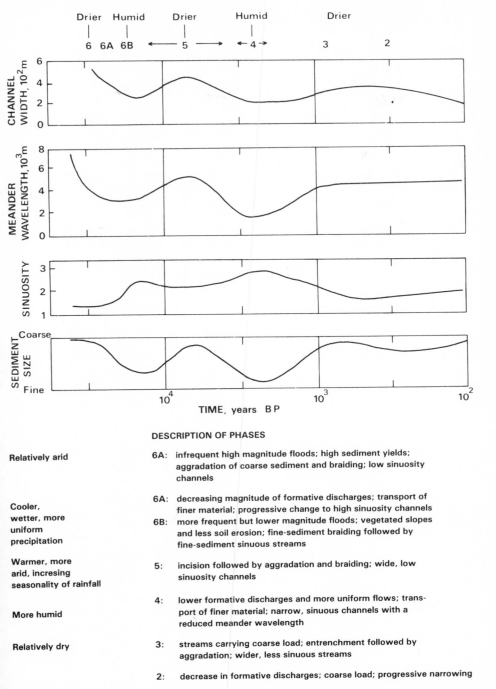

DESCRIPTION OF PHASES

Relatively arid

6A: infrequent high magnitude floods; high sediment yields; aggradation of coarse sediment and braiding; low sinuosity channels

Cooler, wetter, more uniform precipitation

6A: decreasing magnitude of formative discharges; transport of finer material; progressive change to high sinuosity channels

6B: more frequent but lower magnitude floods; vegetated slopes and less soil erosion; fine-sediment braiding followed by fine-sediment sinuous streams

Warmer, more arid, incresing seasonality of rainfall

5: incision followed by aggradation and braiding; wide, low sinuosity channels

More humid

4: lower formative discharges and more uniform flows; transport of finer material; narrow, sinuous channels with a reduced meander wavelength

Relatively dry

3: streams carrying coarse load; entrenchment followed by aggradation; wider, less sinuous streams

2: decrease in formative discharges; coarse load; progressive narrowing

Fig 5.7 Changes in the Colorado River, Texas, over time (after Baker and Penteado-Orellana, 1977).

the directions of change in discharge and load but also on their relative and absolute degrees of change. To take those into account requires much more information than is currently available.

Despite these deficiencies, the rationale does indicate the main adjustments to channel form which might be expected after disturbance. A primary need is for more reliable data on sediment factors in particular. Not surprisingly, one of the best examples of this type of approach comes from Schumm's (1968a) own work on the Riverine Plain of New South Wales where previous channels are particularly well preserved. Three separate phases of channel development were recognized which, in order of increasing age, are: the present Murrumbidgee river system; ancestral rivers which occur as depressions on the alluvial plain and which have been partly destroyed by the present river; and prior streams now infilled with sediment but clearly visible on aerial photographs. Morphological and sedimentological evidence enabled the approximate dimensions of these channels to be estimated (Table 5.7). The source areas for runoff and sediment have remained substantially constant over time but channel characteristics have fluctuated markedly, presumably because of major changes in climatic and hydrologic conditions.

Table 5.7   Morphology of river channels, Riverine Plain, New South Wales (after Schumm, 1968a)

	Width, m	Depth, m	w/d	Sinuosity	Gradient, m m^{-1}
Murrumbidgee River	67	6.4	10	2	0.000133
Ancestral river	140	10.7	13	1.7	0.000151
Prior streams	180	2.7	67	1.1	0.000379

	Meander wavelength, m	Channel silt–clay (M), %	Bankfull discharge, m^3 s^{-1}	Bed load at bankfull, t day^{-1}
Murrumbidgee River	850	25	280	2 000
Ancestral river	210	16	14 400	21 000
Prior streams	5 500	1.6	650	54 000

A late Pleistocene age is ascribed to the prior streams. Although some dispute exists as to the climate at that time, Schumm has assumed relatively arid conditions with a reduced annual discharge but high sediment load, the latter being associated with low vegetation density and large peak flows. Equation (5.13) therefore applies. To transport the large load, prior streams were wide and shallow with a steeper gradient produced principally through a reduced channel sinuosity rather than by incision or aggradation.

With a change to more humid conditions about 3000 BP, discharge increased but sediment load declined. In accordance with equation (5.12), the channel of the ancestral river became deeper and more sinuous, the latter being largely responsible for the lower gradient. Since then both discharge and sediment load have decreased (equation 5.11) to give a present channel which is narrower and more sinuous than its ancestors. Besides illustrating the possible channel adjustments to fluctuating climate, this study shows that, in an area where the valley slope is low, modifications to channel gradient were relatively small over a period of at least 10^4 years and could be accommodated almost entirely by changes to channel sinuosity.

The main purpose of this section was to illustrate a procedure which, despite its various deficiencies, can be used to indicate the broad directions of change in run-off, sediment yield and channel morphology resulting from altered catchment conditions. As set out, the procedure is basically deductive in that it initially requires independent information on those conditions. Because that type of information is rarely available, reconstructions have most often proceeded inductively whereby estimates of former channel characteristics (notably w, d, λ and M) are used to indicate past discharges and climates, a line of reasoning which is less secure. However, the procedure provides one basis for assessing the effects of man's activities on river channels, which, being more recent, can possibly be established with greater certainty.

The effects of man

Over the last 2000 years, and especially the last 300 years, man's activities have had an increasing influence on drainage basins and their constituent channels. The scale of climatic fluctuation has been much less during that period (Figure 5.2) but man's modification of the physical environment may have induced changes similar in scale to those produced by climatic change in the more distant past. Indeed one of the main incentives for taking a longer-term view of stream channel response has been to provide a framework for estimating the effects of man's activities, since they operate through the same basic mechanisms as climatic change. If dangerous or expensive outcomes are to be avoided, the consequences of interference need to be understood.

Two broad types of man-induced change can be identified (Table 5.8). The first includes those changes brought about by direct modification to the channel itself, which often takes the form of engineering works designed to alleviate the effects of

Table 5.8   Types of man-induced change

Direct or channel-phase changes:
    River regulation –
        Water storage by reservoirs
        Diversion of water
    Channel changes –
        Bank stabilization
        Channel straightening
        Stream gravel extraction
Indirect or land-phase changes:
    Land use changes –
        Removal of vegetation, especially deforestation
        Afforestation
        Changes in agricultural practices
        Building construction
        Urbanization
        Mining activity
    Land drainage –
        Agricultural drains
        Storm-water sewerage systems

---

flooding, erosion or deposition. Indirect changes result from activity in extra-channel areas, which modifies discharge and load in the stream and ultimately results in stream channel response. With both types, effects can be transmitted long distances away from the initial change. Two examples have been chosen from Table 5.8 to illustrate some of the dominant influences.

Reservoir development

Dams have been built for the purpose of river regulation over many centuries but the pace of construction has increased dramatically in the last three decades. In North America and Africa up to 20 per cent of total stream runoff is now regulated by reservoirs, with comparable figures for Europe and Asia of 15 and 14 per cent respectively (Beaumont, 1978). The impact of a particular scheme on the fluvial system will vary with the size and purpose of the reservoir and its physical setting but in general both upstream and downstream adjustments can be expected.

Upstream, local base-level is raised to a position at which the water surface inter-sects the original bed, the maximum rise in height being determined by the crest of the dam spillway. With a reduction in capacity and competence for transport, a depositional wedge is constructed and channel gradient locally lowered. Although aggradation seems to take place rapidly at first, its upstream extent may be limited or long delayed (Leopold and Bull, 1979; Figure 4.18C). Lane (1955) cited a Formosan example where the bed slope had adjusted to about half of its original value within eight years, causing a rise in river level which threatened a hydroelec-tric plant 1.3 km upstream of the 13 m high dam. Williams (1978c) reported bed aggradation of 0.3–0.6 m 8 km upstream of a reservoir on the North Platte River opened in 1941. Upstream influences are variable, depending on the sediment transport characteristics and the height of the dam relative to the pre-existing pro-file of the stream.

Most work has been concerned with the downstream effects of reservoir con-struction, of which two have been widely reported: a reduction in the magnitude of flood peaks by amounts ranging from 20 to 75 per cent (Petts, 1979); and a marked decrease in sediment discharge, especially in those reaches immediately below the dam. Thus the downstream patterns of erosion and deposition may be significantly altered with consequences for stream channel response, the particular form of which will depend on the relative changes in discharge and load. In line with pre-vious reasoning, possible adjustments can be suggested (Petts, 1979):

$$Q^0, \ Q_{sb}^- \rightarrow w^\pm, d^+, A_b^+, S^+, s^- \tag{5.14}$$

$$Q^-, Q_{sb}^- \rightarrow w^-, d^\pm, A_b^-, S^\pm, s^\pm \tag{5.15}$$

where A_b is channel capacity (bankfull cross-sectional area).

A common response to the release of sediment-free water below dams is degradation of the channel bed, which may undermine important engineering structures. The degradation which is initiated close to the dam may continue until slope is decreased or channel roughness increased sufficiently to reduce velocity and shear stress below some critical erosional threshold. The relationship between the length and depth of scour and bed slope adjustment is unlikely to be simple, particularly where differential transport leads to bed armouring. The occurrence of coarse lag deposits at some downstream location will tend to inhibit bed adjustment in reaches further upstream.

The primary morphological response to the change in-flow regime seems to be a decrease in channel capacity, brought about principally by a reduction in channel width (equation 5.15). Losses of channel capacity in excess of 50 per cent are not uncommon (Petts, 1979). Since width reduction is largely achieved through the formation of depositional berms and bars which requires the introduction and redistribution of sediment, a favoured location for channel change is below tributary junctions where sediment is imported by non-regulated tributaries. This aggradational phase will tend to lag behind bed degradation because the redistribution of large quantities of sediment may be involved.

Williams (1978c) has studied the changes which have occurred along 480 km of the North Platte and Platte Rivers in Nebraska since the nineteenth century as a result of river regulation schemes, most of which were operational by 1941. With no significant change in climate, both peak discharge and mean annual discharge have declined to 10–30 per cent of their pre-dam values. Sediment loads have also probably decreased but no data are available. The most notable effect has been a large decrease in bankfull width (Figure 5.8A(i)), parts of the previous channel being colonized by vegetation which has helped to stabilize deposits. The most pronounced changes have occurred in the upper 365 km where widths in the 1970s were only 10–20 per cent of their 1865 values. At the Overton station in particular there is some evidence of delay in the narrowing process following flow reduction. Associated with the narrowing, the rivers have tended to become less braided and slightly more sinuous. Data from 12 gauging stations indicate quite large but generally inconsistent changes in bed elevation and channel gradient. In the reach downstream of the largest reservoir (completed in 1941), an initial degradation of 0.6–0.8 m has been followed in the late 1960s by aggradation of 0.4 m (Figure 5.8A(ii)). These fluctuations in bed height probably reflect the complex regulation of water and sediment delivery to the rivers, and suggest that bed degradation may be only an initial response to reservoir development.

The direction and magnitude of channel change are controlled by the extent to which the magnitude–frequency characteristics of the flow and the quantity and calibre of the sediment load are modified. The effects of river regulation will tend to diminish with distance downstream as non-regulated tributaries make an increasing contribution to the flow (Figure 5.8B). Where few tributaries exist, effects may persist for considerable distances. Thus the reduction in sediment discharge along the Nile following the completion of the High Aswan Dam in 1964 has resulted in the erosion not only of the Nile itself but also of coastal areas 965 km downstream (Kashef, 1981). Since many reservoirs are relatively new, Petts (1979) has speculated that a century or more may be required for the full effects to be realized, especially in reaches further downstream. In the planning of regulation schemes, the geomorphologic consequences need to be appreciated if adverse effects are to be avoided.

Land use changes

When dealing with indirect change, the problem is to determine how much alteration of runoff and erosion conditions in extra-channel areas is necessary to produce a given type and amount of stream channel adjustment. Land use change can take various forms but, for illustrative purposes, is considered here as a two-phase process: forest clearance for the purpose of cultivation or grazing, and urbanization. Wolman (1967) has proposed a sequence for the mid-Atlantic region of the United

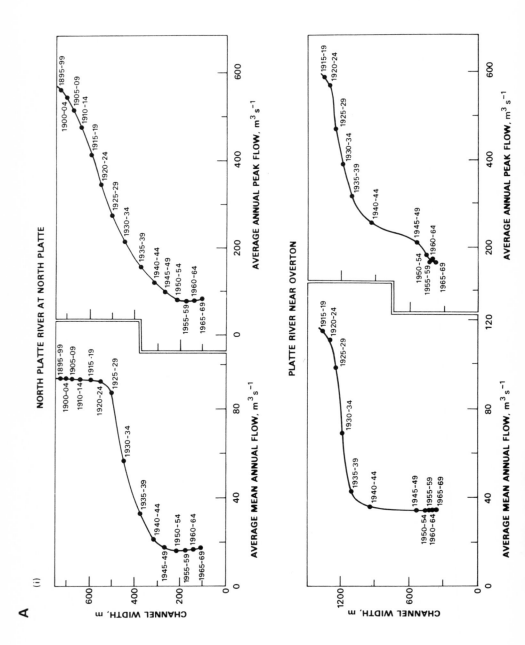

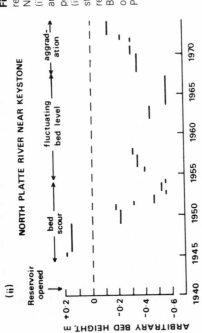

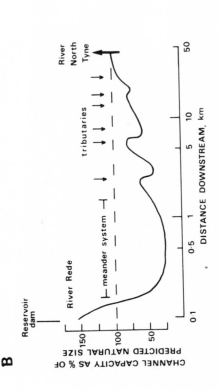

Fig 5.8 A. Channel changes resulting from the regulation of the Platte and North Platte Rivers, Nebraska (after Williams, 1978c):
(i) Changes in channel width with mean annual and annual peak flows averaged over 5-year periods;
(ii) Changes in bed elevation at the gauging station immediately downstream of the largest reservoir.
B. Fluctuations in channel capacity downstream of Catcleugh reservoir, Northumberland (after Petts, 1979).

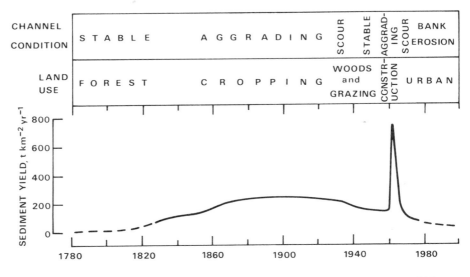

Fig 5.9   Variation in sediment yield over time, Piedmont region, USA (after Wolman, 1967).

States covering these two phases, in which changing land use is related firstly to sediment yield and then to general channel conditions (Figure 5.9).

Forest clearance began in Europe more than 3000 years ago so that any interpretation of channel adjustment faces the problem of differentiating between the relative influences of climatic fluctuation and human activity. The effects of large-scale deforestation may be clearer in areas where European-style farming has been introduced more recently. In the United States the farming era began about 1700 in the Piedmont region (Wolman, 1967) and after 1820 in Wisconsin (Knox, 1977), while the conversion of forest to pasture occurred even later in New Zealand (Bennett and Selby, 1977).

A major result of forest clearance is accelerated soil erosion on hillslopes, associated with which are network extension through gully development and an increase in the sediment supplied to streams. In both the Piedmont and Wisconsin, changes were slow at first but intensified as the farming area expanded particularly into the upper parts of catchments. Much of the eroded sediment is still stored, either as colluvial-sheetwash deposits on hillslopes or as alluvium in flood-plains and channels (Trimble, 1974; Costa, 1975). The conversion of forest to farming land also affects runoff characteristics. Knox (1977) estimated that the magnitude of floods having a recurrence interval of less than 5 years increased by 3–5 times, with the impact being greatest in small watersheds. However, runoff from high intensity rains was less affected.

The higher sediment loads have generally caused channel-bed aggradation and overbank deposition on flood-plains to depths of over 1 m (Meade, 1976), the latter being partly a consequence of the former in that bed aggradation increases the frequency of overbank flows. In line with equations (5.8) and (5.10), channels have tended to become wider, shallower and less sinuous where the influx of coarse material has been appreciable. In the Mangawhara catchment of New Zealand, the channel is narrow and stable in its upper 3 km where the catchment is still forested but rapidly becomes wider and more irregular beyond that point, characteristics which persist downvalley (Bennett and Selby, 1977). There also, channel length has decreased overall from 16.1 km to 13.5 km in 33 years, the decrease in sinuosity being most marked in downstream reaches.

Longitudinal variations in stream channel response have been reported elsewhere. Knox (1977) found that, as a result of increased bed load transport and more frequent flooding, channels in the first 40 km have increased their bankfull widths by more than 100 per cent when compared with their pre-settlement counterparts. In the next 15 km increases in width have usually been less than 40 per cent, while in the lower reaches where bed load transport is less important and changes in flood frequency have been less marked the transport and deposition of finer sediments have tended to produce narrower and deeper cross-sections. Depending on how forest clearance alters the rate and type of sediment supply to streams, channel response may vary from one basin to another or between different parts of the same basin. In areas where fine gravel and sand are readily available as potential bed load, channel aggradation, widening and bar instability are common responses to forest clearance, all of which are associated with braiding.

Wolman's schematic diagram (Figure 5.9) identifies a phase following the farming era which can be associated with a reversion to woods or the introduction of conservation practices designed to alleviate the worst effects of farming. In the Piedmont region the consequent decrease in sediment supply has initiated a period of channel scouring (Trimble, 1974; Costa, 1975). Much of the land in the Savannah River basin that was formerly under crops has reverted to less erosive uses and the river is now actively eroding its bed at least in those parts of the catchment where the main wave of sediment resulting from accelerated erosion has passed through (Meade, 1976). In Maryland incision by the smaller streams has led to the formation of new flood-plains within older ones (Costa, 1975).

Channels can seemingly adjust rapidly to changed conditions at least in the width dimension, although comparisons of past and present channels are largely limited to planimetric properties because of the type of data generally available. However, the response is likely to be complex, with temporal and spatial lags being involved. Thus, for example, if forest clearance is followed by the introduction of conservation measures and the wave of sediment associated with the former has yet to complete its passage through the basin, stream channel response may vary with position depending on whether sediment supply is increasing, constant or declining. Single changes let alone compound ones seldom produce single effects.

In comparison with forest clearance, **urbanization** represents a more localized change in land use but its effects may nevertheless be propagated downstream. In general the creation of impervious surfaces and installation of more efficient drainage systems in urban areas increases both the volume of runoff for a given rainfall (Table 5.9) and the magnitude of flood discharges. As regards sediment yield, urban development can be represented as a two-phase process, a large initial increase when soil is exposed to runoff on construction sites being followed by a decline as sediment sources become more stable in the urban landscape (Figure 5.9).

The more frequent and greater flood discharges associated with urbanization cause channel enlargement downstream (equation 5.6). Comparing urban and rural sites around the town of Catterick in North Yorkshire, Gregory and Park (1976) found that channel capacities were up to 150 per cent larger in the former. Hammer (1972) has evaluated the relative influence of several land use types in pro-

Table 5.9   Relationship between rainfall and direct runoff for pre-urban and urban conditions, Hempstead, Long Island (after Seaburn, 1969)

Rainfall, mm	Direct runoff, mm		Ratio of (2) to (1)
	Pre-urban period (1)	Urban period (2)	
25	1.5	2.2	1.5
50	2.9	6.4	2.2
75	4.2	11.9	2.8
100	5.5	18.5	3.4
125	6.7	26.0	3.9

moting channel change for 78 small basins near Philadelphia (Table 5.10). The results suggest that the degree of channel enlargement is correlated with the age (and type) of urban development. There is a lag in channel adjustment because the effect of a land surface change on flood peaks takes time to influence the channel itself.

No distinction has yet been drawn between the relative contributions of width and depth to the total change in channel capacity. Based upon re-surveys over a 20-year period (1953–1972) of 14 monumented cross-sections in the urbanized catchment of Watts Branch, Maryland (A_d = 9.6 km^2), Leopold (1973) found overall that mean depth had increased by 23 per cent, largely as a result of overbank deposition rather than bed scour, but that bankfull width had decreased by 35 per cent, a response which runs counter to expectation. During the first 12 years urbanization did not markedly alter the frequency of high flows but did induce a higher rate of sediment supply, leading to within-channel deposition and cross-sectional narrowing. Thereafter the number of high flows increased rapidly as the urban area expanded and in 1967 progressive enlargement of the channel began. At two cross-sections the channel area increased by 40 and 62 per cent between 1968 and 1972. When observation ceased the enlargement process may have been incomplete especially as regards channel widening, although the flashy floods associated with urban catchments may not always saturate banks sufficiently to reduce their stability. In any case cross-sectional changes are unlikely to be simple so that single-valued parameters such as width or area may not adequately express the effects (Richards and Wood, 1977).

Table 5.10   Ratio of enlarged channel area to natural channel area in basins less than 13 km^2, assuming that all the basin area is in use as specified (after Hammer, 1972)

Land use	Enlarged channel area/ Natural channel area
Wooded	0.75
Previous developed land	1.08
Impervious area less than 4 years old; unsewered streets and houses	1.08
Cultivation	1.29
Houses more than 4 years old fronted by sewered streets	2.19
Sewered streets more than 4 years old	5.95
Impervious areas more than 4 years old	6.79

Leopold's study illustrates the importance of phasing in channel adjustment. The first few years when sediment supply is higher (Figure 5.9) may be a period of channel contraction and only in the post-construction phase may the increased frequency and magnitude of flood flows produce significant enlargement. Arnold *et al.* (1982) have also observed phased changes in channels affected by urbanization. Once construction was complete, sediment yields declined but discharges remained high, creating an imbalance which led to high rates of bank erosion. That erosion has not only produced channel widening but, by locally increasing the sediment discharge in downstream reaches, has caused pattern instability and a change from meandering to braided. Sinuosity has decreased and slope increased through the meander cut-off process. Part of the River Bollin in Cheshire has also adjusted to a flashier regime by becoming less sinuous, a decrease in sinuosity from 2.41 to 2.34 between 1872 and 1935 being followed by a much sharper decline to 1.4 by 1973 (Mosley, 1975). Rates of change seem to have accelerated in the 1960s with an increase in annual flood maxima, related principally to suburban expansion but also to the renewal of agricultural tile drains.

The main emphasis in the literature has been on the hydrologic rather than the geomorphic impacts of urbanization but the two need not be simply related. Not only is there spatial and temporal lag in response but the character of channel change varies over time with the relative extent to which discharge and load conditions are modified at different stages during the urbanization process. Most of the examples cited above refer to relatively small urban areas in basins of less than 50 km² but larger rivers may not show such marked changes since a smaller proportion of their catchment area is likely to be affected. Despite this scale limitation and the lack of information on the downstream propagation of effects, it is again evident that stream channels can respond relatively rapidly to external disturbance, which has implications for their design and control in the urban landscape.

Postscript

Natural rivers are dynamic entities which adjust their channel form over time to external or internal disturbances. Much of the recent interest in river history stems from a concern with the increasing influence that man's activities are having on the fluvial landscape. Reconstruction of the past is seen not necessarily as an end in itself but as a means of testing models of change which, if verified, can be used to forecast future behaviour. However, the past is imperfectly preserved and reconstructions become more generalized and less reliable over longer timespans. On the other hand, short-term observations of river channel adjustment may represent only the initial response which precedes a more complete transformation as effects are distributed throughout the fluvial system.

Contemporary opinion favours a model of episodic change in which periods of rapid adjustment are separated by periods of relative stability (Schumm, 1977; Brunsden and Thornes, 1979). Considering landforms as a whole, river channels are quite sensitive elements at least in certain dimensions such as channel width. However, major uncertainties remain as to the character of their response:

(i) Relationships between channel form and control variables are far from adequate, especially as regards the influence of the type and quantity of sediment load, but they form a basis for identifying the equilibrium state which might develop under a given set of conditions and which acts as a datum for assessing observed states. Relationships obtained for one environment or type of channel may not apply to another so that empirical results in particular need to be carefully assessed as to their generality.

(ii) To assess the ability of rivers to attain and maintain a characteristic geometry, it is necessary to determine how much alteration in input conditions is required to produce a given type and amount of channel change. Sensitivity to change varies from one environment to another, and from one channel form variable to another (Figure 4.1), in a way that is not completely understood.

(iii) Information is needed on the relaxation paths and times required for the attainment of stability following disruption, with due regard being paid to the rates of adjustment of different form elements. The concept of equilibrium is more difficult to apply where, as in rivers, there are multiple outputs with variable time scales of adjustment.

(iv) The propagation process whereby localized changes are transmitted away from source is poorly understood. In this respect stronger links need to be established between river channel and drainage network processes, wherein consideration is given to the interactions of main streams and tributaries of varying relative size.

The stage has yet to be reached when the changes in runoff and sediment yield resulting from direct or indirect human interference can be effectively related to the magnitude and direction of river channel response. Equations (5.6)–(5.13) represent a first step toward that end. River channels are three-dimensional phenomena with various degrees of freedom whose adjustment reflects a multi-linked chain of complex interactions (Figure 1.1).

References

ABBOTT, J.E. and FRANCIS, J.R.D. 1977: Saltation and suspension trajectories of solid grains in a water stream. *Philosophical Transactions of the Royal Society* 284A, 225–54.

ABRAHAMS, A.D. 1972: Drainage densities and sediment yields in eastern Australia. *Australian Geographical Studies* 10, 19–41.

—— 1975: Topologically random channel networks in the presence of environmental controls. *Bulletin of the Geological Society of America* 86, 1459–62.

—— 1976: Evolutionary changes in link lengths: further evidence for stream abstraction. *Transactions of the Institute of British Geographers New Series* 1, 225–30.

—— 1977: The factor of relief in the evolution of channel networks in mature drainage basins. *American Journal of Science* 277, 626–46.

—— 1980: Divide angles and their relation to interior link lengths in natural channel networks. *Geographical Analysis* 12, 157–71.

ABRAHAMS, A.D. and CAMPBELL, R.N. 1976: Source and tributary-source link lengths in natural channel networks. *Bulletin of the Geological Society of America* 87, 1016–20.

ACKERS, P. and CHARLTON, F.G. 1970a: Dimensional analysis of alluvial channels with special reference to meander length. *Journal of Hydraulics Research* 8, 287–316.

—— 1970b: The slope and resistance of small meandering channels. *Proceedings of the Institution of Civil Engineers* 47, Supplementary Paper 7362-S, 349–70.

ADAMS, R.M. 1965: *Land behind Baghdad*. Chicago: University of Chicago Press.

AGHASSY, J. 1973: Man-induced badlands topography. In Coates, D.R. (ed.), *Environmental Geomorphology and Landscape Conservation, volume 3* (Stroudsberg, Pa.: Dowden, Hutchinson & Ross), 124–36.

ALEXANDER, C.S. and NUNNALLY, N.R. 1972: Channel stability on the lower Ohio River. *Annals of the Association of American Geographers* 62, 411–17.

ALEXANDER, D. 1979: Simulation of channel morphology: problems and prospects. *Progress in Physical Geography* 3, 544–72.

ANDERSON, M.G. and BURT, T.P. 1978: Analysis of spatial water quality and stream networks in the southern Cotswolds during and after the drought of 1976. *Earth Surface Processes* 3, 59–70.

ANDERSON, M.G. and CALVER, A. 1977: On the persistence of landscape features formed by a large flood. *Transactions of the Institute of British Geographers New Series* 2, 243–54.

—— 1980: Channel plan changes following large floods. In Cullingford, Davidson and Lewin 1980, 43–52.

ANDREWS, E.D. 1979: Scour and fill in a stream channel, East Fork River, western Wyoming. *United States Geological Survey Professional Paper* 1117, 49pp.

—— 1980: Effective and bankfull discharges of streams in the Yampa river basin, Colorado and Wyoming. *Journal of Hydrology* 46, 311–30.

ANTROPOVSKIY, V.I. 1972: Criterial relations of types of channel processes. *Soviet Hydrology: Selected Papers* 5, 371–81.

ARNOLD, C.L., BOISON, P.J. and PATTON, P.C. 1982: Sawmill Brook: an example of rapid geomorphic change related to urbanization. *Journal of Geology* 90, 155–66.

BAGNOLD, R.A. 1956: The flow of cohesionless grains in fluids. *Philosophical Transactions of the Royal Society* 249A, 235–97.

—— 1960: Some aspects of the shape of river meanders. *United States Geological Survey Professional Paper* 282E, 135–44.

—— 1966: An approach to the sediment transport problem from general physics. *United States Geological Survey Professional Paper* 4221, 37pp.

—— 1977: Bed load transport by natural rivers. *Water Resources Research* 13, 303–12.

—— 1980: An empirical correlation of bedload transport rates in flumes and natural rivers. *Proceedings of the Royal Society* 372A, 453–73.

BAKER, V.R. 1973: Paleohydrology and sedimentology of Lake Missoula flooding in eastern Washington. *Geological Society of America Special Paper* 144, 79pp.

—— 1977: Stream-channel response to floods, with examples from central Texas. *Bulletin of the Geological Society of America* 88, 1057–71.

—— 1978: Adjustment of fluvial systems to climate and source terrain in tropical and subtropical environments. In Miall, A.D. (ed.), *Fluvial Sedimentology* (Calgary: Canadian Society of Petroleum Geologists), Memoir 5, 211–30.

BAKER, V.R. and PENTEADO-ORELLANA, M.M. 1977: Adjustment to Quaternary climatic change by the Colorado River in central Texas. *Journal of Geology* 85, 395–422.

BAKER, V.R. and RITTER, D.F. 1975: Competence of rivers to transport coarse bedload material. *Bulletin of the Geological Society of America* 86, 975–8.

BATHURST, J.C. 1978: Flow resistance of large-scale roughness. *Journal of the Hydraulics Division American Society of Civil Engineers* 104, HY12, 1587–604.

BATHURST, J.C., THORNE, C.R. and HEY, R.D. 1979: Secondary flow and shear stress at bends. *Journal of the Hydraulics Division American Society of Civil Engineers* 105, HY10, 1277–95.

BEAUMONT, P. 1978: Man's impact on river systems: a world-wide view. *Area* 10, 38–41.

BECKINSALE, R.P. 1969: River regimes. In Chorley, R.J. (ed.), *Introduction to Physical Hydrology* (London: Methuen), 176–92.

BEGIN, Z.B. 1981: Stream curvature and bank erosion: a model based on the momentum equation. *Journal of Geology* 89, 497–504.

BEGIN, Z.B., MEYER, D.F. and SCHUMM, S.A. 1981: Development of longitudinal profiles of alluvial channels in response to base-level lowering. *Earth Surface Processes and Landforms* 6, 49–68.

BENNETT, J.R. and SELBY, M.J. 1977: Induced channel instability and hydraulic geometry of the Mangawhara stream, New Zealand. *Journal of Hydrology (New Zealand)* 16, 134–47.

BENNETT, R.J. 1976: Adaptive adjustment of channel geometry. *Earth Surface Processes* 1, 131–50.

BLUCK, B.J. 1976: Sedimentation in some Scottish rivers of low sinuosity. *Transactions of the Royal Society of Edinburgh* 69, 425–56.

BLYTH, K. and RODDA, J.C. 1973: A stream length study. *Water Resources Research* 9, 1454–61.

BRADLEY, W.C., FAHNESTOCK, R.K. and ROWEKAMP, E.T. 1972: Coarse sediment transport by flood flows on Knik River, Alaska. *Bulletin of the Geological Society of America* 83, 1261–84.

BRIDGE, J.S. 1977: Flow, bed topography, grain size and sedimentary structure in open channel bends: a three-dimensional model. *Earth Surface Processes* 2, 401–16.

BROTHERTON, D.I. 1979: On the origin and characteristics of river channel patterns. *Journal of Hydrology* 44, 211–30.

BROWN, F.R. 1963: Cavitation in hydraulic structures: problems created by cavitation phenomena. *Journal of the Hydraulics Division American Society of Civil Engineers* 89, HY1, 99–116.

BRUNSDEN, D. 1980: Applicable models of long term landform evolution. *Zeitschrift für Geomorphologie*, Supplement 36, 16–26.

BRUNSDEN, D. and THORNES, J.B. 1979: Landscape sensitivity and change. *Transactions of the Institute of British Geographers New Series* 4, 463–84.

BRUSH, L.M. 1961: Drainage basins, channels, and flow characteristics of selected streams in central Pennsylvania. *United States Geological Survey Professional Paper* 282F, 145–81.

BUNTING, B.T. 1961: The role of seepage moisture in soil formation, slope development and stream initiation. *American Journal of Science* 259, 503–18.

BURKHAM, D.E. 1972: Channel changes of the Gila River in Safford valley, Arizona, 1846–1970. *United States Geological Survey Professional Paper* 655G, 24pp.

CALLANDER, R.A. 1978: River meandering. *Annual Review of Fluid Mechanics* 10, 129–58.

CALVER, A. 1978: Modelling drainage headwater development. *Earth Surface Processes* 3, 233–41.

CARLSTON, C.W. 1963: Drainage density and streamflow. *United States Geological Survey*

Professional Paper 422C, 8pp.
—— 1965: The relation of free meander geometry to stream discharge and its geomorphic implications. *American Journal of Science* 263, 864–85.
—— 1966: The effect of climate on drainage density and streamflow. *Bulletin of the International Association of Scientific Hydrology* 11, 62–9.
—— 1968: Slope-discharge relations for eight rivers in the United States. *United States Geological Survey Professional Paper* 600D, 45–7.
—— 1969: Downstream variations in the hydraulic geometry of streams: special emphasis on mean velocity. *American Journal of Science* 267, 499–510.
CHANG, H.H. 1979a: Geometry of rivers in regime. *Journal of the Hydraulics Division American Society of Civil Engineers* 105, HY6, 691–706.
—— 1979b: Minimum stream power and river channel patterns. *Journal of Hydrology* 41, 303–27.
—— 1980: Geometry of gravel streams. *Journal of the Hydraulics Division American Society of Civil Engineers* 106, HY9, 1443–56.
CHARLTON, F.G., BROWN, P.M. and BENSON, R.W. 1978: The hydraulic geometry of some gravel rivers in Britain. *Hydraulics Research Station Report* IT 180, 48pp.
CHERKAUER, D.S. 1972: Longitudinal profiles of ephemeral streams in southeastern Arizona. *Bulletin of the Geological Society of America* 83, 353–66.
—— 1973: Minimization of power expenditure in a riffle–pool alluvial channel. *Water Resources Research* 9, 1613–28.
CHIEN, N. 1961: The braided stream of the lower Yellow River. *Scientia Sinica* 10, 734–54.
CHITALE, S.V. 1973: Theories and relationships of river channel patterns. *Journal of Hydrology* 19, 285–308.
CHORLEY, R.J. 1969: The drainage basin as the fundamental geomorphic unit. In Chorley, R.J. (ed.), *Introduction to Physical Hydrology* (London: Methuen), 37–59.
CHORLEY, R.J. and KENNEDY, B.A. 1971: *Physical Geography: a Systems Approach*. London: Prentice-Hall.
CHORLEY, R.J. and MORGAN, M.A. 1962: Comparison of morphometric features, Unaka Mountains, Tennessee and North Carolina, and Dartmoor, England. *Bulletin of the Geological Society of America* 73, 17–34.
CHURCH, M. 1978: Palaeohydrological reconstructions from a Holocene valley fill. In Miall, A.D. (ed.), *Fluvial Sedimentology* (Calgary: Canadian Society of Petroleum Geologists), Memoir 5, 743–72.
—— 1980: *On the Equations of Hydraulic Geometry*. Vancouver: Department of Geography, University of British Columbia.
CHURCH, M. and KELLERHALS, R. 1978: On the statistics of grain size variation along a gravel river. *Canadian Journal of Earth Sciences* 15, 1151–60.
CHURCH, M. and MARK, D.M. 1980: On size and scale in geomorphology. *Progress in Physical Geography* 4, 342–90.
COFFMAN, D.M., KELLER, E.A. and MELHORN, W.N. 1972: New topologic relationship as an indicator of drainage network evolution. *Water Resources Research* 8, 1497–505.
COLBY, B.R. 1963: Fluvial sediments – A summary of source, transportation, deposition, and measurement of sediment discharge. *United States Geological Survey Bulletin* 1181A, 47pp.
—— 1964: Sand discharge and mean-velocity relationships in sandbed streams. *United States Geological Survey Professional Paper* 462A, 47pp.
COOKE, R.U. and REEVES, R.W. 1976: *Arroyos and Environmental Change in the American South-West*. Oxford: Clarendon Press.
COSTA, J.E. 1974: Response and recovery of a Piedmont watershed from tropical storm Agnes, June 1972. *Water Resources Research* 10, 106–12.
—— 1975: Effects of agriculture on erosion and sedimentation in Piedmont province, Maryland. *Bulletin of the Geological Society of America* 86, 1281–6.
CULLINGFORD, R.A., DAVIDSON, D.A. and LEWIN, J. (eds.) 1980: *Timescales in Geomorphology*. Chichester: Wiley-Interscience.
DACEY, M.F. and KRUMBEIN, W.C. 1976: Three growth models for stream channel networks.

Journal of Geology 84, 153–63.

DANIEL, J.F. 1971: Channel movement of meandering Indiana streams. *United States Geological Survey Professional Paper* 732A, 18pp.

DANSGAARD, W.S., JOHNSEN, S.J., CLAUSEN, H.B. and LANGWAY, C.C. 1971: Climatic record revealed by the Camp Century Ice Core. In Turekian, K.K. (ed.), *The Late Cenozoic Glacial Ages* (New Haven: Yale University Press), 37–56.

DAVIES, T.R. and SUTHERLAND, A.J. 1980: Resistance to flow past deformable boundaries. *Earth Surface Processes* 5, 175–9.

DAVIS, W.M. 1899: The geographical cycle. *Geographical Journal* 14, 481–504.

DAY, D.G. 1980: Lithologic controls on drainage density: a study of six small rural catchments in New England, NSW. *Catena* 7, 339–51.

DEIGAARD, R. and FREDSŒ, J. 1978: Longitudinal grain sorting by current in alluvial streams. *Nordic Hydrology* 9, 7–16.

DENDY, F.E. and BOLTON, G.C. 1976: Sediment-yield-runoff-drainage area relationships in the United States. *Journal of Soil and Water Conservation* 31, 264–6.

DEVDARIANI, A.S. 1967: The profile of equilibrium and a regular regime. *Soviet Geography* 8, 168–83.

DE VRIES, J.J. 1976: The groundwater outcrop-erosion model: evolution of the stream network in the Netherlands. *Journal of Hydrology* 29, 43–50.

DOUGLAS, I. 1967: Man, vegetation and the sediment yield of rivers. *Nature* 215, 925–8.

DOZIER, J. 1976: An examination of the variance minimization tendencies of a supraglacial stream. *Journal of Hydrology* 31, 359–80.

DUNKERLEY, D.L. 1977: Frequency distributions of stream link lengths and the development of channel networks. *Journal of Geology* 85, 459–69.

DUNNE, T. 1979: Sediment yield and land use in tropical catchments. *Journal of Hydrology* 42, 281–300.

—— 1980: Formation and controls of channel networks. *Progress in Physical Geography* 4, 211–39.

DUNNE, T. and DIETRICH, W.E. 1980: Experimental investigation of Horton overland flow on tropical hillslopes – 2. Hydraulic characteristics and hillslope hydrographs. *Zeitschrift für Geomorphologie*, Supplement 35, 60–80.

DUNNE, T. and LEOPOLD, L.B. 1978: *Water in Environmental Planning.* San Francisco: W.H. Freeman.

DURY, G.H. 1970: A resurvey of part of the Hawkesbury River, New South Wales, after 100 years. *Australian Geographical Studies* 8, 121–32.

—— 1976: Discharge prediction, present and former, from channel dimensions. *Journal of Hydrology* 30, 219–46.

EINSTEIN, H.A. 1950: The bedload function for sediment transportation in open channel flows. *United States Department of Agriculture Technical Bulletin* 1026, 70pp.

EINSTEIN, H.A. and BARBAROSSA, N.L. 1952: River channel roughness. *Transactions of the American Society of Civil Engineers* 117, 1121–46.

EINSTEIN, H.A. and SHEN, H.W. 1964: A study of meandering in straight alluvial channels. *Journal of Geophysical Research* 69, 5239–47.

EMMETT, W.W. 1970: The hydraulics of overland flow on hillslopes. *United States Geological Survey Professional Paper* 662A, 68pp.

—— 1975: The channels and waters of the Upper Salmon River area, Idaho, *United States Geological Survey Professional Paper* 870A, 116pp.

EMMETT, W.W. and LEOPOLD, L.B. 1965: Downstream pattern of riverbed scour and fill. *United States Department of Agriculture Miscellaneous Publication* 970, 399–409.

ENGELUND, F. 1974: Flow and bed topography in channel bends. *Journal of the Hydraulics Division American Society of Civil Engineers* 100, HY11, 1631–48.

ENGELUND, F. and SKOVGAARD, O. 1973: On the origin of meandering and braiding in alluvial streams. *Journal of Fluid Mechanics* 57, 289–302.

EVERITT, B.L. 1968: Use of the cottonwood in an investigation of the recent history of a flood-plain. *American Journal of Science* 266, 417–39.

FAHENSTOCK, R.K. 1963: Morphology and hydrology of a glacial stream – White River,

Mount Rainier, Washington. *United States Geological Survey Professional Paper* 422A, 70pp.

FAULKNER, H. 1974: An allometric growth model for competitive gullies. *Zeitschrift für Geomorphologie*, Supplement 21, 76–87.

FENTON, J.D. and ABBOTT, J.E. 1977: Initial movement of grains on a stream bed: the effect of relative protrusion. *Proceedings of the Royal Society* 352A, 523–37.

FERGUSON, R.I. 1973: Channel pattern and sediment type. *Area* 5, 38–41.

—— 1975: Meander irregularity and wavelength estimation. *Journal of Hydrology* 26, 315–33.

—— 1976: Disturbed periodic model for river meanders. *Earth Surface Processes* 1, 337–47.

—— 1979: River meanders: regular or random? In Wrigley, N. (ed.), *Statistical Applications in the Spatial Sciences* (London: Pion), 229–41.

—— 1981: Channel forms and channel changes. In Lewin, J. (ed.), *British rivers* (London: George Allen & Unwin), 90–125.

FLINT, J.J. 1973: Development of headward growth of channel networks. *Bulletin of the Geological Society of America* 84, 1087–94.

—— 1974: Stream gradient as a function of order, magnitude and discharge. *Water Resources Research* 10, 969–73.

—— 1976: Link slope distribution in channel networks. *Water Resources Research* 12, 645–54.

—— 1980: Tributary arrangements in fluvial systems. *American Journal of Science* 280, 26–45.

FOLEY, M.G. 1978: Scour and fill in steep, sandy-bed ephemeral streams. *Bulletin of the Geological Society of America* 89, 559–70.

—— 1980: Bed-rock incision by streams. *Bulletin of the Geological Society of America* 91, Part 2, 2189–213.

FOURNIER, F. 1960: Debit solide des cours d'eau. Essai d'estimation de la perte en terre subie par l'ensemble du globe terrestre. *International Association of Scientific Hydrology Publication* 53, 19–22.

FRIEDKIN, J.F. 1945: A laboratory study of the meandering of alluvial rivers. *United States Waterways Experimental Station*, Vicksburg, Mississippi, 40pp.

GHOSH, A.K. and SCHEIDEGGER, A.E. 1970: Dependence of stream link lengths and drainage areas on stream order. *Water Resources Research* 6, 336–40.

GILBERT, G.K. 1877: *Report on the geology of the Henry Mountains*. Washington, DC: United States Geological Survey, Rocky Mountain Region.

GILMAN, K. and NEWSON, M.D. 1980: *Soil Pipes and Pipeflow – a Hydrological Study in Upland Wales*. Norwich: Geobooks.

GLOCK, W.S. 1931: The development of drainage systems: a synoptic view. *Geographical Review* 21, 475–82.

GOLE, C.V. and CHITALE, S.V. 1966: Inland delta building activity of Kosi River. *Journal of the Hydraulics Division American Society of Civil Engineers* 92, HY2, 111–26.

GORYCKI, M.A. 1973: Hydraulic drag: a meander-initiating mechanism. *Bulletin of the Geological Society of America* 84, 175–86.

GOUDIE, A.S. 1972: *The concept of Post-Glacial progressive desiccation*. Research Paper 4. Oxford: School of Geography.

GRAF, W.H. 1971: *Hydraulics of sediment transport*. New York: McGraw-Hill.

GRAF, W.L. 1977: The rate law in fluvial geomorphology. *American Journal of Science* 277, 178–91.

GREGORY, K.J. 1976: Drainage networks and climate. In Derbyshire, E. (ed.), *Geomorphology and Climate* (Chichester: Wiley-Interscience), 289–315.

GREGORY, K.J. and GARDINER, V. 1975: Drainage density and climate. *Zeitschrift für Geomorphologie* 19, 287–98.

GREGORY, K.J. and PARK, C.C. 1976: Stream channel morphology in north-west Yorkshire. *Revue de Géomorphologie Dynamique* 25, 63–72.

GREGORY, K.J. and WALLING, D.E. 1968: The variation of drainage density within a catchment. *Bulletin of the International Association of Scientific Hydrology* 13, 61–8.

—— 1973: *Drainage Basin Form and Process: a Geomorphological Approach.* London: Edward Arnold.

GRIFFITHS, G.A. 1979: Recent sedimentation history of the Waimakariri River, New Zealand. *Journal of Hydrology (New Zealand)* 18, 6–28.

GRIMSHAW, D.L. and LEWIN, J. 1980: Source identification for suspended sediments. *Journal of Hydrology* 47, 151–62.

GROVE, J.M. 1972: The incidence of landslides, avalanches and floods in western Norway during the Little Ice Age. *Arctic and Alpine Research* 4, 131–8.

GUPTA, A. and FOX. H. 1974: Effects of high-magnitude floods on channel form: a case study in Maryland Piedmont. *Water Resources Research* 10, 499–509.

HACK, J.T. 1957: Studies of longitudinal stream profiles in Virginia and Maryland. *United States Geological Survey Professional Paper* 294B, 97pp.

—— 1965: Postglacial drainage evolution and stream geometry in the Ontonagon area, Michigan. *United States Geological Survey Professional Paper* 504B, 40pp.

HACK, J.T. and GOODLETT, J.C. 1960: Geomorphology and forest ecology of a mountain region in the Central Appalachians. *United States Geological Survey Professional Paper* 347, 66pp.

HAIBLE, W.W. 1980: Holocene profile changes along a California coastal stream. *Earth Surface Processes* 5, 249–64.

HAMMER, T.R. 1972: Stream channel enlargement due to urbanization. *Water Resources Research* 8, 1530–40.

HARRISON, S.S. and CLAYTON, L. 1970: Effects of ground-water seepage on fluvial processes. *Bulletin of the Geological Society of America* 81, 1217–26.

HARVEY, A.M. 1969: Channel capacity and the adjustment of streams to hydrologic regime. *Journal of Hydrology* 8, 82–98.

—— 1975: Some aspects of the relations between channel characteristics and riffle spacing in meandering streams. *American Journal of Science* 275, 470–8.

HAYNES, C.V. 1968: Geochronology of late Quaternary alluvium. In Morrison, R.B. and Wright, H.E. (eds.), *Means of Correlation of Quaternary Successions* (Salt Lake City: University of Utah Press), 591–631.

HEEDE, B.H. 1981: Dynamics of selected mountain streams in the Western United States of America. *Zeitschrift für Geomorphologie* 25, 17–32.

HELLEY, E.J. 1969: Field measurement of the initiation of large bed particle motion in Blue Creek near Klamath, California. *United States Geological Survey Professional Paper* 562G, 19pp.

HENDERSON, F.M. 1963: Stability of alluvial channels. *Transactions of the American Society of Civil Engineers* 128, 657–86.

HEY, R.D. 1976: Geometry of river meanders. *Nature* 262, 482–4.

—— 1978: Determinate hydraulic geometry of river channels. *Journal of the Hydraulics Division American Society of Civil Engineers* 104, HY6, 869–85.

—— 1979: Flow resistance in gravel-bed rivers. *Journal of the Hydraulics Division American Society of Civil Engineers* 105, HY4, 365–79.

HEY, R.D. and THORNE, C.R. 1975: Secondary flows in river channels. *Area* 7, 191–5.

HICKIN, E.J. 1974: The development of river meanders in natural river channels. *American Journal of Science* 274, 414–42.

HICKIN, E.J. and NANSON, G.C. 1975: The character of channel migration on the Beatton River, north-east British Columbia, Canada. *Bulletin of the Geological Society of America* 86, 487–94.

HILL, A.R. 1973: Erosion of river banks composed of glacial till near Belfast, Northern Ireland. *Zeitschrift für Geomorphologie* 17, 428–42.

HJULSTRÖM, F. 1935: Studies of the morphological activity of rivers as illustrated by the River Fyris. *Bulletin of the Geological Institute University of Uppsala* 25, 221–527.

HOLEMAN, J.N. 1968: The sediment yield of major rivers of the world. *Water Resources Research* 4, 737–47.

HONG, L.B. and DAVIES, T.R.H. 1979: A study of stream braiding. *Bulletin of the*

Geological Society of America 90, Part 2, 1839–59.

HOOKE, J.M. 1977: The distribution and nature of changes in river channel patterns: the example of Devon. In Gregory, K.J. (ed.), *River channel changes* (Chichester: Wiley-Interscience), 265–80.

—— 1979: An analysis of the processes of river bank erosion. *Journal of Hydrology* 42, 39–62.

—— 1980: Magnitude and distribution of rates of river bank erosion. *Earth Surface Processes* 5, 143–57.

HOOKE, R. Le B. 1975: Distribution of sediment transport and shear stress in a meander bend. *Journal of Geology* 83, 543–66.

HORTON, R.E. 1933: The role of infiltration in the hydrologic cycle. *Transactions of the American Geophysical Union* 14, 446–60.

—— 1945: Erosional development of streams and their drainage basins: hydrophysical approach to quantitative morphology. *Bulletin of the Geological Society of America* 56, 275–370.

HOWARD, A.D. 1971a: Simulation of stream networks by headward growth and branching. *Geographical Analysis* 3, 29–50.

—— 1971b: A simulation model of stream capture. *Bulletin of the Geological Society of America* 82, 1355–76.

—— 1980: Thresholds in river regimes. In Coates, D.R. and Vitek, J.D. (eds.) *Thresholds in Geomorphology* (Boston: George Allen & Unwin), 227–58.

—— 1982: Equilibrium and time scales in geomorphology: application to sand-bed alluvial streams. *Earth Surface Processes and Landforms* 7, 303–25.

HOWARD, A.D., KEETCH, M.E. and VINCENT, C.L. 1970: Topological and geometrical properties of braided streams. *Water Resources Research* 6, 1674–88.

HOWE, G.M., SLAYMAKER, H.O. and HARDING, D.M. 1967: Some aspects of the flood hydrology of the upper catchments of the Severn and Wye. *Transactions of the Institute of British Geographers* 41, 33–58.

HUDSON, N.W. 1971: *Soil Conservation*. London: Batsford.

HUGHES, D.J. 1977: Rates of erosion on meander arcs. In Gregory, K.J. (ed.), *River Channel Changes* (Chichester: Wiley-Interscience), 193–206.

HUNG, C.S. and SHEN, H.W. 1976: Stochastic models of sediment motion on flat bed. *Journal of the Hydraulics Division American Society of Civil Engineers* 102, HY12, 1745–59.

IKEDA, H. 1970: On the longitudinal profiles of the Asake, Mitaki and Utsube Rivers, Mie Prefecture. *Geographical Review of Japan* 43, 148–59.

INMAN, D.L. and NORDSTROM, C.E. 1971: On the tectonic and morphologic classification of coasts. *Journal of Geology* 79, 1–21.

JAMES, W.R. and KRUMBEIN, W.C. 1969: Frequency distributions of stream link lengths. *Journal of Geology* 77, 544–65.

JARVIS, R.S. 1976: Classification of nested tributary basins in analysis of drainage basin shape. *Water Resources Research* 12, 1151–64.

—— 1977: Drainage network analysis. *Progress in Physical Geography* 1, 271–95.

JARVIS, R.S. and SHAM, C.H. 1981: Drainage network structure and the diameter-magnitude relation. *Water Resources Research* 17, 1019–27.

JOHNSON, R.H. and PAYNTER, J. 1967: The development of a cutoff on the River Irk at Chadderton, Lancashire. *Geography* 52, 41–9.

JONES, J.A.A. 1981: *The Nature of Soil Piping: a Review of Research*. Norwich: Geobooks.

JONES, O.T. 1924: The longitudinal profiles of the Upper Towy drainage system. *Quarterly Journal of the Geological Society of London* 80, 568–609.

KASHEF, A.-A.I. 1981: Technical and ecological impacts of the High Aswan Dam. *Journal of Hydrology* 53, 73–84.

KELLER, E.A. 1971: Areal sorting of bed load material: the hypothesis of velocity reversal. *Bulletin of the Geological Society of America* 82, 753–6.

—— 1972: Development of alluvial stream channels: a five-stage model. *Bulletin of the Geological Society of America* 83, 1531–6.

—— 1978: Pools, riffles, and channelization. *Environmental Geology* 2, 119–27.

KELLER, E.A. and MELHORN, W.N. 1973: Bedforms and fluvial processes in alluvial stream channels: selected observations. In Morisawa, M. (ed.), *Fluvial Geomorphology* (Binghamton NY: New York State University Publications in Geomorphology), 253–83.

—— 1978: Rhythmic spacing and origin of pools and riffles. *Bulletin of the Geological Society of America* 89, 723–30.

KELLERHALS, R., CHURCH, M. and BRAY, D.I. 1976: Classification of river processes. *Journal of the Hydraulics Division American Society of Civil Engineers* 102, HY7, 813–29.

KIRKBY, A.V.T. and KIRKBY, M.J. 1974: Surface wash at the semi-arid break of slope. *Zeitschrift für Geomorphologie*, Supplement 21, 151–76.

KIRKBY, M.J. 1971: Hillslope process-response models based on the continuity equation. *Institute of British Geographers, Special Publication* 3, 15–30.

—— 1976: Tests of the random network model, and its application to basin hydrology. *Earth Surface Processs* 1, 197–212.

—— 1977: Maximum sediment efficiency as a criterion for alluvial channels. In Gregory, K.J. (ed.), *River Channel Changes* (Chichester: Wiley-Interscience), 429–42.

—— 1978: Implications for sediment transport. In Kirkby, M.J. (ed.), *Hillslope Hydrology* (Chichester: Wiley-Interscience), 325–63.

KIRKBY, M.J. and CHORLEY, R.J. 1967: Throughflow, overland flow and erosion. *Bulletin of the International Association of Scientific Hydrology* 12, 5–21.

KLIMEK, K. 1974: The retreat of alluvial river banks in the Wisloka valley (South Poland). *Geographia Polonica* 28, 59–75.

KNIGHTON, A.D. 1972: Changes in a braided reach. *Bulletin of the Geological Society of America* 83, 3813–22.

—— 1973: Riverbank erosion in relation to streamflow conditions, River Bollin-Dean, Cheshire. *East Midland Geographer* 6, 416–26.

—— 1974: Variation in width-discharge relation and some implications for hydraulic geometry. *Bulletin of the Geological Society of America* 85, 1069–76.

—— 1975: Variations in at-a-station hydraulic geometry. *American Journal of Science* 275, 186–218.

—— 1976: Stream adjustment in a small Rocky Mountain basin. *Arctic and Alpine Research* 8, 197–212.

—— 1977: Alternative derivation of the minimum variance hypothesis. *Bulletin of the Geological Society of America* 88, 364–6.

—— 1979: Comments on log-quadratic relations in hydraulic geometry. *Earth Surface Processes* 4, 205–10.

—— 1980a: Comment on 'Drainage network power' by K.J. Gregory. *Water Resources Research* 16, 1128–9.

—— 1980b: Longitudinal changes in size and sorting of stream-bed material in four English rivers. *Bulletin of the Geological Society of America* 91, 55–62.

—— 1981a: Asymmetry of river channel cross-sections: Part I. Quantitative indices. *Earth Surface Processes and Landforms* 6, 581–8.

—— 1981b: Local variations of cross-sectional form in a small gravel-bed stream. *Journal of Hydrology (New Zealand)* 20, 131–46.

—— 1981c: Channel form and flow characteristics of supraglacial streams, Austre Okstindbreen, Norway. *Arctic and Alpine Research* 13, 295–306.

—— 1982: Asymmetry of river channel cross-sections: Part II. Mode of development and local variation. *Earth Surface Processes and Landforms* 7, 117–31.

KNOX, J.C. 1972: Valley alluviation in south-western Wisconsin. *Annals of the Association of American Geographers* 62, 401–10.

—— 1977: Human impacts on Wisconsin stream channels. *Annals of the Association of American Geographers* 67, 323–42.

KOMURA, S. 1976: Hydraulics of slope erosion by overland flow. *Journal of the Hydraulics Division American Society of Civil Engineers* 102, HY10, 1573–86.

KRIGSTRÖM, A. 1962: Geomorphological studies of sandur plains and their braided rivers in Iceland. *Geografiska Annaler* 44, 328–46.

KRINITZSKY, E.L. 1965: Geological influences on bank erosion along meanders of the lower

Mississippi River. *United States Army Corps of Engineers, Engineer Waterways Experimental Station*, Reports 12-15, 30pp.

KUENEN, P.H. 1956: Experimental abrasion of pebbles. 2. Rolling by current. *Journal of Geology* 64, 336–68.

LACEY, G. 1929: Stable channels in alluvium. *Proceedings of the Institution of Civil Engineers* 229, 259–384.

LaMARCHE, V.C. 1966: An 800-year history of stream erosion as indicated by botanical evidence. *United States Geological Survey Professional Paper* 550D, 83–6.

LAMB, H.H. 1977: *Climate: Present, Past and Future. Volume 2 Climatic History and the Future*. London: Methuen.

LANE, E.W. 1953: Design of stable channels. *Proceedings of the American Society of Civil Engineers* 79, 280-1 – 280-31.

—— 1955: The importance of fluvial morphology in hydraulic engineering. *Proceedings of the American Society of Civil Engineers* 81, 1–17.

—— 1957: A study of the shape of channels formed by natural streams flowing in erodible material. *MRD Sediment Series 9, United States Army Engineer Division, Missouri River, Corps Engineers, Omaha, Nebraska*, 1–106.

LANGBEIN, W.B. 1964a: Geometry of river channels. *Journal of the Hydraulics Division American Society of Civil Engineers* 90, HY2, 301–12.

—— 1964b: Profiles of rivers of uniform discharge. *United States Geological Survey Professional Paper* 501B, 119–22.

—— 1965: Geometry of river channels: closure of discussion. *Journal of the Hydraulics Division American Society of Civil Engineers* 91, HY3, 297–313.

LANGBEIN, W.B. and LEOPOLD, L.B. 1964: Quasi-equilibrium states in channel morphology. *American Journal of Science* 262, 782–94.

—— 1966: River meanders – theory of minimum variance. *United States Geological Survey Professional Paper* 422H, 15pp.

—— 1968: River channel bars and dunes – theory of kinematic waves. *United States Geological Survey Professional Paper* 422L, 19pp.

LANGBEIN, W.B. and SCHUMM, S.A. 1958: Yield of sediment in relation to mean annual precipitation. *Transactions of the American Geophysical Union* 39, 1076–84.

LARONNE, J.B. and CARSON, M.A. 1976: Interrelationships between bed morphology and bed-material transport for a small, gravel-bed channel. *Sedimentology* 23, 67–85.

LARRAS, J. 1968: Problèmes d'hydraulique fluviale. *Annales des Ponts et Chaussées* 138, 195–209.

LAWSON, J.D. and O'NEILL, I.C. 1975: Transport of materials in streams. In Chapman, T.G. and Dunin, F.X. (eds.), *Prediction in catchment hydrology* (Canberra: Australian Academy of Science), 165–202.

LEE, L.J. and HENSON, B.L. 1977: The interrelationships of the longitudinal profiles and channel pattern for the Red River. *Journal of Hydrology* 35, 191–201.

LEEDER, M.R. 1979: 'Bedload' dynamics: grain-grain interactions in water flows. *Earth Surface Processes* 4, 229–40.

LEOPOLD, L.B. 1951: Rainfall frequency: an aspect of climatic variation. *Transactions of the American Geophysical Union* 32, 347–57.

—— 1973: River channel change with time: an example. *Bulletin of the Geological Society of America* 84, 1845–60.

LEOPOLD, L.B., BAGNOLD, R.A., WOLMAN, M.G. and BRUSH, L.M. 1960: Flow resistance in sinuous or irregular channels. *United States Geological Survey Professional Paper* 282D, 111–34.

LEOPOLD, L.B. and BULL, W.B. 1979: Base level, aggradation, and grade. *Proceedings of the American Philosophical Society* 123, 168–202.

LEOPOLD, L.B. and EMMETT, W.W. 1976: Bedload measurements, East Fork River, Wyoming. *Proceedings of the National Academy of Sciences* 73, 1000–4.

LEOPOLD, L.B., EMMETT, W.W. and MYRICK, R.M. 1966: Channel and hillslope processes in a semi-arid area, New Mexico. *United States Geological Survey Professional Paper* 352G, 153–253.

LEOPOLD, L.B. and LANGBEIN, W.B. 1962: The concept of entropy in landscape evolution. *United States Geological Survey Professional Paper* 500A, 20pp.

LEOPOLD, L.B. and MADDOCK, T. 1953: The hydraulic geometry of stream channels and some physiographic implications. *United States Geological Survey Professional Paper* 252, 57pp.

LEOPOLD, L.B. and MILLER, J.P. 1956: Ephemeral streams – hydraulic factors and their relation to the drainage net. *United States Geological Survey Professional Paper* 282A, 36pp.

LEOPOLD, L.B. and WOLMAN, M.G. 1957: River channel patterns – braided, meandering and straight. *United States Geological Survey Professional Paper* 282B, 39–85.

—— 1960: River meanders. *Bulletin of the Geological Society of America* 71, 769–94.

LEOPOLD, L.B., WOLMAN, M.G. and MILLER, J.P. 1964: *Fluvial Processes in Geomorphology.* San Francisco: W.H. Freeman.

LEWIN, J. 1976: Initiation of bed forms and meanders in coarse-grained sediment. *Bulletin of the Geological Society of America* 87, 281–5.

—— 1978: Floodplain geomorphology. *Progress in Physical Geography* 2, 408–37.

LEWIS, L.A. 1969: Some fluvial geomorphic characteristics of the Manati Basin, Puerto Rico. *Annals of the Association of American Geographers* 59, 280–93.

LI, R.-M., SIMONS, D.B. and STEVENS, M.A. 1976: Morphology of cobble streams in small watersheds. *Journal of the Hydraulics Division American Society of Civil Engineers* 102, HY8, 1101–17.

LIMERINOS, J.T. 1970: Determination of the Manning coefficient from measured bed roughness in natural channels. *United States Geological Survey Water-Supply Paper* 1898B, 47pp.

LISLE, T. 1979: A sorting mechanism for a riffle-pool sequence. *Bulletin of the Geological Society of America* 90, Part 2, 1142–57.

LUKE, J.C. 1974: Special solutions for nonlinear erosion problems. *Journal of Geophysical Research* 79, 4035–40.

LUSBY, G.C. 1979: Effects of converting sagebrush cover to grass on the hydrology of small watersheds at Boco Mountain, Colorado. *United States Geological Survey Water-Supply Paper* 1532J, 36pp.

MACKIN, J.H. 1948: Concept of the graded river. *Bulletin of the Geological Society of America* 59, 463–512.

—— 1956: Cause of braiding by a graded river. *Bulletin of the Geological Society of America* 67, 1717–18.

MADDOCK, T. 1969: The behavior of straight open channels with movable beds. *United States Geological Survey Professional Paper* 622A, 70pp.

MADDUMA BANDARA, C.M. 1974: Drainage density and effective precipitation. *Journal of Hydrology* 21, 187–90.

MARCUS, A. 1980: First-order drainage basin morphology – definition and distribution. *Earth Surface Processes* 5, 389–98.

MEADE, R.H. 1976: Sediment problems in the Savannah River basin. In Dillman, B.L. and Stepp, J.M. (eds.), *The Future of the Savannah River* (Clemson, South Carolina: Water Resources Research Institute), 105–29.

MELTON, M.A. 1957: An analysis of the relations among elements of climate, surface properties, and geomorphology. *Office of Naval Research, Geography Branch, Project NR 389-042, Technical Report* 11, 102pp.

—— 1958: Correlation structure of morphometric properties of drainage systems and their controlling agents. *Journal of Geology* 66, 442–60.

MEYBECK, M. 1976: Total mineral dissolved transport by world major rivers. *Hydrological Sciences Bulletin, International Association of Scientific Hydrology* 21, 265–84.

MIALL, A.D. 1977: A review of the braided-river depositional environment. *Earth Science Reviews* 13, 1–62.

MILLER, J.P. 1958: High mountain streams; effects of geology on channel characteristics and bed material. *New Mexico State Bureau of Mines and Mineral Resources, Memoir* 4, 51pp.

MILLER, J.P. and WENDORF, F. 1958: Alluvial chronology of the Tesuque Valley, New

Mexico. *Journal of Geology* 66, 177–94.

MILLER, V.C. 1975: Lateral tributary capture in the Montalban area, Spain. *The ITC-Journal* 2, 230–5.

MILLS, H.H. 1979: Downstream rounding of pebbles – a quantitative review. *Journal of Sedimentary Petrology* 49, 295–302.

MILNE, J.A. 1982: Bed-material size and the riffle-pool sequence. *Sedimentology* 29, 267–78.

MOCK, S.J. 1971: A classification of channel links in stream networks. *Water Resources Research* 7, 1558–66.

—— 1976: Topological properties of some trellis pattern channel networks. *United States Army Cold Regions Research and Engineering Laboratory, CRREL Report* 76–46, 59pp.

MORGAN, R.P.C. 1972: Observations on factors affecting the behaviour of a first-order stream. *Transactions of the Institute of British Geographers* 56, 171–86.

—— 1977: Soil erosion in the United Kingdom: field studies in the Silsoe area, 1973–75. *National College of Agricultural Engineering, Silsoe, Occasional Paper* 4, 41pp.

MORISAWA, M.E. 1964: Development of drainage systems on an upraised lake floor. *American Journal of Science* 262, 340–54.

MOSLEY, M.P. 1974: Experimental study of rill erosion. *Transactions of the American Society of Agricultural Engineers* 17, 909–13.

—— 1975: Channel changes on the River Bollin, Cheshire, 1872–1973. *East Midlands Geographer* 6, 185–99.

NANSON, G.C. 1980: A regional trend to meander migration. *Journal of Geology* 88, 100–8.

NANSON, G.C. and YOUNG, R.W. 1981: Downstream reduction of rural channel size with contrasting urban effects in small coastal streams of southeastern Australia. *Journal of Hydrology* 52, 239–55.

NEVINS, T.H.F. 1969: River training – the single thread channel. *New Zealand Engineering*, December, 367–73.

NEWSON, M.D. 1978: Drainage basin characteristics, their selection, derivation and analysis for a flood study of the British Isles. *Earth Surface Processes* 3, 277–93.

NIXON, M. 1959: A study of the bankfull discharges of rivers in England and Wales. *Proceedings of the Institution of Civil Engineers* 12, 157–75.

NORDIN, C.F. and BEVERAGE, J.P. 1965: Sediment transport in the Rio Grande New Mexico. *United States Geological Survey Professional Paper* 462F, 35pp.

NORDIN, C.F., MEADE, R.H., CURTIS, W.F., BOSIO, N.J. and LANDIM, P.M.B. 1980: Size distribution of Amazon River bed sediment. *Nature* 286, 52–3.

NOVAK, I.D. 1973: Predicting coarse sediment transport: the Hjulström curve revisited. In Morisawa, M. (ed.), *Fluvial Geomorphology* (Binghamton NY: New York State University Publications in Geomorphology), 13–25.

ONESTI, L.J. and MILLER, T.K. 1978: Topological classifications of drainage networks: an evaluation. *Water Resources Research* 14, 144–8.

ONISHI, Y., SUBHASH, C. and KENNEDY, J.F. 1976: Effects of meandering in alluvial streams. *Journal of the Hydraulics Division American Society of Civil Engineers* 102, HY7, 899–917.

OSTERKAMP, W.R. 1978: Gradient, discharge, and particle-size relations of alluvial channels in Kansas, with observations on braiding. *American Journal of Science* 278, 1253–68.

—— 1980: Sediment-morphology relations of alluvial channels. *Proceedings of the Symposium on Watershed Management, American Society of Civil Engineers, Boise 1980*, 188–99.

PARK, C.C. 1977: World-wide variations in hydraulic geometry exponents of stream channels: an analysis and some observations. *Journal of Hydrology* 33, 133–46.

PARKER, G. 1976: On the cause and characteristic scales of meandering and braiding in rivers. *Journal of Fluid Mechanics* 76, 457–80.

—— 1979: Hydraulic geometry of active gravel rivers. *Journal of the Hydraulics Division American Society of Civil Engineers* 105, HY9, 1185–201.

PARKER, G. and PETERSON, A.W. 1980: Bar resistance of gravel-bed streams. *Journal of the Hydraulics Division American Society of Civil Engineers* 106, HY10, 1559–75.

PARKER, R.S. 1977: Experimental study of drainage basin evolution and its hydrologic implications. *Colorado State University, Fort Collins, Colorado, Hydrology Papers* 90, 58pp.

PATTON, P.C. and BAKER, V.R. 1977: Geomorphic response of central Texas streams to catastrophic rainfall and runoff. In Doehring, D.O. (ed.), *Geomorphology in Arid Regions* (Binghamton NY: New York State University Publications in Geomorphology), 189–217.

PATTON, P.C. and SCHUMM, S.A. 1975: Gully erosion, northern Colorado: a threshold phenomenon. *Geology* 3, 88–90.

PEARCE, A.J. 1976: Magnitude and frequency of erosion by Hortonian overland flow. *Journal of Geology* 84, 65–80.

PENNING-ROWSELL, E.G. and TOWNSHEND, J.R.G. 1978: The influence of scale on the factors affecting stream channel slope. *Transactions of the Institute of British Geographers New Series* 3, 395–415.

PETTS, G.E. 1977: Channel response to flow regulation: the case of the River Derwent, Derbyshire. In Gregory, K.J. (ed.), *River Channel Changes* (Chichester: Wiley-Interscience), 145–64.

—— 1979: Complex response of river channel morphology to reservoir construction. *Progress in Physical Geography* 3, 329–62.

PICKUP, G. 1976a: Alternative measures of river channel shape and their significance. *Journal of Hydrology (New Zealand)* 15, 9–16.

—— 1976b: Adjustment of stream-channel shape to hydrologic regime. *Journal of Hydrology* 30, 365–73.

PICKUP, G. and RIEGER, W.A. 1979: A conceptual model of the relationship between channel characteristics and discharge. *Earth Surface Processes* 4, 37–42.

PICKUP, G. and WARNER, R.F. 1976: Effects of hydrologic regime on magnitude and frequency of dominant discharge. *Journal of Hydrology* 29, 51–75.

POPOV, I.V. 1964: Hydromorphological principles of the theory of channel processes and their use in hydrotechnical planning. *Soviet Hydrology* 1964, 158–95.

PRICE, R.J. and HOWARTH, P.J. 1970: The evolution of the drainage system (1904–1965) in front of Breidamerkurjökull, Iceland. *Jökull* 20, 27–37.

QUICK, M.C. 1974: Mechanism for streamflow meandering. *Journal of the Hydraulics Division American Society of Civil Engineers* 100, HY6, 741–53.

RANA, S.A., SIMONS, D.B. and MAHMOOD, K. 1973: Analysis of sediment sorting in alluvial channels. *Journal of the Hydraulics Division American Society of Civil Engineers* 99, HY11, 1967–80.

RAUDKIVI, A.J. 1976: *Loose boundary hydraulics*. Oxford: Pergamon Press. 2nd edition.

RENDELL, H. and ALEXANDER, D. 1979: Note on some spatial and temporal variations in ephemeral channel form. *Bulletin of the Geological Society of America* 90, 761–72.

RHODES, D.D. 1977: The b-f-m diagram: graphical representation and interpretation of at-a-station hydraulic geometry. *American Journal of Science* 277, 73–96.

—— 1978: World-wide variations in hydraulic geometry exponents of stream channels: an analysis and some observations – comments. *Journal of Hydrology* 39, 193–7.

RICHARDS, K.S. 1973: Hydraulic geometry and channel roughness – a non-linear system. *American Journal of Science* 273, 877–96.

—— 1976a: Channel width and the riffle-pool sequence. *Bulletin of the Geological Society of America* 87, 883–90.

—— 1976b: The morphology of riffle-pool sequences. *Earth Surface Processes* 1, 71–88.

—— 1977: Channel and flow geometry. *Progress in Physical Geography* 1, 65–102.

RICHARDS, K.S. and WOOD, R. 1977: Urbanization, water redistribution, and their effect on channel processes. In Gregory, K.J. (ed.), *River Channel Changes* (Chichester: Wiley-Interscience), 369–88.

RITTER, D.F., KINSEY, W.F. and KAUFFMAN, M.E. 1973: Overbank sedimentation in the Delaware River Valley during the last 6000 years. *Science* 179, 374–5.

ROSE, J., TURNER, C., COOPE, G.R. and BRYAN, M.D. 1980: Channel changes in a lowland river catchment over the last 13,000 years. In Cullingford, Davidson and Lewin 1980, 159–75.

RUBEY, W.W. 1952: Geology and mineral resources of the Hardin and Brussels quadrangles (in Illinois). *United States Geological Survey Professional Paper* 218, 175pp.

RUHE, R.V. 1952: Topographic discontinuities of the Des Moines lobe. *American Journal of Science* 250, 46–56.

RUNDQUIST, L.A. 1975: A classification and analysis of natural rivers. *Colorado State University, Fort Collins, Colorado, PhD Thesis (unpublished)*, 377pp.

SCHEIDEGGER, A.E. 1970: *Theoretical Geomorphology*. Berlin: Springer-Verlag. 2nd Edition.

SCHEIDEGGER, A.E. and LANGBEIN, W.B. 1966: Probability concepts in geomorphology. *United States Geological Survey Professional Paper* 500C, 14pp.

SCHICK, A.P. 1974: Formation and obliteration of desert stream terraces – a conceptual analysis. *Zeitschrift für Geomorphologie*, Supplement 21, 88–105.

SCHUMM, S.A. 1956: The evolution of drainage systems and slopes in badlands at Perth Amboy, New Jersey. *Bulletin of the Geological Society of America* 67, 597–646.

—— 1960: The shape of alluvial channels in relation to sediment type. *United States Geological Survey Professional Paper* 352B, 17–30.

—— 1963a: A tentative classification of alluvial river channels. *United States Geological Survey Circular* 477, 10pp.

—— 1963b: Sinuosity of alluvial rivers on the Great Plains. *Bulletin of the Geological Society of America* 74, 1089–100.

—— 1967: Meander wavelength of alluvial rivers. *Science* 157, 1549–50.

—— 1968a: River adjustment to altered hydrologic regimen – Murrumbidgee River and paleochannels, Australia. *United States Geological Survey Professional Paper* 598, 65pp.

—— 1968b: Speculations concerning paleohydrologic controls of terrestrial sedimentation. *Bulletin of the Geological Society of America* 79, 1573–88.

—— 1969: River metamorphosis. *Journal of the Hydraulics Division American Society of Civil Engineers* 95, HY1, 255–73.

—— 1971: Fluvial geomorphology: the historical perspective. In Shen, H.W. (ed.), *River Mechanics*, volume 1 (Fort Collins, Colorado: H.W. Shen), 4–1 – 4–30.

—— 1973: Geomorphic thresholds and complex response of drainage systems. In Morisawa, M. (ed.), *Fluvial Geomorphology* (Binghamton NY: New York State University Publications in Geomorphology), 299–309.

—— 1977: *The Fluvial System*. New York: Wiley-Interscience.

—— 1980: Some applications of the concept of geomorphic thresholds. In Coates, D.R. and Vitek, J.D. (eds.), *Thresholds in Geomorphology* (Boston: George Allen & Unwin), 473–85.

SCHUMM, S.A. and KHAN, H.R. 1972: Experimental study of channel patterns. *Bulletin of the Geological Society of America* 83, 1755–70.

SCHUMM, S.A. and LICHTY, R.W. 1963: Channel widening and flood-plain construction along Cimarron River in south-western Kansas. *United States Geological Survey Professional Paper* 352D, 71–88.

—— 1965: Time, space, and causality in geomorphology. *American Journal of Science* 263, 110–19.

SCHUMM, S.A. and PARKER, R.S. 1973: Implications of complex response of drainage systems for Quaternary alluvial stratigraphy. *Nature* 243, 99–100.

SCHUMM, S.A. and STEVENS, M.A. 1973: Abrasion in place: a mechanism for rounding and size reduction of coarse sediments in rivers. *Geology* 1, 37–40.

SEABURN, G.E. 1969: Effects of urban development on direct runoff to East Meadow Brook, Nassau County, Long Island, New York. *United States Geological Survey Professional Paper* 627B, 14pp.

SEDIMENTATION SEMINAR, H.N. Fisk Laboratory of Sedimentology 1977: Magnitude and frequency of transport of solids by streams in the Mississippi basin. *American Journal of Science* 277, 862–75.

SHAHJAHAN, M. 1970: Factors controlling the geometry of fluvial meanders. *Bulletin of the International Association of Scientific Hydrology* 15, 13–24.

SHEN, H.W. and KOMURA, S. 1968: Meandering tendencies in straight alluvial channels. *Journal of the Hydraulics Division American Society of Civil Engineers* 94, HY4, 997–1016.

SHIELDS, A. 1936: Anwendung der Ähnlichkeitsmechanik und der Turbulenzforschung auf die Geschiebebewegung. *Mitteilung der preussischen Versuchsanstalt für Wasserbau und Schiffbau* 26, Berlin.

SHIMANO, Y. 1975: A study of Hack's law on the relationship between drainage areas and mainstream lengths. *Geographical Review of Japan* 48, 85–97.

SHREVE, R.L. 1966: Statistical law of stream numbers. *Journal of Geology* 74, 17–37.

—— 1967: Infinite topologically random channel networks. *Journal of Geology* 75, 178–86.

—— 1974: Variation of mainstream length with basin area in river networks. *Water Resources Research* 10, 1167–77.

—— 1975: The probabilistic-topologic approach to drainage-basin geomorphology. *Geology* 3, 527–9.

SIMONS, D.B., LI, R.-H., ALAWADY, M.A. and ANDREW, J.W. 1979: Report on: Connecticut River streambank erosion study, Massachusetts, New Hampshire and Vermont. *Colorado State University Research Institute, Fort Collins, Colorado, Report CSU-213*, 256pp.

SIMONS, D.B. and RICHARDSON, E.V. 1966: Resistance to flow in alluvial channels. *United States Geological Survey Professional Paper* 422J, 61pp.

SIMONS, D.B., RICHARDSON, E.V. and HAUSHILD, W.H. 1963: Some effects of fine sediment on flow phenomena. *United States Geological Survey Water-Supply Paper* 1498G, 46pp.

SMART, J.S. 1968: Statistical properties of stream lengths. *Water Resources Research* 4, 1001–14.

—— 1972: Channel networks. *Advances in Hydroscience* 8, 305–46.

—— 1978: The analysis of drainage network composition. *Earth Surface Processes* 3, 129–71.

—— 1981: Link lengths and channel network topology. *Earth Surface Processes and Landforms* 6, 77–9.

SMART, J.S. and WALLIS, J.R. 1971: Cis and trans links in natural channel networks. *Water Resources Research* 7, 1346–8.

SMART, J.S. and WERNER, C. 1976: Applications of the random model of drainage basin composition. *Earth Surface Processes* 1, 219–34.

SMITH, D.G. 1976: Effect of vegetation on lateral migration of anastomosed channels of a glacier meltwater river. *Bulletin of the Geological Society of America* 87, 857–60.

SMITH, N.D. 1970: The braided stream depositional environment: comparison of the Platte River with some Silurian clastic rocks, north-central Appalachians. *Bulletin of the Geological Society of America* 81, 2993–3014.

—— 1971: Transverse bars and braiding in the lower Platte River, Nebraska. *Bulletin of the Geological Society of America* 82, 3407–20.

SMITH, T.R. 1974: A derivation of the hydraulic geometry of steady-state channels from conservation principles and sediment transport laws. *Journal of Geology* 82, 98–104.

SMITH, T.R. and BRETHERTON, F.P. 1972: Stability and the conservation of mass in drainage basin evolution. *Water Resources Research* 8, 1506–29.

SONG, C.C.S. and YANG, C.T. 1980: Minimum stream power: theory. *Journal of the Hydraulics Division American Society of Civil Engineers* 106, HY9, 1477–87.

SPEIGHT, J.G. 1967: Spectral analysis of meanders of some Australian rivers. In Jennings, J.N. and Mabbutt, J.A. (eds.), *Landform Studies from Australia and New Guinea* (Cambridge: Cambridge University Press), 48–63.

STANLEY, D.J., KRINITZSKY, E.L. and COMPTON, J.R. 1966: Mississippi river bank failure. *Bulletin of the Geological Society of America* 77, 859–66.

STATHAM, I. 1977: *Earth Surface Sediment Transport*. Oxford: Clarendon Press.

STEVENS, M.A., SIMONS, D.B. and RICHARDSON, E.V. 1975: Non-equilibrium river form. *Journal of the Hydraulics Division American Society of Civil Engineers* 101, HY5, 557–66.

STEWART, J.H. and LaMARCHE, V.C. 1967: Erosion and deposition produced by the flood of December 1964 on Coffee Creek, Trinity County, California. *United States Geological Survey Professional Paper* 422K, 22pp.

STODDART, D.R. 1978: Geomorphology in China. *Progress in Physical Geography* 2, 187–236.

STRAHLER, A.N. 1952: Hypsometric (area-altitude) analysis of erosional topography. *Bulletin of the Geological Society of America* 63, 1117–42.

—— 1957: Quantitative analysis of watershed geomorphology. *Transactions of the American Geophysical Union* 38, 913–20.

TANNER, W.F. 1960: Helicoidal flow, a possible cause of meandering. *Journal of Geophysical Research* 65, 993–5.

TASK COMMITTEE FOR PREPARATION OF SEDIMENT MANUAL 1971a: Sediment transportation mechanics: H. Sediment discharge formulas. *Journal of the Hydraulics Division American Society of Civil Engineers* 97, HY4, 523–67.

—— 1971b: Sediment transportation mechanics: Q. Genetic classification of valley sediment deposits. *Journal of the Hydraulics Division American Society of Civil Engineers* 97, HY1, 43–53.

TASK FORCE ON FRICTION FACTORS IN OPEN CHANNELS 1963: Friction factors in open channels: Progress report. *Journal of the Hydraulics Division American Society of Civil Engineers* 89, HY2, 97–143.

THORNE, C.R. and HEY, R.D. 1979: Direct measurements of secondary currents at a river inflexion point. *Nature* 280, 226–8.

THORNE, C.R. and TOVEY, N.K. 1981: Stability of composite river banks. *Earth Surface Processes and Landforms* 6, 469–84.

THORNES, J.B. 1974: Speculations on the behaviour of stream channel width. *London School of Economics, Graduate School of Geography Discussion Paper* 49, 17pp.

TINKLER, K.J. 1970: Pools, riffles, and meanders. *Bulletin of the Geological Society of America* 81, 547–52.

TRIMBLE, S.W. 1974: *Man-Induced Soil Erosion on the Southern Piedmont 1700–1900.* Ankeny, Iowa: Soil Conservation Society of America.

—— 1975: Denudation studies: Can we assume stream steady state? *Science* 188, 1207–8.

TROUTMAN, B.M. 1980: A stochastic model for particle sorting and related phenomena. *Water Resources Research* 16, 65–76.

TWIDALE, C.R. 1964: Erosion of an alluvial bank at Birdwood, South Australia. *Zeitschrift für Geomorphologie* 8, 189–211.

VANONI, V.A. 1978: Predicting sediment discharge in alluvial channels. *Water Supply and Management* 1, 399–417.

VANONI, V.A. and NOMICOS, G.N. 1960: Resistance properties of sediment-laden streams. *Transactions of the American Society of Civil Engineers* 125, 1140–67.

WALKER, H.J. and ARNBORG, L. 1966: Permafrost and ice-wedge effect on riverbank erosion. In *Proceedings Permafrost International Conference, 1963* (Washington, DC), 164–71.

WALLING, D.E. and KLEO, A.H.A. 1979: Sediment yields of rivers in areas of low precipitation: a global view. In *The Hydrology of Areas of Low Precipitation* (Washington DC: International Association of Hydrological Sciences), Proceedings of the Canberra Symposium, December 1979, IAHS-AISH Publication 128, 479–93.

WEBB, B.W. and WALLING, D.E. 1982: The magnitude and frequency characteristics of fluvial transport in a Devon drainage basin and some geomorphological implications. *Catena* 9, 9–24.

WENDLAND, W.M. and BRYSON, R.A. 1974: Dating climatic episodes of the Holocene. *Quaternary Research* 4, 9–24.

WERRITTY, A. 1972: The topology of stream networks. In Chorley, R.J. (ed.), *Spatial Analysis in Geomorphology* (London: Methuen), 167–96.

WHEELER, D.A. 1979: The overall shape of longitudinal profiles of streams. In Pitty, A.F. (ed.), *Geographical Approaches to Fluvial Processes* (Norwich: Geobooks), 241–60.

WHITE, W.R., MILLI, H. and CRABBE, A.D. 1973: Sediment transport: an appraisal of available methods. Volume 2 Performance of theoretical methods when applied to flume and field data. *Hydraulics Research Station Report* INT 119, 54pp.

WHITTAKER, J.G. and JAEGGI, M.N.R. 1982: Origin of step-pool systems in mountain streams. *Journal of the Hydraulics Division American Society of Civil Engineers* 108, HY6, 758–73.

WILCOCK, D.N. 1967: Coarse bedload as a factor determining bed slope. *Publication of the International Association of Scientific Hydrology* 75, 143–50.

—— 1971: Investigation into the relations between bedload transport and channel shape. *Bulletin of the Geological Society of America* 82, 2159–76.

WILLIAMS, G.P. 1978a: Hydraulic geometry of river cross-sections – theory of minimum variance. *United States Geological Survey Professional Paper* 1029, 47pp.

—— 1978b: Bankfull discharge of rivers. *Water Resources Research* 14, 1141–58.

—— 1978c: The case of the shrinking channels – the North Platte and Platte Rivers in Nebraska. *United States Geological Survey Circular* 781, 48pp.

WILSON, L. 1973: Variations in mean annual sediment yield as a function of mean annual precipitation. *American Journal of Science* 273, 335–49.

WISE, S.M. 1980: Caesium-137 and Lead-210: A review of the techniques and some applications in geomorphology. In Cullingford, Davidson and Lewin 1980, 109–27.

WOLMAN, M.G. 1955: The natural channel of Brandywine Creek, Pennsylvania. *United States Geological Survey Professional Paper* 271, 56pp.

—— 1959: Factors influencing erosion of a cohesive river bank. *American Journal of Science* 257, 204–16.

—— 1967: A cycle of sedimentation and erosion in urban river channels. *Geografiska Annaler* 49A, 385–95.

WOLMAN, M.G. and BRUSH, L.M. 1961: Factors controlling the size and shape of stream channels in coarse uncohesive sands. *United States Geological Survey Professional Paper* 282G, 183–210.

WOLMAN, M.G. and GERSON, R. 1978: Relative scales of time and effectiveness of climate in watershed geomorphology. *Earth Surface Processes* 3, 189–208.

WOLMAN, M.G. and LEOPOLD, L.B. 1957: River flood plains: some observations on their formation. *United States Geological Survey Professional Paper* 282C, 87–109.

WOLMAN, M.G. and MILLER, J.P. 1960: Magnitude and frequency of forces in geomorphic processes. *Journal of Geology* 68, 54–74.

WOMACK, W.R. and SCHUMM, S.A. 1977: Terraces of Douglas Creek, northwestern Colorado: an example of episodic erosion. *Geology* 5, 72–6.

WOODYER, K.D. 1968: Bankfull frequency in rivers. *Journal of Hydrology* 6, 114–42.

YALIN, M.S. 1971: On the formation of dunes and meanders. *Proceedings of the 14th International Congress of the International Association for Hydraulic Research* 3, Paper C13, 1–8.

—— 1972: *Mechanics of Sediment Transport*. Oxford: Pergamon Press.

YANG, C.T. 1971a: Potential energy and stream morphology. *Water Resources Research* 7, 311–22.

—— 1971b: On river meanders. *Journal of Hydrology* 13, 231–53.

—— 1971c: Formation of riffles and pools. *Water Resources Research* 7, 1567–74.

—— 1976: Minimum unit stream power and fluvial hydraulics. *Journal of the Hydraulics Division American Society of Civil Engineers* 102, HY7, 919–34.

YATSU, E. 1955: On the longitudinal profile of the graded river. *Transactions of the American Geophysical Union* 36, 655–63.

ZAGWIJN, W.H. 1975: Variations in climate as shown by pollen analysis, especially in the Lower Pleistocene of Europe. In Wright, A.E. and Moseley, F. (eds.), *Ice Ages: Ancient and Modern* (Liverpool: Seel House Press), 137–52.

ZASLAVSKY, D. and SINAI, G. 1981: Surface hydrology: I – Explanation of phenomena; II – Distribution of raindrops; III – Causes of lateral flow; IV – Flow in sloping, layered soil; V – In-surface transient flow. *Journal of the Hydraulics Division American Society of Civil Engineers* 107, HY1, 1–93 (I – 1–16; II – 17–36; III – 37–52; IV – 53–64; V – 65–93).

ZELLER, J. 1967: Meandering channels in Switzerland. *Publication of the International Association of Scientific Hydrology* 75, 174–86.

ZERNITZ, E.R. 1932: Drainage patterns and their significance. *Journal of Geology* 40, 498–521.

Index

Numbers in italic refer to figures; bold numbers indicate pages of particular relevance